Amateur Arts in the UK

The Policy Studies Institute (PSI) is Britain's leading independent research organisation undertaking studies of economic, industrial and social policy, and the workings of political institutions.

PSI is a registered charity, run on a non-profit basis, and is not associated with any political party, pressure group or commercial interest.

PSI attaches great importance to covering a wide range of subject areas with its multi-disciplinary approach. The Institute's 30+ researchers are organised in teams which currently cover the following programmes:

Family Finances
Health Studies and Social Care
Innovation and New Technology
Quality of Life and the Environment
Social Justice and Social Order
Employment Studies
Arts and the Cultural Industries
Information Policy
Education

This publication arises from the Arts programme and is one of over 30 publications made available by the Institute each year.

Information about the work of PSI, and a catalogue of available books can be obtained from:
Marketing Department, PSI
100 Park Village East, London NW1 3SR
Telephone: 071-387 2171; Fax: 071-388 0914

Amateur Arts in the UK

Robert Hutchison and Andrew Feist

Policy Studies Institute, London

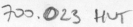

The publishing imprint of the independent
POLICY STUDIES INSTITUTE
100 Park Village East, London NW1 3SR
Telephone: 071-387 2171; Fax: 071-388 0914

ISBN 0 85374 533 1
A CIP catalogue record of this book is available from the British Library.
9 8 7 6 5 4 3 2 1
PSI Report No. 726

How to obtain PSI publications
All bookshop and individual orders should be
sent to PSI's distributors:
BEBC Ltd
9 Albion Close, Parkstone
Poole, Dorset, BH12 2LL
Books will normally be despatched in 24 hours.
Cheques should be made payable to BEBC Ltd.
Credit card and telephone/fax orders may be placed
on the following freephone numbers:
FREEPHONE: 0800 262260 FREEFAX: 0800 262266

Booktrade Representation (UK & Eire)
Book Representation Ltd
P O Box 17, Canvey Island
Essex SS8 8HZ

PSI Subscriptions
PSI Publications are available on subscription.
Further information from PSI's subscription agent:
Carfax Publishing Company Ltd
Abingdon Science Park, P O Box 25
Abingdon OX14 3UE

Laserset by Policy Studies Institute
Printed in Great Britain by Billing & Sons Ltd, Worcester

Contents

List of tables in main text

List of figures

Foreword

The performing arts, and students of music in particular, are the principal focus of my working days, and in my leisure hours I have long been concerned with the opportunities for amateur activity. Many amateurs become professionals; many professionals work with amateurs. In such an interdependent process it has always seemed important to me to view amateurs and professionals as complementary, of equal value though with different ways of working.

When in 1989 the Carnegie UK Trust invited me to chair its special Conference in Edinburgh to focus on the Arts and Crafts for Amateurs I was pleased to accept. That successful Conference came about because of the inquiries by Sir Ian Hunter into the possibility of a Council for the Amateur and the Trust's concern for the deteriorating position of many amateur agencies. The 50 representatives of national arts agencies present voted for a UK Steering Committee to make more detailed inquiries into the role played by amateurs in the cultural life of our country and especially in the arts and crafts.

As part of its work the steering committee, known as the Voluntary Arts Network, decided to ask the Policy Studies Institute to research into amateur arts in the UK. We are enthused and challenged by the results in this report. The case studies describe the vast range of activity and the repeated aim of high standards by amateur participants in many different types of organisation. Statistics and tables alone can often appear cold but the report and its conclusions chart the breadth and depth of amateur activity in the UK often in difficult circumstances and often under-funded especially by the statutory authorities. The report also presents the scope for increased activity in the future.

The Voluntary Arts Network committee wishes to thank the Trustees and Officers of the Baring Foundation and the Calouste

Gulbenkian Foundation for sharing with the Carnegie UK Trust in the promotion of this important report and the Policy Studies Institute, and Robert Hutchison and Andrew Feist in particular, for undertaking the study.

Sir David Lumsden
Principal, The Royal Academy of Music
Chairman, The Voluntary Arts Network Steering Committee

Acknowledgements

The authors are most grateful to the Carnegie United Kingdom Trust and the Gulbenkian and Baring Foundations which have financed the study, and to the members of the Steering Committee of the Voluntary Arts Network, who helped to initiate the project and who have offered support, advice and guidance at every stage. Those who have provided information and/or who have consented to be interviewed are too numerous to mention. But we have received excellent co-operation and help from hundreds of people involved in the amateur arts. We offer our thanks to all of them. Jill Ebrey made a particularly useful contribution to the area study in Stoke-on-Trent and Newcastle-under-Lyme, and Russell Jones was singularly helpful in facilitating the survey of members of the National Federation of Music Societies.

We have also had a number of discussions with those involved in the National Inquiry into the Arts and the Community, which is complementary to, and has been conducted in parallel with, our research (see Chapter 2); in particular we would like to thank Gabriel Chanan for his constructive comments on our efforts.

Andrew Feist has been responsible for the area studies in Aberdeen, Exeter, the London Borough of Lewisham and Teignbridge, and Robert Hutchison for those in Powys, Stoke-on-Trent and Newcastle- under-Lyme, and Telford.

Robert Hutchison
Andrew Feist

September 1991

Summary of report

1. The amateur and professional arts are intertwined and inder-dependent; the term 'amateur' is not unambiguously separated from 'professional'; rather than a clear amateur/professional divide, there is a complex amateur/professional continuum or spectrum of ambition, accomplishment and activity.

2. It can be estimated from the *General Household Survey* that just under 1.8 million individuals are regularly involved in amateur music and drama. Of these, around one-third are organised in relatively formal groups, societies, or other forms of voluntary association. From a survey conducted by Research Services of Great Britain for the Arts Council, it can be estimated that 3.7 million people in the U.K. regularly practise photography, 3.0 million regularly practise one or more of the textile crafts, and 1.8 million are regularly involved in painting and drawing. Only a small minority of these are involved in amateur arts groups.

3. A total of 775,000 people aged 16 and over are regularly involved in all kinds of 'formal' amateur arts and crafts groups. This does not include members of film societies, enrolments in adult education classes, or those involved in the arts in women's institutes, townswomen's guilds and young farmers' clubs. Nor does it include members of jazz, rock and pop groups.

4. National 'umbrella' organisations, whose memberships consist largely of affiliated groups, are an important feature of the structure of the amateur arts. 28 of the main 'umbrella' organisations in the

performing arts, crafts and photography, have a combined individual membership of around 448,000.

5. Most amateur arts groups are not affiliated to any national organisation. Only 42 per cent of responding societies in the seven areas studied were found to be members of a national 'umbrella' body.

6. The past 25 years has seen a marked growth in the number of specialist national interest groups for individual amateur and professional artists and craftspeople. Of 27 such national organisations of craftspeople, with a combined membership of over 40,000, 17 have been founded since 1967.

7. The 16 to 19 age group has the highest percentage involved in the amateur arts. Participation rates for amateur music and drama fall thereafter, stabilise throughout middle-age, and decline further in old age. Participation in the textile crafts follow a contrary pattern, with participation rates generally increasing with age. Overall, participation rates are highest amongst students in full-time education, 11 per cent of whom were active in the arts in the 4 weeks before interview.

8. Sparsely populated rural areas contain a higher number of amateur groups per head of population and a higher percentage of population engaged in formal amateur arts groups than is the case in urban areas.

9. Although some forms of amateur arts activity – for instance, drama and light opera – exist on a national scale, others have particularly strong roots in particular regions. However art forms traditionally associated with one or more regions are now being practised in many parts of the UK, and there is evidence of the growing popularity of artistic forms and styles from overseas. This has led to an even greater diversity in amateur arts activities.

10. Amateur arts groups are largely self-financing, usually through a mixture of membership subscriptions, box office income, donations and fund-raising. Direct public funding is minimal. Local authorities spent an estimated £3.5 million on grants to amateur organisations in England and Wales in 1990/91.

11. Attendances at amateur opera and drama performances are estimated to have totalled about 12 million in 1989/90, which is more than annual attendances at London's West End theatre. Concerts promoted by choirs and orchestras affiliated to the National Federation of Music Societies recorded total attendances over 1 million.

The importance of the amateur arts

12. Like the professional arts, the importance of the amateur arts can be put in five main ways: the social dimension; as a form of recreation; as a means of personal development; the psychological importance of the arts; and their economic importance. The social and psychological importance of the amateur arts, including their importance for exploring and expressing personal and cultural identity, as well as their importance for personal development, need underlining in our technocratic age.

13. In some areas of arts activity, including many of the arts activities of ethnic minorities, the distinction between 'professionals' and 'amateurs' is either irrelevant or inappropriate. But there are numerous ways in which full-timers and part-timers, amateurs and professionals, have collaborated to their mutual advantage. Such collaboration often acts as a form of informal training of professionals at various stages of their careers.

14. It seems likely that the amateur sector generates far more opportunities for professional work than it displaces.

15. In mainly rural areas, the amateur arts are frequently the sole form of arts activity.

16. The amateur arts are essential to the preservation and development of traditional art forms and are vital to the promotion of cultural diversity.

17. The amateur arts tend to be a more integral part of everyday life than professional performances and exhibitions.

Policy issues and recommendations

18. Consideration of how best to support the amateur arts should be a major component of the National Arts Strategy.

19. Arts funding bodies need to develop and implement a coherent set of policies for supporting and evaluating programmes that involve people in practising the arts, and programmes that enhance cultural diversity.

20. With the Central Council for Amateur Theatre, the Arts Council of Great Britain (ACGB) should encourage and support financially the establishment of a Drama Association of England to fulfil in England the functions undertaken by the Drama Association of Wales in the Principality.

21. Local government support for the arts – including the amateur arts – needs to be more carefully monitored and good practice among local authorities that give appropriate and consistent support to the amateur arts needs to be widely publicised.

22. Independent studies are needed (a) of what is happening to the arts in education (including adult education) and (b) of the longer-term benefits of encouraging participation in the arts at a young age.

23. 'Adult education' and the 'amateur arts' are overlapping categories. Liberal adult education is under severe threat both from the attrition in local government expenditure and from the proposals contained in the White Paper, *Education and Training for the 21st Century*.

1 Introduction

Arts and crafts practised for the love of them, or for the challenge that they offer, for enjoyment, for self-expression and self-development, for celebration and other sound social reasons, or practised in order to produce something beautiful, are integral to cultural life in any society. In the United Kingdom the arts and crafts practised by amateurs are taken for granted by some, despised by others, and ignored by many more. Yet the arts never have been, and never will be, the monopoly of full-time specialists.

However, there have been too many barriers of exclusion to serious participation in, and appreciation of, the arts and crafts. These barriers have been barriers of class, education and 'professional exclusiveness', as well as psychological barriers. For example, those lacking in self- confidence have excluded themselves from activities that, but for the lack of self-confidence, they might enjoy. Indeed one of the qualities that the arts enable us to explore is our own self-confidence. The growth of many forms of professional/amateur collaboration in the arts has done something to break down social and psychological barriers, as well as providing less experienced or accomplished artists with sources of inspiration and examples of technical and imaginative achievement.

However, the growth of professional/amateur collaboration should not obscure the powerful influence of major social factors – class, gender, ethnicity – in the way that the arts are financed, practised, and enjoyed. Practising the arts in a purposeful and satisfying manner calls for a good deal of time as well as the appropriate facilities. The time and facilities needed, as well as the economic backing to promote work effectively, are more readily available to some social groups than others.

For example, the social and economic changes in developed countries in the last 300 years have expressed themselves in the creation of two types of social space: the public world, peopled largely by men, and the private or domestic sphere, which has been more the province of women and children. The ways in which the arts and crafts have been produced and valued have reflected this dichotomy, and the ability of women to succeed in the arts has been crucially influenced by access (or lack of it) to appropriate training. Similarly, the relative lack of qualified members of the Asian and Afro-Caribbean communities in the professions concerned with organising and promoting the arts has made it easier for a relatively uncritical Eurocentric approach to dominate national consciousness in general, and arts policy in particular.

There is no full consideration in this report of questions of equal opportunities or of the multicultural nature of the United Kingdom. But the report is written conscious of the importance of these issues for arts research and for the formulation and implementation of arts policies. It is primarily a statistical, rather than a sociological report, but we note with interest the remark by Ruth Finnegan in her masterly work, *The Hidden Musicians, Music-making in an English town*, that music cannot be explained (or explained away) 'as the creation of class divisions or manipulation', nor is it in any simple way 'predictable from people's social and economic background, or even, in most cases, their age'.

However, along with all the other arts and crafts, music can be seen as having a central part in the social structure and processes of our life today. The amateur arts are a way of life for tens of thousands of people and a vital recreational activity for many millions more.

This study sets out to establish a picture of the amateur arts and crafts in the UK – how they are organised and funded, the numbers of adults involved in arts and crafts activities, with references to regional differences and differences between urban and rural areas. We have taken an inclusive view of the arts and crafts – those art forms and craft categories in regular receipt of subsidy from the Arts and Crafts Councils and Regional Arts Associations (now Regional Arts Boards) have all been included in the study. To save repetition, the word 'arts' should be taken to include the crafts, photography, film and video.

One hundred different types and styles of dancing are on offer in adult education classes in inner London in 1991-2; the support for and practice of these diverse styles throughout the UK needs a separate study, as does the fast-changing rock and pop music scene. Dancing and rock and pop music are immensely popular; we have not neglected them altogether, but nor have we done them any kind of justice.

Indeed two researchers, each contracted to work for 65 days on research into the amateur arts, cannot hope to give a comprehensive account when faced with such a vast and colourful kaleidoscope of amateur arts organisations and activities.

We were asked by the Voluntary Arts Network Steering Committee to examine the extent of activity in the amateur arts; to look at the role of volunteers in supporting arts activities of all kinds; to conduct detailed studies in a number of areas; to investigate the nature and extent of public funding for the amateur arts in England, Scotland, Wales and Northern Ireland; and to be mindful of the changes going on in adult education and the youth service.

The approaches and methods that we adopted included the following:

1. Detailed studies in seven areas – five in England, one each in Scotland and Wales. The seven areas were selected to be broadly representative – in social and economic terms – of the UK as a whole. This aspect of the research included sending self-completion questionnaires to all the amateur arts groups that could be identified in those areas.

2. Self-completion questionnaires sent to the principal national organisations concerned with the amateur arts. In the case of twelve of the organisations, follow-up interviews were also arranged with the directors or administrators.

3. Surveys of policies towards, and funding of, the amateur arts by the four main Arts Councils in the UK, the Crafts Council, the fifteen Regional Arts Associations in England and Wales, and a sample of local authorities.

4. A comprehensive questionnaire survey of clubs and societies affiliated to the National Federation of Music Societies.

5. A sample survey of local art clubs and societies.

6. Surveys of national interest groups of craftspeople, visual artists and musicians.

7. Sample surveys of the arts and crafts activities of Young Farmers' Clubs, Women's Institutes and Townswomens' Guilds.

8. A survey of poetry competitions.

Professor Finnegan points out that in the arts the term 'amateur' is not unambiguously separated from 'professional', and that rather than a clear amateur/professional divide there is a complex amateur/professional continuum or spectrum of accomplishment and activity; serious participants in the arts put very different interpretations on the terms 'amateur' and 'professional'. We develop the idea of a continuum in Chapter 2, which also includes a discussion of amateur arts activity in relation to other forms of participatory arts and crafts activity: youth arts, adult education, and community arts.

Chapter 3 draws on a number of surveys as well as our own to provide a picture of the extent of involvement by the adult population in amateur arts and crafts activities. Chapters 4-8 report on our surveys of the principal nationally organised specialist interest groups whose members include both 'professionals' and 'amateurs', and of those bodies which seek to promote the interests of local groups at the national level. The involvement in the arts and crafts of Young Farmers' Clubs, Women's Institutes and Townswomen's Guilds are described in Chapter 8.

The next three chapters (Chapters 9-11) report on three different ways in which the amateur arts are supported through public institutions and public money. Chapters 12 and 13 are about professional/amateur collaboration in music and drama. Chapter 14 is a brief description of the Royal National Eisteddfod of Wales, perhaps the largest amateur arts event in Europe, but one that partly depends for its organisation on a core group of professional administrators.

Much creative activity is, by its nature, a largely solitary process. There is, for example, a huge amount of creative writing going on in the UK, and some indications of the extent of this are given in Chapter 15.

The reports of the seven area studies follow the chapter of Conclusions and Recommendations. The first four appendices provide more detailed statistical information, including the results of surveys of members of the National Federation of Music Societies and of local art clubs and societies.

In addition to being actively involved as an artist or artistic director, there are many other ways of being involved in the arts, both amateur and professional. The tens of thousands of volunteers involved in the organisation and administration of arts activities, in selling tickets, stewarding events, or acting as guides or security staff at museums and galleries, form another kind of bridge between the amateur and professional worlds and make an indispensable contribution to cultural life. Appendix E looks at the role of volunteers in a range of arts organisations, including those heavily involved in various kinds of professional/amateur collaboration.

As the new Regional Arts Boards find their feet, and the National Arts Strategy is formulated, and as concern about the future of local government and of adult education reaches a new phase, we offer some facts, figures, thoughts and recommendations to help inform the debate about the future of arts policy.

It is hoped that this report will lead to more serious consideration of how opportunities to practise and enjoy the arts, to raise the aspirations of amateur artists and to learn from other practitioners, and to encourage personal development and the development of social networks and community celebrations through the arts, can be enhanced.

2 Participation in the arts: definitions and concepts

The terms 'arts' and 'amateur' have powerful, and to some extent, forbidding resonances. The arts are disciplined forms of enquiry and expression through which feelings and ideas about experience can be organised and communicated. The definitions of what constitute 'the arts' differ from one country to another and from one century to another. Cooking, architecture, gardening, radio and television – all 'arts' in their different ways – are excluded from the definition of the arts used in this report, but origami and embroidery are included. Arguably one of the most disabling aspects of European cultures has been the historic divide between the fine arts and the applied arts – a division that is itself a by-product of the gradual devaluing of manual labour. The crafts need different kinds of attention and support to those given to other art forms. Indeed the health of a society may be partially judged by the extent to which creative manual work is celebrated.

According to the research organisation Mass Observation, an arts activity is felt by the general public 'to have a classical quality, to be "old fashioned" and to be something "passed down"'. Mass Observation found that photography is not thought to be an art, because it is seen as something that 'anyone can do'.[1] Clearly what Eric Midwinter has called 'the elitist bar',[2] the sense that the arts are not an immediate and relevant and direct part of day-to-day living, is still very real.

Amateurs are, from the Latin root, people who love what they do and do it for its own sake. Yet nowadays the term amateur is nearly always used pejoratively. The steady drip, drip of condescension set in years ago. As the third Arts Council chairman, Lord Clark, said of the first Arts Council chairman, John Maynard Keynes, 'he was not the man for wandering minstrels and amateur theatricals... he believed in excellence'.[3] Yet excellence and the amateur theatre were never mutually exclusive categories. For over half a century, the guiding spirit of the Questors Theatre, Ealing was Alfred Emmet. In its obituary for Emmet *The Independent* wrote

> Questors was never about a little clique of self-admiring enthusiasts gratifying their own egos. For all his benign exterior, Emmet applied rigorous standards of excellence and accomplishment to all their activities, whether it was the all-important nurturing of young talents or laying bricks in another extension to the theatre. Nobody was allowed to rest on their laurels.[4]

Such a description is not only applicable to some amateur theatre companies, but to amateur organisations as well as individuals working across the range of the amateur arts and crafts. But, of course, a great deal of amateur work is self-indulgent, derivative, mediocre, slipshod or worse. What is it then that separates the professional from the amateur, and how useful are these categories?

The most common distinction made between professionals and amateurs in the arts is that the former practise their art for a living, or at least aim to make it their prime source of income. A review of Hilary Spurling's biography of Paul Scott began:

> One morning in 1950, when Paul Scott was sitting on the lavatory after breakfast, his wife Penny slid an envelope under the door. It was a BBC contract offering him 90 guineas for a radio play he had recently written, and its arrival marked the end to years of disappointment as a would-be writer and the beginning of success which was to culminate in his winning the Booker Prize in 1978 – the year of his death – and in the posthumous triumph of the TV *Raj Quartet*. 'You could say', Scott admitted later, 'that an amateur went into the closet and a professional emerged'.[5]

But 'professional' cannot be satisfactorily defined solely by reference to income. For few of those practitioners whom most people would acknowledge as professionals in fact earn a full-time living from their art. Ann Jellicoe has suggested that 'professionals are those who have professed, have taken a religious vow' and points to several advantages of using professionals in community plays:

1. They are trained and have learnt the discipline of their art.

2. They have (or should have) measured themselves against the highest standards.

3. Their training and talent have given them the freedom to be bold and innovatory if they wish. Equally, it allows them to be extremely economical and to eliminate. It is usually the mark of an amateur designer that they try and put/leave too much in.

4. They have a full-time commitment and responsibility to the work.[6]

These qualities of professionals are important, but there are other characteristics that often distinguish a fully professional from an amateur approach to the arts. It is clear also that, even within the cultures of the United Kingdom, the distinction between amateurs and professionals needs to be drawn differently across the different craft and art forms. Partly this is a matter of economics. For example, there are thousands of lace-makers in the UK, and about 500 teachers recognised by the Lace Guild, but partly because lace-making is such a time-consuming activity, only a handful who make much of a living from their work. In some art forms the distinction between professionals and amateurs is otiose – the Poetry Society and the Arvon Foundation (which organises a range of creative writing courses) use the decidedly flexible term 'established writer' in preference to trying to draw invidious distinctions between professional and amateur poets or novelists.

In many non-European cultures the distinction often breaks down altogether or is completely irrelevant. The organising director of the Black Arts Alliance has expressed 'doubt that there is an equivalent to "amateur" in any Black language'.[7] Many of the traditional dance and music forms from the Indian sub-continent have their basis in religious belief – artistic aspirations may be high, but the business of being paid for accomplished work is sometimes seen as a threat rather than as an aspiration. The problem of classification and its effect upon one ethnic arts group was forcefully put several years ago by Jatinder Verma of the Tara Arts Group:

> Tara's current round of applications to local authorities, the Arts Council and Greater London Arts, has revealed a glaring inability on the part of these funding sources to appreciate the nature of the group.

Over and over again, attempts have been made to categorise us as either 'professional' or 'amateur' or 'community arts'. Tara is an Asian theatre group, drawing upon the resources and skills of the community in London and is held together by two full-time workers. Clearly it is not a 'professional' group, except in terms of standards of presentation. Nor is it an 'amateur' group. Which amateur group has a consistent programme of touring productions throughout the year, productions which are toured around the country? And Tara is not a 'community arts' group either; only two of its twenty members are full-time workers, and the group works solely within the medium of drama. It is a failure to accept this structure as a viable one that has been our major obstacle to receiving adequate – rather than subsistence – levels of subsidy from arts-funding sources.[8]

Tara's work has changed considerably in recent years, but this quotation illustrates the principal problem in embarking on any study of the amateur arts and crafts in the United Kingdom; it is impossible to put a ring-fence around a set of individuals or organisations and label them 'amateur artists'. The social and economic bases of arts activity are forever changing, and artists practise with varying aspirations and skills. However, in most art forms it is possible to identify a broad continuum of practitioners and organisations, from the unashamedly frivolous and inward-looking to those seeking to be judged by the highest international standards, and expecting financial rewards commensurate with considerable talents and immense experience.

The parameters in Figure 1 are perhaps useful in helping to distinguish between amateurs and professionals in most art forms. In addition to persistence – a key quality – fully fledged professionals are likely to possess many or all of the attributes at the right-hand side of the spectra, while the more self-satisfied and unambitious of amateurs will probably possess many or all of the attributes to the left. The important point is that most serious practitioners of the arts will probably place themselves at different points along these axes, and that those positions will differ at different periods of their lives. All artists begin as children; and since children have few of the techniques, worries or opportunities of full-time professionals, it might be said that all artists begin as amateurs.

Figure 1 The amateur/professional continuum

Negative income from arts employment	Income	All income from arts employment
Self-taught	Training	Fully professionally trained
Unimportant	Artistic aspirations	High
Spare time/hobby	Time allocated	Full-time
Not taken seriously	Status of art form in society	Considered as prof. occupation
Limited	Experience	Considerable
Imitative and derivative	Content and style	Original
Recreational	General approach	Creative/ business-like

Four approaches to participation in the arts

Despite what is said above, there is an identifiable set of practices and organisations that form the heartlands of the adult amateur arts – the affiliated organisations of the Central Council for Amateur Theatre, the local art clubs and societies reported on in Appendix D, the world of traditional music and folk dance, eisteddfodau and the organisations in membership of the Welsh Amateur Music Federation and the National Federation of Music Societies. All these, and much else besides, clearly fall within the purview of this report.

But the amateur arts can be seen, and should be seen, in relation to the three other broad approaches to organised participation in the arts: through youth arts work, through adult education, and through community arts.

'The "arts" are a dead letter for the majority of young people' argues Paul Willis in a study which points to the informality of the everyday culture of the young.[9] Dick Chamberlain, himself a former youth and community worker, makes a similar point, though in slightly less exaggerated terms: 'The kinds of things that young people are expressing through various forms – like street dance, graffiti, fanzines, bhangra and rap – cut across accepted definitions of what is seen as art'.[10] This is not the place for an involved argument about the prevalence and nature of working-class youth sub-cultures. But Ruth Finnegan's observations on rock bands are worth recording:

> A large proportion of band members were between 16 and 21, as were many of their audiences, but... these were individuals and groups with many *different* interests, musical tastes and backgrounds, not necessarily with a great deal of sympathy for, or interest in, each other's ideas or way of life or necessarily too concerned with each other's ages. Furthermore, other young people locally were keen on other pursuits, both other forms of music (classical, brass bands, operatic) and such activities as drama, sports or photography. Judged in relation to young people's active commitments in Milton Keynes, the privileged position sometimes assumed for rock music as constituting either 'youth culture' in general or a series of differentiated youth 'sub-cultures' or 'counter-cultures' looks more like a wishful creation of the commercial recording outlets or the academic theorists than an exact description of actual grass-roots practice.[11]

Though large numbers of young people are actively involved in a great variety of differentiated forms of pop and rock music, young people's interests and concerns are just as varied – perhaps more so – than those of the adult population.

Most youth clubs and youth arts activities are voluntarily-run, and only a minority of youngsters have continuing contact with the youth service provided by local authorities. The youth service is gradually coming to terms with the fact that the arts can have relevance to all young people. But our case studies reflected the fact that 'youth arts work is often marginalised and dependent on peripheral, short-term funding'.[12] As a report on *Youth Work and the Performing Arts* by Her Majesty's Inspectors put it: 'Financial resourcing for youth arts work presents a varied and mostly unsatisfactory picture' and 'few existing youth clubs, even in larger centres, can satisfy the accommodation needs of specialist art work for long'.[13] Nevertheless, there has been a considerable growth in many kinds of youth arts work – not least youth theatre (see Appendix C).

The involvement of the formal adult education sector in supporting the amateur arts has stronger roots, but is perhaps under an even bigger threat from pressures on local government expenditure than youth service work is. Local education authorities are far and away the largest providers of adult education. A range of approaches to the arts in adult education classes is well-established, and provides hundreds of thousands of people each year with an introduction to, or a continuation of, practising and developing work in their chosen craft or art form. Part of the importance of adult education is that it offers a relatively unintimidating way for people to get involved in a craft or art relatively late in life. There is a certain amount of overlap and cross-over between 'adult education' and the 'amateur arts' – but in her study of the crafts in adult education, Cherry Ann Knott pointed out that 'although students generally took their part-time courses very seriously, disappointingly few developed their craft involvement far beyond this, unless specifically encouraged to do so'. However, 'in lace-making, hand knitting, machine knitting, glass engraving, crochet/macramé and metalwork, more than 20 per cent of the students spent more than ten hours at their craft between classes each week'. Of the total sample of 1,086 students, only 86 (8 per cent) belonged to any craft guild or society. More is said about the present state of adult education in Chapter 11, but in summing up the benefits for adults learning a craft in a part-time way, Cherry Ann Knott says that students value the lack of pressure and the relative freedom in their learning:

> Perhaps above all they value the 'sharing' dimension of adult education. The sharing includes not only the passing on of the tutor's enthusiasm and expertise to the students, but also the continual process of interchange between the students.[14]

It is the 'process of interchange' as well as the processes of developing skills and self-confidence that are important in all aspects of the participatory arts, not least in community arts, a phrase that entered the currency of the arts world about 20 years ago.

'Community arts' has been deployed as a general term for forms of creative expression in which all the community could take part. The community arts movement has shared a continuing concern to democratise the arts and make them more a part of common experience. Community artists have been involved in every art form and have worked with almost every age group. Although there has been a great deal of participatory arts activity under the heading 'community arts' over the last 20 years, 'community' is a word that, at best, lacks precision. As Raymond Williams pointed out, it is a term that 'seems never to be used unfavourably',[15] and it continues to be widely used by many attempting to add an extra coating of worthiness to whatever activity they are engaged upon. Communities can be either geographical entities or they can be communities of interest – in other words they can be neighbourhoods or networks. While it is true that some territorial communities are larger than neighbourhoods and that not all communities of interest are satisfactorily described as networks, these 'N-words' are perhaps somewhat sharper-edged in their meanings than the warm-bath term 'community'.

The National Inquiry into Arts and the Community was set up in April 1990 to carry out a study of arts activities which increase local involvement, participation in and access to the arts. The aim is to review this widespread but little-coordinated movement, assess its growth and significance, and make recommendations on its future role and support. The Inquiry will publish its findings early in 1992.

Referring to the PSI study of the amateur arts as complementary to their own investigations, the National Inquiry researchers, in an Interim Statement, argue that

> Whilst watertight definitions are probably impossible, these two types of arts activity, amateur on the one hand and community-oriented on the other, are distinct both in purpose and practice, each playing an important and greatly under-recognised role in contemporary society.
>
> Each has a strong presence in many localities and hence a large but little-recognised national presence; and there are some types of activity and venue where both can be found side by side. But they are usually different in purpose. Amateur arts is primarily the practice of arts activity for its own sake. Community-oriented arts is arts with additional social purposes. These include personal development and social cohesion; expressing or reinterpreting cultural, religious or ethnic affiliations; articulating feelings about social issues or local problems; and stimulating or contributing to local action, democracy and change.[16]

Three points should be made about the above statement:

First, amateur arts are not 'primarily the practice of arts activity for its own sake.' The amateur arts, like all human activities, are practised for a rich mixture of motives, one aspect of which may be a relatively 'pure' love of the activity for its own sake.

Secondly, although 'stimulating or contributing to local action, democracy and change' may not be a pronounced part of much amateur arts and crafts activity, all the 'additional social purposes' ascribed above to 'community-oriented arts' can be found, in greater or lesser degrees, in the main streams and tributaries of the amateur arts. Many of those heavily involved in the amateur arts are consciously and explicitly concerned with personal development as well as social cohesion. But, in general terms, there *is* a difference of emphasis between the two categories; 'social concern' tends to be a more fundamental element of 'community arts' than of much 'amateur arts'.

So thirdly, while 'amateur arts' and 'community arts' can usually be distinguished both in purpose and practice, there is also some degree of overlap between the categories, and there are certainly some types of activity where both 'community arts' and 'amateur arts' can be found side by side.

The principal distinction between amateur arts and community arts is that amateur arts activities tend to be self-motivated and self-organised (entirely or largely by volunteers), community arts programmes and projects tend to be initiated, or at least facilitated, by those paid to take initiatives, whether community artists, animateurs, community workers, local government officers or others.

This distinction is neither hard nor fast, but it is broadly applicable. It is also the case that while it would be a caricature to describe all amateur artists and craftspeople as 'middle-class', there is a middle-class bias in much of the amateur arts. By contrast, community arts initiatives – some of which derive from or are closely related to political campaigning – tend to be taken with relatively disadvantaged groups (for example, the unemployed, disabled people, single parents) and/or in relatively disadvantaged areas (for example, bleak housing estates).

There are plenty of exceptions to these general rules. Some community dance work has taken place in higher education establishments – not exactly bastions of underprivilege. What is interesting is the way that the community arts movement of the 1970s can be seen to have metamorphosed into a wider spectrum of different approaches and initiatives in the different art forms in the 1980s and 1990s. Community plays, discussed later in the report, provide one example. Some community plays can be seen as community arts initiatives which involve members of amateur drama societies. Again, during the 1980s a number of dance and mime animateur posts were established in different areas. They were set up initially with Arts Council funding in partnership with Regional Arts Associations, local authorities and, more recently, other partners such as the Sports Council, the youth service or social services. Lucy Perman of the Community Dance and Mime Foundation writes:

> The animateurs work with a range of different community groups in their location, setting up workshops, bringing in professional companies, organising festivals and other events, setting up youth groups, etc. The work varies depending on the individual animateur, the area and community and the expectations of the different funding bodies. For example, some animateurs focus more on work with young people, or people with disabilities, others have a more education-biased brief. More recently the posts tend to be called 'community dance worker', 'dance development worker' or 'dancer-in-residence'.[17]

To take another example, over the last two decades writers' groups have emerged from youth arts work, from adult education classes, as self-organised amateur groups, or as a result of community arts initiatives (or from some combination of more than one of these approaches). Regional Arts Associations have done something to encourage such groups; for example, Mark Illis is currently being funded by Southern Arts and Berkshire County Council to foster writers' groups in Berkshire. And, with a change of Literature Director in the 1980s, the Arts Council finally recognised community publications as Literature and their authors as Writers.[18]

The genesis of the considerable number of writers' groups dotted around Britain helps to show that there can never be a completely neat and tidy classification of arts activities. The four broad approaches to encouraging and organising active participation in the arts discussed in this chapter do overlap. While the distinction between 'community arts' and 'amateur arts' can often be made in terms of intentions and the sources of new initiatives, once a production or programme of arts activities is under way, these distinctions, and their limited importance, tend to melt away.

What is important is that everybody, at each stage of their lives, should have excellent local opportunities to practise and enjoy the arts, and that people should be encouraged to exercise their imaginative powers and to develop their talents and capabilities to the full. If these things are to happen, some of the long-standing barriers to participation in the arts need to be further broken down, and a much stronger commitment to youth arts, adult education, community arts and the amateur arts demonstrated at every level of government.

References

1. Mass Observation, *Arts in London: A Qualitative Research Study*, 1990, p.39.

2. Eric Midwinter, *Creating chances: Arts by Older People*, Centre for Policy in Ageing, 1990, p.34.

3. Quoted in Harold Baldry, *The Case for the Arts*, Secker and Warburg, 1981, p.15.

4. *The Independent*, 23 January 1991.

5. Andrew Motion, 'The Secrets of the Closet', *The Observer*, 11 November 1990.

6. Ann Jellicoe, *Community Plays*, Methuen, 1987, p.147.

7. Letter from SuAndi, Black Arts Alliance, 11 April 1991.

8. Walter Baker, *The Arts of Ethnic Minorities*, Commission for Racial Equality, 1985, p.30.

9. Paul Willis, *Common Culture*, Open University Press, 1990.

10. Dick Chamberlain, *Intention to Reality, Developing Youth Arts Policy*, Youth Clubs UK Publications, 1991, p.9.

11. Ruth Finnegan, *The Hidden Musicians, Music-making in an English town*, Cambridge University Press, 1989, pp.122-3.

12. Nick Randell and Simon Myhill (eds.), *Kaleidoscope – Arts Work that Works*, Youth Clubs UK Publications, 1989, Introduction.

13. HM Inspectors, *Youth Work and the Performing Arts*, Department of Education and Science, 1988, pp.7-8.

14. Cherry Ann Knott, *'I Can't Wait for Wednesday', The Crafts in Adult Education*, Crafts Council, 1987, pp.53, 59.

15. Raymond Williams, *Keywords*, Fontana/Croom Helm, 1976.

16. National Inquiry into the Arts and the Community, 'Interim Statement on the Trend of the Findings', July 1991, mimeo.

17. Letter from Lucy Perman, 8 May 1991.

18. Alastair Thomson, 'Community Publishing', *Adults Learning*, September 1990.

3 National perspective: the pyramid of activity

Five categories of amateur activity have been identified:
* voluntary associations which are affiliated to national 'umbrella' organisations;
* voluntary associations which function outside the 'umbrella' networks;
* more informal groups which do not function as voluntary associations;
* individual amateur artists and craftspeople involved in some kind of tuition;
* individuals working in isolation.

The most easily identifiable amateur activity is that in organised formal associations, which are themselves members of one of the multitude of national 'umbrella' organisations. As we move from the first category to the fifth, so it becomes harder to identify the numbers of individuals participating on a regular basis. But in only a few instances do 'umbrella' organisations have a comprehensive national membership; outside the 'umbrella' based groups are a large number of amateur organisations which exist without reference to any national body. If this report was to concern itself only with the activities of the 'umbrella' bodies, it would miss a large part of group-based amateur arts participation. Furthermore, although some amateur arts organisations move in and out of 'umbrella' membership, a number of categories of amateur groups, such as that of student societies, function largely outside the 'umbrella' networks. The survey of National Federation of Music Societies (NFMS) members has found that only 1 per cent of choirs and no orchestras were student societies;

and yet student activity in amateur music and drama are higher than levels found in any other social group.

Local groups and national organisations

PSI conducted a survey of nationally organised predominantly or entirely amateur arts organisations whose memberships consist largely of affiliated groups. Not all these 'umbrella' organisations have mutually exclusive memberships. For instance, some choirs are members of both the NFMS and the National Association of Choirs (NAC). Within some art forms – drama is one example – there are a variety of specialist umbrella bodies which are themselves members of a unifying national body – an 'umbrella of umbrellas' such as the Central Council for Amateur Theatre (CCAT). In 1990, the 'umbrella' bodies surveyed had about 10,780 member groups with an estimated individual membership of 552,000. Table 3.1 lists the principal organisations, with details of their memberships.

One of the purposes of undertaking the surveys of amateur arts organisations in the 7 case study areas was to assess the extent to which amateur groups existed unaffiliated to any national body of amateur groups. In all of the study areas a high proportion of performing and non-performing groups were found to exist outside of the auspices of the 'umbrella' bodies. For the 7 areas combined, groups affiliated to 'umbrellas' accounted for only 44 per cent of performing groups and 39 per cent of other groups.

There are no national organisations in England dedicated to promoting the interests of local art clubs and societies. In June 1991 a short questionnaire was sent from PSI to 180 local art clubs and societies selected at random from a list, provided by the Artists Publishing Company, of 1,077 such clubs and societies. The results of the survey are given in Appendix D.

30 of the 85 respondents (35 per cent) are affiliated to a local or regional association – 13 to a local arts council or arts association, 9 to a regional federation of art societies and 8 to a Regional Arts Association. But none is affiliated to a national organisation.

3.1 Umbrella organisations: group and individual membership(a)

	Group membership			Est. individual membership
	1980	1985	1990	1990
Performing groups				
Music				
British Association of Barbershop Singers	..	..	53	1,900
British Association of Symphonic Bands and Wind Ensembles	na	280	421	12,600
British Federation of Brass Bands	300	850	850	25,500
Handbell Ringers of Great Britain	390	520	570	2,830
Ladies Association of British Barbershop Singers	..	..	42	1,600
National Association of Choirs	186	235	300	15,000
National Federation of Music Societies (b)	..	..	990	66,620
National Operatic and Dramatic Association(c)	1,210	1,394	1,900	114,000
Welsh Amateur Music Federation	200	250	300	18,000
Total			5,426	258,050
Drama				
Drama Association of Wales	..	..	172	5,000
Little Theatre Guild of Great Britain	..	..	65	7,600
Northern Amateur Drama Association	..	..	20	1,500
Scottish Community Drama Assn	293	262	224	7,500
Total			481	21,600
Youth music and drama				
British Federation of Young Choirs	na	83	130	8,250
National Association of Youth Orchestras	..	..	110	20,000
National Association of Youth Theatres	na	60	350	17,500
Total			590	45,750
Traditional and folk arts				
English Folk Dance and Song Society	..	..	250(d)	5,800
The Morris Federation	79	131	258	4,000

The Morris Ring	155	165	185	5,500
Open Morris	..	..	70	1,500
Royal Scottish Country Dance Society(e)	..	..	539	28,037
Royal Scottish Pipe Band Association	..	..	400	12,000
Traditional Music and Song Association of Scotland	..	..	50	..
Welsh Folk Dance Society	32	44	30	..
Total			1,782	56,837

Visual arts and crafts groups

Association of Guilds of Weavers, Spinners & Dyers	40	83	95	5,376
Embroiderers' Guild	..	..	152	11,000
Photographic Alliance of Great Britain	..	..	1,150	47,000
Institute of Amateur Cinematographers	..	..	300	2,500
Total			1,697	65,876

Other groups

British Federation of Film Societies	545	343	287	55,000
National Federation of Music Societies (music promoting societies only)	..	..	266	36,380
Federation of Recorded Music Societies	..	..	250	12,500
Total			803	103,880

(a) Excludes 'umbrella' groups for festivals (the British Federation of Music Festivals, National Drama Festivals Association and Royal National Eisteddfod of Wales).

(b) 1990 figures refer only to music promoting societies affiliated to the NFMS, which are included under 'other' groups.

(c) Approximately two-thirds of the membership of NODA is comprised of operatic, light opera and musical societies; the remainder are drama societies.

(d) The English Folk Dance and Song Society has group members although the majority of the membership is made up of individual affiliations.

(e) Figures refer to worldwide membership.

Informal groupings

Much arts activity – for example, much pop, rock, jazz and country music – is practised and performed in groups that do not trouble themselves with the formalities of voluntary associations. Rock and pop music groups do not usually operate with formal membership conditions or written constitutions. Nevertheless, the membership of such groups is sometimes rigidly controlled. At the same time a huge variety of arts activities are informally organised. For example, the women's movement has helped to generate networks and informal groups of women active in different art forms; events for charity are sometimes organised by *ad hoc* informal groupings; and a great deal of arts activity goes on among and between families and friends.

Not all amateur arts participation is group based. The fourth and fifth categories identified are those which relate to the activities of individuals. Individual participation in the arts is the hardest to measure in statistical terms, but it is also the most widespread. The survey in 1991 of arts and crafts activities conducted by Research Surveys of Great Britain for the Arts Council of Great Britain has provided fresh evidence of the extent of involvement in arts and crafts activities (see below).

3.2 Case study areas: membership of 'umbrella' organisations

Numbers of groups in each area affiliated and not affiliated to national 'umbrella' organisations

	Aberdeen		Exeter		Lewisham		Powys	
	Perf.[a]	Other[b]	Perf.	Other	Perf.	Other	Perf.	Other
'Umbrella'	14	3	13	5	7	5	10	7
Not affiliated	14	9	17	4	7	3	15	8
Total	28	12	30	9	14	8	25	15

	Stoke		Teignbridge		Telford		Total	
	Perf.	Other	Perf.	Other	Perf.	Other	Perf.	Other
'Umbrella'	11	5	12	4	5	2	72	31
Not affiliated	16	9	14	10	10	6	93	49
Total	27	14	26	14	15	8	165	80

(a) The 'umbrella' organisations are those listed in Table 3.1.

(b) 'Perf.' covers all performing arts groups – music, drama, opera, folk dance; 'Other' includes visual arts and crafts groups, writers groups, film societies, cinema clubs and music promoting societies.

Adult education and the amateur arts

The network of adult and continuing education classes and courses underpins a whole range of amateur participation in arts and crafts activities.

There is some overlap between adult education classes and the free-standing societies identified in the first two levels of amateur activity. However, the findings of the case study surveys revealed that comparatively few groups existed under the auspices of an adult education institute. The nationwide survey of members of the National Federation of Music Societies confirmed this (see Appendix B). For more on adult education and the arts see Chapter 11.

The individual amateur artist

The base of the pyramid of amateur arts activities is made up of individual practitioners acting in isolation.

Useful information on the extent to which individuals engage in the arts and crafts can be drawn from various general population surveys undertaken over the last 5 years. Up until 1986, the *General Household Survey*, the annual inter-departmental survey of a representative sample of the adult population undertaken by the Office of Population Censuses and Surveys, carried questions on participation in three relevant categories in the four weeks prior to interview: dancing, amateur music and drama, and dressmaking/needlework/knitting. Inevitably, such surveys do not tend to specify the number of individuals active within each of the five different levels identified above. But they do reveal something about the general characteristics of amateur artists and the overall extent of activity.[1]

1986 was the last year that comparable questions on participation were asked. Non-professional performing artists are a particularly active group. The findings of the *General Household Survey 1986* (GHS) reveal that the average participant in amateur music and drama participated 11 times in the four weeks prior to interview. Whilst this figure does seem exceptionally high, it can be largely explained in terms of the nature of amateur performing: it requires a degree of regular commitment.

The description of amateur arts participants as highly active individuals was confirmed in the findings of work carried out as part of *The Economic Importance of the Arts* study. In Ipswich, 81 per cent of those who claimed to be 'engaged' in the amateur arts over the previous 12 months had participated in the 4 weeks before interview.[2]

Table 3.3 shows rates of arts participation over recent years. Since 1977, there has been a marked decline in the percentage of the population claiming to have danced in the four weeks prior to interview. And whilst the percentage of respondents involved in dressmaking, etc has also fallen slightly over the period, there was a one per cent increase in respondents who had been involved in 'amateur music and drama' in 1986.

3.3 Percentage of adult population participating in music, drama, dancing and textile crafts in the 4 weeks before interview

	Percentage of adult population			
	1977	1980	1983	1986
Amateur music/drama(a)	3	3	3	4
Dancing	15	14	11	11
Dressmaking/needlework/ knitting	29	28	27	27

Source: *General Household Survey 1986*, HMSO, 1989.

(a) Excluding classes.

In 1991, the Arts Council of Great Britain commissioned Research Surveys of Great Britain (RSGB) to incorporate a series of questions on participation in the arts in their regular Omnibus surveys. The survey findings provide an additional source of statistics on the extent of participation in the arts amongst the general population. The survey results are based on face-to-face interviews undertaken between 12 June and 7 July 1991 with 7,919 adults aged 16 and over. The questionnaire included a number of questions about types of arts participation. Respondents were presented with a list of 52 arts and crafts and asked: 'In which of these activities, if any, do you take an active part at all nowadays but *not* as a full-time profession?' Respondents were also asked about whether their activity was regular, occasional or very infrequent, although it was not specified what constituted 'regular' or 'infrequent' involvement.

53 per cent of respondents claimed that they took an active part in some form of performing arts (including all kinds of dancing), craft

Figure 2 Percentage of adult population involved in arts and crafts activities(a)

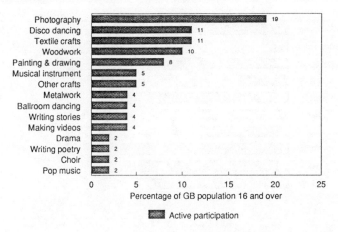

Percentage of GB population 16 and over

Active participation

Source: Arts Council of Great Britain, *RSGB Omnibus Arts Survey – Report on a Survey on Arts and Cultural Activities in GB*, August 1991.

(a) The following categories recorded participation rates of 1 per cent: Scottish dancing; English dancing; folk dancing; other dancing/ballet; sculpture; making films; pottery; jewellery-making; gospel; orchestral music; folk music; Country and Western; electro-acoustics; rock music; and Reggae.

Figure 3 Frequency of participation amongst active participants

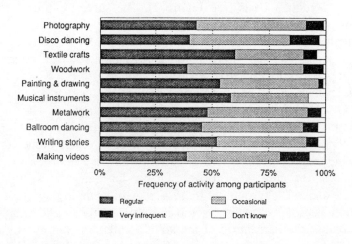

Frequency of activity among participants

Regular   Occasional

Very Infrequent   Don't know

Source: See Figure 2

Figure 4 Individuals involved in selected arts and crafts activities, by gender

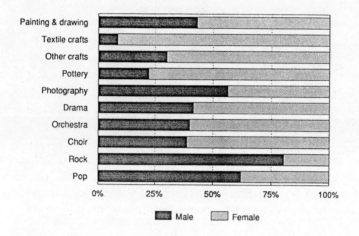

Source: See Figure 2.

(including woodwork and metalwork) or visual arts. A more detailed breakdown of the statistics is given in Figure 2. The findings are broadly in line with the results of the *General Household Survey*. Of all forms of participation, photography was the most widespread, with 19 per cent of the adult population active. Of these, 43 per cent were active on a regular basis (see Figure 3). The survey confirms the widespread popularity of painting and drawing; 8 per cent (the equivalent of 3.7 million people in the UK) claimed to be active, and of these just under half were so on a regular basis. But whereas photography was dominated by male practitioners, women were in the majority in the practice of painting and drawing, pottery and the textile crafts. Other sex differences show up in the performing arts. The male domination of rock and pop music, which is remarked on elsewhere in this report, is evident, but choirs, and to a lesser extent orchestras, have a higher proportion of female participants (see Figure 4).

The RSGB findings confirm one of Ruth Finnegan's observations, about the social background of those who participate in pop groups. Far from being dominated by those from largely working class backgrounds, the percentage of the adult population claiming to be actively involved in pop music was found to be 2 per cent of each social class.

Age

Overall participation rates in amateur music and drama are highest in the 16-19 age group (7 per cent), after which they fall and remain constant for all ages up to and including 45 to 59 year olds. Predictably, participation rates decline further with old age. Only 3 per cent of 60 to 69 year olds and 1 per cent of 70 year olds had participated in amateur music/drama in the four weeks before interview. The pattern of overall declining participation with age, temporarily arrested during middle age, is repeated for dance. It is interesting to note that a broadly contrasting pattern of initial increasing participation with age exists for attenders at theatre, ballet and opera. So, in the live arts at least, involvement in the 16-19 age group is twice as likely to be through 'participation' as attending. As we will consider later, participation at a young age has been found to be an important indicator of future attendance at performing arts events.

A different picture emerges for those engaged in dressmaking/needlework/knitting. Participation rates increase consistently with age, from 16 per cent of 16-19 year olds to 32 per cent of 60-69 year olds, only declining for the oldest group, those aged 70 or over.

3.4   Participation in music, drama, dancing and textile crafts in the 4 weeks before interview, by age, 1986

						Percentage of persons aged 16 and over	
	16-19	20-24	25-29	30-44	45-59	60-69	70 & over
Amateur music/ drama(a)	7	4	4	4	4	3	1
Dancing	25	21	10	10	10	6	3
Dressmaking/needle- work/knitting	16	22	27	29	31	32	24
Attenders at theatre/ opera/ballet	3	5	7	6	7	5	3

Source: *General Household Survey 1986*, HMSO, 1989.

(a) Excluding classes.

Since creativity lives and grows off experience, new initiatives are needed to encourage and enable participation in the arts by older people. At the same time, many classical music societies remain deeply concerned about the effects of an ageing membership – a subject of anxiety for both the NFMS and NAC. The NFMS Strategic Plan notes

> The Federation is prone to attracting a middle-aged and ageing membership and audience... societies will have to be aware of the potential danger in ignoring the age range of their target membership and audience.[3]

As societies age, so their memberships tend to age with them, and given the underlying social motivation of much arts participation, this can make them less attractive socially to younger newcomers. One member of another music 'umbrella' claimed simply that it was 'bloody difficult to interest young people'. Inevitably, inertia can set in. Bernard Robinson, in his descriptive account of amateur music societies, sees ageing as

> one problem [that] affects all societies sooner or later, and I know of no perfect solution. What is to happen to the old friends, past pillars of the Society, still enjoying themselves and anxious to go on helping, but now falling behind in technique and energy?... if the Society acquires the reputation of collecting experienced but ageing members, particularly in the key positions, then young people will not be attracted and the Society must eventually collapse.[4]

The ageing picture is unevenly spread. For some time now there has been concern that the long-term decline in church and school singing (accompanied by the expansion in instrumental teaching in schools – see Table 4.1) has served to reduce the number of young people with choral training joining choirs. Evidence of such a decline comes from a survey commissioned by the British Federation of Young Choirs (BFYC). The survey findings, based on a 33 per cent response to a 10,000-sample postal questionnaire survey of primary and secondary schools in the maintained and independent sectors, revealed that three-quarters of secondary schools felt there had been a decline in the quantity of choral singing over the last 10 years and 86 per cent no longer offered choral singing as part of the curriculum.[5]

A recent article in *The Independent* painted a particularly gloomy picture of the effect on ageing on the future of Welsh male voice choirs.[6] Evidence from the Welsh Amateur Music Federation's surveys of its societies' memberships gives a clear indication of the relatively ageing profile of Welsh male voice choirs. Only 6 per cent of the membership of 96 choirs were under 30 in 1991; 63 per cent were between 30 and 59; and 32 per cent were over 60. Moreover, whilst the figures are not strictly comparable, a similar survey of 64 choirs undertaken in 1982 gave 11 per cent of membership under 30, 72 per cent of membership between 30 and 59, and only 17 per cent over 60 (see Table 3.5). One reason why male voice choirs tend to be elderly is that tuition in part singing has declined with the decline of chapel-going.

3.5 Welsh Amateur Music Federation: male voice choirs' membership, by age, 1982 and 1991(a)

	Under 30		30-59		60 & over		Total
South East(b)							
1991	111	(5)	1,479	(62)	803	(34)	2,393 (100)
West(c)							
1991	128	(6)	1,324	(62)	682	(32)	2,134 (100)
North(d)							
1991	106	(8)	862	(65)	368	(28)	1,336 (100)
All(e)							
1982	457	(11)	2,993	(72)	688	(17)	4,138 (100)
1991	345	(6)	3,665	(63)	1,853	(32)	5,863 (100)

Source: Welsh Amateur Music Federation.

(a) Percentages are given in brackets.

(b) Number in sample: 38.

(c) Number in sample: 33.

(d) Number in sample: 25.

(e) Number in sample: 1982, 64; 1991, 96.

But if the average age of the typical Welsh male voice choir is increasing steadily, the same cannot be said of brass bands. For 65 brass bands giving details of the age structure of their playing members in 1991, 65 per cent of their membership was under 30; 31 per cent were aged 30 to 59 and only 4 per cent were 60 and over. Comparative figures for 1982 reveal only a small change in the age structure of the membership over the period (Table 3.6).

3.6   Welsh Amateur Music Federation: brass band membership, by age 1982 and 1991(a)

	Under 30	30-59	60 & over	Total
South East(b)				
1982	875 (64)	410 (30)	81 (6)	1,366 (100)
1991	780 (66)	361 (30)	46 (4)	1,187 (100)
West(c)				
1982	446 (76)	130 (22)	10 (2)	586 (100)
1991	356 (61)	191 (33)	39 (7)	586 (100)
North(d)				
1982	405 (70)	157 (27)	13 (2)	575 (100)
1991	349 (67)	161 (31)	10 (2)	520 (100)
All(e)				
1982	1,726 (68)	697 (28)	104 (4)	2,527 (100)
1991	1,485 (65)	713 (31)	95 (4)	2,293 (100)

Source: Welsh Amateur Music Federation.

(a) Percentages are given in brackets.

(b) Bands in sample: 1982, 42; 1991, 33.

(c) Bands in sample: 1982, 17; 1991, 17.

(d) Bands in sample: 1982, 15; 1991, 15.

(e) Bands in sample: 1982, 74; 1991, 65.

One explanation of the younger age profiles of many brass bands is the existence of strong family ties within the bands' memberships. David Johnson, secretary of the British Federation of Brass Bands, felt that generally there was little shortage of young and talented players wanting to join brass bands. In Johnson's own band, the vast majority were under 24. But with so much emphasis on achieving quality and competitive success, many brass bands have little room for 'passengers'. As a result, there tends to be a greater degree of selectivity in the acceptance and placing of new younger players. As Ruth Finnegan noted in Milton Keynes, the musical director of a brass band wields a considerable degree of power in the band's day-to-day running.[7]

Socio-economic group

As with attendance at the theatre, ballet and opera, participation rates in amateur music and drama are greater in the higher socio-economic groups. But there are important differences between the two.

For amateur music and drama, participation rates are highest amongst full-time students, with 11 per cent of respondents participating in the 4 weeks before interview. Nor can this figure be explained away simply in terms of the number of individuals engaged in vocational arts courses; student participation in music and drama goes well beyond those registered for vocational courses. For the last year that the Department of Education and Science identified students in higher education undertaking all arts courses – music, drama, art

3.7 **Participation in music, drama, dancing, textile crafts and attending the performed arts in the 4 weeks before interview, by socio-economic group, 1986**

Great Britain   *Percentages of persons aged 16 and over*

	Amateur music/ drama(a)	Dancing	Dressmaking/ needlework/ knitting(b)	Attending theatre/ ballet/opera
Professional	7	9	52	14
Employers/managers	5	10	52	8
Intermediate and junior non-manual	5	12	51	8
Skilled manual and own account non-professional	2	9	49	3
Semi-skilled manual and personal service	2	11	46	2
Unskilled manual	1	6	41	2
Full-time student	11	24	33	8
Total	4	11	48	5

Source: *General Household Survey 1986*, HMSO, 1989.

(a) Excluding classes.

(b) Women only.

and design – as a discrete category (1984), they accounted for 4,400 out of the full-time university population of 256,000 (less than 2 per cent). Even taking into account the polytechnics and colleges, the figure for music, drama, art and design courses was only 7 per cent of the total student population. Full-time students have more leisure time than the working population; the GHS reveals that under the general heading 'open air outings, sight-seeing and entertainment', full-time students are more active than any other socio-economic group. However, whatever the reason – financial or social – the figures show that full-time students are more inclined to spend their free time creatively in the fields of music and drama rather than as part of the audience for the performed arts.[8]

3.8 **Participants in amateur music and drama and attenders at the theatre, ballet or opera in the four weeks prior to interview, by socio-economic group, 1986**

Great Britain   *Percentages of those involved*

	Participants in amateur music and drama(a)	Attending theatre/ ballet/opera	Total population
Professional	6	9	3
Employers and managers	17	18	13
Intermediate and junior non-manual	43	46	32
Skilled manual and own account non-professional	12	12	22
Semi-skilled manual and personal service	11	8	21
Unskilled manual	2	2	6
Full-time students	10	5	3
Total(b)	100	100	100

Source: *General Household Survey 1986*, HMSO, 1989.

(a) Excludes classes.

(b) Excludes members of Armed Forces, those who have never worked and those whose job was inadequately described.

Findings from the *General Household Survey*, and surveys conducted in Glasgow and Ipswich as part of *The Economic*

Importance of the Arts study indicate that involvement in the amateur arts is greater amongst the higher socio-economic groups. According to the 1986 *General Household Survey*, 7 per cent of 'professionals', and 5 per cent of 'employers/managers'and those in 'intermediate and junior non-manual' occupations had been involved in amateur music or drama in the 4 weeks before the interview (Table 3.7).

But, although those involved in the amateur arts are more likely to come from the higher socio-economic groups, the pattern of participation is less skewed than for those who claim to have *attended* the theatre, ballet and opera in the previous 4 weeks. Around 6 per cent of those participating in amateur music and drama are classified as 'professionals'. By contrast, 9 per cent of those attending the theatre, ballet and opera were similarly classified (Table 3.8).

But if the statistics point to the dominance of the higher socio-economic groupings, these figures confirm that involvement in the amateur arts is certainly not the preserve of one class. Ruth Finnegan's work in Milton Keynes found that different forms of music were not, by and large, the sole preserve of particular socio-economic groupings. Whilst some of the more formally arranged activities were drawn largely from the middle classes, other groups were of mixed composition:

> Contrary to some expectations, the findings on local musicians and their backgrounds in Milton Keynes in the early 1980s did *not* reveal any clear class-dominated patterns for involvement in music generally... Many of those engaged in classical music *were* from reasonably affluent, educated, and privileged families, but certainly not all....neither rock music nor brass bands could be said to be exclusively or even primarily 'working class'; nor was folk music (indeed, if anything, it was mainly favoured by the highly educated practitioners); while jazz and operatic activities were particularly heterogeneous in terms of social and economic background.[9]

However, those active in music-making were more frequently bonded by similarities in their family backgrounds. Many came from households where practical involvement in music was an established part of daily life. Ruth Finnegan felt that whilst social class was not irrelevant, as a means of defining the way people were involved in amateur music, it was unhelpful. The concept of *musical family* was a far more important factor determining the nature and extent of involvement in music-making than any concept of class.

Some statistical evidence can be found to underline the importance of parental influence as a means of stimulating active participation by children. As part of the Glasgow and Ipswich *Economic Importance of the Arts* surveys, residents with children between 5 and 15 years were asked which arts activities their children took part in outside school. These indicated that whilst

> the usual social differences were apparent... the most influential factor in determining a child's involvement in the arts outside school was parental interest. Children whose parents were not actively engaged in amateur activity were very unlikely to be involved in the arts at home. In the survey not a single case occurred of a child playing an instrument or singing in a choir outside school when the parents were not also engaged.[10]

So it would appear that active participation in the arts is in large part a consequence of parental interest. But the importance of child participation may well carry a greater significance for the professional arts. Research, largely conducted in Canada and the United States, has established a link between active child participation in the arts and attendance at performed arts events in later life. William Morrison and Edwin West examined a range of variables amongst those currently attending professional arts events in Ontario. Their findings suggest two things. Whilst exposure to the arts as a child as part of an arts audience was found to be a poor indicator of involvement in the arts in later life, active participation was found to be closely correlated. Morrison and West concluded that

> empirical results give the strongest indication yet that provincial and state arts councils should expand programs which encourage child participation... the arts councils should also consider the many local groups in existence especially those involving young people... Since amateur groups offer considerable potential for encouraging child participation.[11]

Additional work by Laura Dobson and Edwin West on the characteristics of the theatre audience in Atlanta has suggested more specifically that adult attendance is most closely related to child participation in non-school related arts activities.[12] This brings us back to Ruth Finnegan's point that participation in music is engendered through (musical) families, in which case 'child participation' is not the key variable in determining future attendance, it is parental interest and subsequent child participation. The key question then becomes: what are the influences which create first generation arts participants?

Regional variations in activity

The seven case study areas were chosen deliberately to cover differing parts of Great Britain in order to allow any regional variations in the nature of participation to show through. But one of the striking characteristics of the case study findings is the degree of consistency in the range of groups identified. Dramatic and light operatic companies, orchestras, choirs, art, craft and photography groups were found in all seven areas. Of course the number found in each area varied. But whilst some of the amateur arts are practised from Land's End to John O'Groats and from London to Derry, some are more closely linked with traditional art forms, and the practice of these does tend to have strong national and regional dimensions. One only has to look at the range of specialist 'umbrella' organisations in Scotland to get some of the flavour of the regional dimensions of the amateur arts.

But just as the amateur arts in the UK have become increasingly internationalised – the rapid growth of the barbershop movement provides one example – so the regional and national art forms have spread around the UK. Membership of the Southern Counties Amateur Bands' Association increased from 31 bands to 72 over the ten year period 1980/1 to 1990/1.[13] As the case studies reveal, the brass band movement is not an isolated example. The Exeter Branch of the Royal Scottish Country Dance Society was established in 1969. One of the morris dance clubs in Lewisham – Tylers Men – practise traditional Welsh dance; and the Bon Accord Cloggies, an Aberdeen-based group formed in 1982, practices traditional clog dancing from the north-east and north-west England. The increasing mobility of the population, better communications, and to some extent the facilitating role of national 'umbrellas' are likely to have played a part in the spread of traditional art forms from their base regions (although neither Tylers Men or the Bon Accord Cloggies were affiliated to national organisations).

The traditional cultures of Scotland, Wales and Northern Ireland remain very strong. But are there significant regional patterns to the levels of amateur arts activity in England (where over 80 per cent of the population of the United Kingdom live)? The information gathered in the case study regions and what is known about the regional spread of membership for some of the principal 'umbrella' organisations provides some insight into regional differences. There is certainly evidence of a continued regional bias in some art forms. But there are also indications of an urban/rural differential.

Table 3.9 sets out the group membership figures for 1990 by standard region of England for some of the main 'umbrella' organisations, adjusted to give figures per million population. Although the analysis of brass bands is based on the location of the rehearsal room, the membership of the NFMS, NAC and groups listed in the *Folk Directory 1990/1* is based on the contact address held by the 'umbrella' organisation or listed in the relevant publication. This use of contact addresses to locate groups may be one factor influencing the particularly low figures for Greater London (see Appendix A).

3.9   Membership of selected 'umbrella' organisations by standard region of England, 1990(a)

England   *Societies per million resident population*

	NODA	BFBB	NAC	EFDSS	Choirs	Orch-estras	Music clubs	All NFMS	Total
						NFMS			
North (3.1)	34.5	15.9	14.0	26.7	13.0	1.6	6.5	21.1	112.3
Yorks./Humber (4.9)	38.9	15.4	14.0	29.6	9.9	3.6	5.5	19.0	116.8
East Midlands (4.0)	25.3	16.0	7.5	32.8	10.0	3.0	5.3	18.3	99.5
East Anglia (2.0)	31.8	10.3	1.0	41.1	12.7	2.4	10.8	25.9	110.0
London (6.8)	6.8	0.7	0.7	14.5	10.2	3.0	2.5	15.7	38.6
Rest of South East (10.6)	38.6	9.3	1.7	40.7	23.3	7.2	11.8	42.2	126.8
South West (4.7)	42.3	17.6	1.3	53.1	17.6	3.7	6.2	27.5	141.9
West Midlands (5.2)	28.0	6.5	8.0	26.6	10.5	3.8	3.6	18.0	89.1
North West (6.4)	34.8	9.7	6.6	27.1	7.5	1.7	3.9	13.2	91.8

(a) Population figures, in millions, are given in brackets.

(b) Bands/societies, listed in directories rather than groups affiliated to the umbrella organisations.

The distribution of societies reflects a range of separate influences. The membership of the National Association of Choirs has traditionally been dominated by northern-based choirs and this is clearly reflected in the figures. But, as has been observed, the geographical focus of the brass band movement has shifted somewhat, and with 9.3 bands per million resident population in the South East (excluding London), this is just below the equivalent figure for the North West (9.7). But ranging from 15.4 to 17.6 bands per million population, it is Yorkshire and Humberside, the East Midlands, the North, and the South West regions which have a markedly higher number of bands relative to the resident population.

Of all the classifications listed in the table, it is the National Operatic and Dramatic Association (NODA) which has the most evenly distributed membership. The appeal of amateur operatics (opera, operetta and musical comedy make up an estimated two-thirds of NODA's membership) would appear to be a truly national phenomenon. Excluding London, which will be considered later, the number of societies ranged from 25.3 per million in the East Midlands to 42.3 per million in the South West.

Only for the members of the National Federation of Music Societies is there a particularly strong south-eastern bias. For all categories of membership of the NFMS, it is the South East which has the highest numbers of members relative to population. These figures exclude London, but if the calculations are reworked, and London is included, the South East is still the region with the highest recorded figure (31.9 societies per million population) within the categories of NFMS membership.

In general, the London area records some of the lowest figures for societies per million population; only for NFMS choirs and orchestras is London not ranked last. There are some obvious explanations for this. The low figures for bands and NAC members can in part be explained by historical and cultural differences. The low figure for NFMS music clubs (only 2.5 per million) owes something to the professional music scene in London. NODA also record relatively few London-based members, although this is partly a consequence of the way in which London societies have been identified (see Appendix A). The situation in London is part of a much wider picture which shows that there are considerably more amateur arts in rural than in urban areas. A more detailed regional analysis, by county, given in

Appendix A, reveals that, with the exception of Humberside, it is the metropolitan areas which have the lowest number of societies per million population. Conversely, areas of low population density such as Cornwall and Cumbria record some of the highest figures (251.8 and 210.5 respectively). This general situation was confirmed by the case study findings, once appropriate adjustments had been made to the distorting effect of student societies (see Table 3.10).

3.10 Case study groups by area

	Groups identified	Of which student groups	Total less student groups	Groups per 100,000 resident pop.
Aberdeen	46	7	39	18.5
Exeter	64	17	47	45.9
Lewisham	39	5	34	18.8
Powys	66	–	66	56.5
Stoke/Newcastle	78	3	75	20.5
Teignbridge	59	1	58	52.4
Telford	29	–	29	21.0

How can the urban/rural difference be explained? The case studies provide some answers. The prevalence of amateur arts organisations in Teignbridge was in part a function of the human geography of the area. Each small town had its own set of amateur arts organisations, and many of the smaller villages also had their own dramatic societies and pantomimes.

Variations in the provision of adult education might be another contributory factor. The England-wide survey of courses at adult education centres (1985/6), undertaken jointly by the Department of Education and Science and the National Institute for Adult and Continuing Education, analysed class types by London, other metropolitan areas and non-metropolitan areas (Table 3.11).

In 1985/6 London had more than double the national average of arts and crafts adult education courses per head of population; but the figure for metropolitan districts outside London (425 courses per

3.11 Arts and crafts based adult education courses, 1985/6(a)

England   *Thousands*

		Districts		
	London	Other metropolitan	Non-metropolitan	Total
Needlework and handicrafts	3.8	2.5	7.3	13.9
Art	3.8	1.6	6.7	12.2
Music, speech and drama(b)	1.8	0.5	1.2	3.5
Total arts and crafts	9.4	4.7	15.2	29.5
Arts and crafts courses per million resident population	1,400	425	510	620

Source: Department of Education and Science

(a) Figures are actuals for 80 responding LEAs out of the 97 surveyed. The figures in the total column do not equal the sum of the other columns due to rounding.

(b) Excludes dance which is included under 'sport and physical education'.

million population) was actually below the equivalent figure for non-metropolitan districts. So adult education provision, at least in terms of LEA-run courses, could not explain fully the figures for metropolitan-located societies outside London.[14]

References

1. *General Household Survey 1986*, HMSO, 1989.

2. John Myerscough, *The Economic Importance of the Arts in Ipswich*, PSI, 1988, p.112.

3. 'NFMS Three Year Strategic Plan' 1991-1993, nd, p.13.

4. Bernard Robinson, *An Amateur in Music*, Countryside Books, 1985, p.64.

5. 'Singing in schools survey – findings', British Federation of Young Choirs, January 1991; Andrew Fairbairn, 'Classroom singing', *County Councils Gazette*, May 1991.

6. 'You can't stop Welshmen singing, can you?', *The Independent*, 3 June 1991.

7. Ruth Finnegan, *The Hidden Musicians, Music-making in an English town*, Cambridge University Press, 1989.

8. Department of Education and Science, Statistical Bulletin, *Student numbers in higher education – Great Britain 1975 to 1987*, 4/89, March 1989; *General Household Survey 1986*, HMSO.

9. Finnegan, *op.cit.*, pp.312-14.

10. John Myerscough, *The Economic Importance of the Arts in Britain*, PSI, 1988, p.125.

11. William Morrison and Edwin West, 'Child Exposure to the Performing Arts: The Implications for Adult Demand', *Journal of Cultural Economics*, Vol.10, No.1, June 1986, pp.17-24.

12. Laura Dobson and Edwin West, 'Performing Arts Subsidies and Future Generations' in Harry Hillman-Chartrand, Claire McCaughey and William Hendon (eds.) *Cultural Economics 88: A Canadian Perspective*, Association for Cultural Economics, 1989.

13. *Directory of British Brass Bands*, Volume 3, 1980/81 and Volume 6, 1990/1.

14. Department of Education and Science, Statistical Bulletin, *Survey of Adult Education Centres in England 1985/6: Enrolments, Courses, Hours of Tuition and Subjects of Study*, 10/88, August 1988.

4   Music and folk dance

In amateur music, the classical, operatic, brass band and folk worlds are largely populated by societies which function as voluntary associations – they have written constitutions, annual general meetings and elected officers. This chapter deals primarily with the characteristics of the national federations which exist to represent their members' interests at the national level. But it has to be remembered that these four areas do not make up the totality of amateur music participation.

Ruth Finnegan's study of music-making in Milton Keynes breaks down music participation into seven categories. To the four listed above must be added country and western; jazz; and pop and rock. These seven worlds of local music 'were distinguishable not just by their differing musical styles but also by other social conventions: in the people who took part, their values, their shared understandings and practices, modes of production and distribution, and the social organisation of their collective musical activities'.[1] Whilst, as Ruth Finnegan points out, these musical worlds are by no-means mutually exclusive categories of participation, in that people may be involved in more than one area at any point in time, the headings provide a framework for analysis.

Whilst recognising the significance of jazz, pop, rock, and country and western as vital aspects of amateur participation in music, from the point of view of this report they present something of a dilemma. Firstly, the term 'amateur' has more complicated associations with large sections of the jazz, pop and country music worlds. In her review of bands in Stoke-on-Trent and Newcastle-under-Lyme, Jill Ebrey noted that, for most of the bands, the term 'amateur... seems to hold little currency'.[2] Furthermore, the concept of federations representing specific strands of local music at a national level, which characterises so much amateur music making, has no real equivalent in jazz, pop and rock. The only national organisation for performing jazz artists is the Association of British Jazz Musicians, with around 100 members. But since membership of the Musicians' Union is itself a condition of membership, this is in effect a fully professional body.

National 'umbrella' organisations in music

But although some segments of the amateur music world are not covered by national federations, classical music, brass bands, music theatre and folk music and dance are organised through a whole range of bodies, some of which have highly specialist memberships. The one attempt to establish an all-embracing national body for amateur music – the Amateur Music Association – failed to attract public funds and consequently collapsed.

National federations of local music societies divide historically into two groups. The National Federation of Music Societies (NFMS), the National Association of Choirs (NAC), the National Operatic and Dramatic Association (NODA) and the British Federation of Music Festivals (BFMF) all pre-date the Second World War. The oldest of the four, NODA, was established in 1899 with 'the express purpose of bringing together members of operatic and dramatic societies for their mutual assistance and combined benefit'.

The NFMS, inaugurated in February 1935, aimed to promote amateur choral and orchestral societies, to provide information, and to allow societies to liaise over music hire, concert dates and tours by musicians. The NFMS consists of three categories of member society: choral societies, orchestras and music clubs. Whilst there is some overlap between the memberships of the NFMS and the NAC, the two organisations started out with somewhat different objectives. The NAC, which has traditionally had a largely northern-based membership, was originally set up to represent choirs in relation to competitive festivals. Its membership was – and still is – largely made up of standard mixed, male or women's choirs, which usually give unaccompanied performances. By contrast, the choral membership of the NFMS is geared more towards choral *societies* and the serious classical repertoire. Both the NFMS and NODA have succeeded in building memberships well in excess of 1,000 groups.

Whilst the older national organisations have maintained and generally expanded their memberships, new 'umbrella' bodies have been established over the last 30 years, to represent what are increasingly segmented musical interest groups. One recent example is the setting up of the British Bluegrass Music Association in 1991. Two other examples of the growing diversity and specialisation of British participatory music are the growth of the barbershop quartet movement and symphonic wind bands. The British Association of Barbershop Singers (BABS) was set up in 1974 'to perpetuate and promote the style of four-part harmony singing known as barbershop (defined by the use of a lead singer singing the melody line with tenor above and bass and baritone below)'. Two years later, the Ladies Association of British Barbershop Singers (LABBS) was established with 7 British clubs as founder members. The establishmeht of both barbershop organisations is symptomatic of the increasing internationalisation of musical forms. The British Association of Symphonic Bands and Wind Ensembles (BASBWE) celebrated its tenth birthday in 1991. The growth in the number of wind ensembles has in part been a function of the growth in peripatetic music teaching and the increased popularity of certain woodwind instruments. The figures for Associated Board examination entrants for clarinet and flute over the 15 year period 1974-1989 provide one indicator of this trend. By 1989, flute and clarinet candidates accounted for 16 per cent of all examinees, double the percentage entered in 1974 (see Table 4.1). The symphonic wind band has provided a particularly appropriate performing vehicle for this expanded population of practitioners. BASBWE estimate that there are now some 200,000 wind players of school age and it recently set up an Education Trust to further their development.

A second feature of the move towards more specialist 'umbrella' organisations, and one which has parallels in drama, has been the establishment of national organisations devoted to youth activity. The UK has developed a strong international reputation for producing good youth orchestras. The National Association of Youth Orchestras (NAYO) was set up in 1961. Apart from acting as a forum for national, regional, county and local youth orchestras, since 1980 the NAYO has organised annual Festivals of British Youth Orchestras for member (and guest) orchestras. In 1990, these ran simultaneously in Glasgow and Edinburgh, providing a total of 42 concerts. Whilst not

4.1 Candidates entered for Associated Board examinations: 1974 and 1989, Britain and Ireland

	Candidates (000s) (grades I-VIII)		Percentages (grades I-VIII)	
	1974	1989	1974	1989
Piano	102	140	48	41
Violin	24	36	11	10
Other strings	7	13	3	4
Flute	5	28	3	8
Clarinet	11	27	5	8
Other wind	3	6	1	2
Trumpet	4	7	2	2
Other brass	5	12	3	3
Other instruments	2	9	1	3
Singing	3	5	1	2
Theory	46	61	22	18
Total	211	345	100	100

Source: Associated Board of the Royal Schools of Music.

competitive, these festivals do incorporate the Novello Youth Orchestra award for performances of contemporary works. The British Federation of Young Choirs (BFYC) was founded in 1983 and aims to stimulate and encourage young people to sing, principally through the running of choral events and training courses for their teachers. In 1990, courses were run for advanced conducting, choral jazz and vocal technique; national and regional singing days were also staged. The Federation was also responsible for commissioning some substantial research into the state of choral singing in schools, and since 1985 has organised an annual award for choral conducting.

Not all of the 'umbrella' organisations established over the last thirty years fall neatly into the category of either youth-orientated or specialist music bodies. The British Federation of Brass Bands (BFBB) and the Welsh Amateur Music Federation (WAMF) both date from the late 1960s but represent established parts of the amateur music movement. Measured in terms of its total income, WAMF is

4.2 Principal music 'umbrellas': date of foundation, group membership and staffing, 1990

	Date	Group members	Headquarters paid staff Full-time	Part-time	Regular volunteers
NODA	1899	1,900	4	2	..
NAC	1920	300	–	-	22
BFMF	1921	300	1	2	..
NFMS	1935	1,256	2	-	6
NAYO	1961	110	-	2	15
WAMF	1968	300	1	1	-
BFBB	1969	850	-	-	8
BABS	1974	53	-	-	30
BASBWE	1981	421	-	-	25
BFYC	1983	150	1	2	15

the largest of the music 'umbrellas'. It receives over three-quarters of its income from the Welsh Arts Council. WAMF's membership falls into 9 categories, of which the largest is male voice choirs (92 groups in 1991). Choral societies, mixed choruses and ladies/youth choirs account for a further 87 member societies. There are also 65 brass bands, 47 amateur operatic societies, 4 orchestras, 4 wind bands and 2 folk music clubs affiliated to WAMF in 1991.

The Scottish Amateur Music Association (SAMA) dates from 1958. SAMA is not an 'umbrella' organisation as such, but runs a variety of national courses for musicians. In April 1991, the second Scots Song Recital Competition was organised; the aim of this venture is to widen singers' knowledge of the vast wealth of Scotland's traditional songs.

What is immediately apparent from Table 4.3 is the disparity in the distribution of public funding. Nevertheless three 'umbrellas' – NODA, BFMF and the British Federation of Young Choirs (BFYC) succeeded in raising sufficient income from other sources to employ full-time paid staff. NODA achieves this through the income generated from its trading arm and a high level of income from subscriptions; the long-established British Federation of Music Festivals receives a regular income from investments.

4.3 Principal music 'umbrellas': income 1989/90

£ thousands

	Central funding	Local auth. funding	Subscriptions	Sponsorship	Other	Total
NODA	-	-	65.0	-	39.0(a)	104.0
NAC	-	-	3.3	-	0.7	4.0
RSPBA(b)	-	-	16.7	2.6	23.8	43.1
NFMS	12.0	-	43.0	-	22.0	77.0
WAMF	106.5	-	7.5	15.0	2.5	131.5
BFBB	-	-	1.7	-	2.6	4.3
BABS	-	-	29.6	-	6.5	36.1
BASBWE	0.9	-	9.7	-	6.9	17.5
BFYC	-	-	4.2	-	74.9(c)	79.1

(a) Net profit from trading arm.

(b) Excludes income generated through the World Pipe Band Championships, which included £19,000 of sponsorship and a grant of £25,000 from Glasgow District Council.

(c) Consisting mainly of sponsorship, grants and donations of £68,440.

Services

As has already been stated, an 'umbrella' organisation can be broadly defined as a body which seeks to promote the interests of local groups at the national level. Some of the music 'umbrellas' run education and training initiatives, distribute grants and organise competitions. Those 'umbrellas' which are themselves run by volunteers are inevitably more restricted in the services that they can provide. Table 4.4 sets out how the range of services differs between 'umbrella' bodies.

Specific services were important in attracting and maintaining membership for a number of 'umbrella' organisations. The NFMS list some 16 services which have wide variations in take-up – 90 per cent use the insurance scheme; 60 per cent the Performing Right Scheme; but only 15 per cent are members of the music hire scheme.

Tim Evans at NODA believed that the practical services offered, in terms of buying scores through NODA's trading arm and a tailored insurance scheme (the latter being taken up by some two-thirds of member societies), were high among the initial reasons for prompting

4.4   Services offered by principal music 'umbrellas'

	Grants	Insu- rance	Publi- cations	Training	Library	National events
NODA	No	Yes	Yes	Yes	Yes	Yes
NAC	No	Yes	Yes	No	Yes	No
NFMS	Yes(a)	Yes	Yes	Yes	Yes(b)	Yes
NAYO	No	No	Yes	No	No	Yes
WAMF	Yes	No	Yes	Yes	Yes	Yes
BFBB	No	No	Yes	No	No	Yes
BABS	No	Yes	Yes	Yes	No	Yes
BASBWE	No	Yes	Yes	Yes	No	Yes
BFYC	Yes	No	Yes	Yes	No	Yes

(a) In Scotland only.

(b) Music exchange scheme.

societies to join. The library service, however, had become less well patronised, partly reflecting the improved provision in this area by public libraries. NODA provides some opportunities for training through the running of an operatic and technical summer school.

As Table 4.4 shows, the majority of the larger music 'umbrellas' are involved in the provision of training of some kind. The running of training courses was considered by most of the 'umbrellas' as the most effective way of improving performing standards. BABS run a 4-day Harmony College as well as chorus director and quartet coaching schools. The British Federation of Young Choirs organises a range of coaching courses for singers and choir trainers. But as Russell Jones of the NFMS pointed out, ultimately the issue of raising standards lay within the control of individual societies.

Only three of the 'umbrella' organisations are responsible for the distribution of grants to members, and the direct grant-giving role of the NFMS is now limited to Scottish societies. Until 1985, the NFMS had received a grant from the Arts Council of Great Britain for distribution to member societies. In that year, however, it passed on this role to the English Regional Arts Associations (RAAs). This has not brought about a sudden drop in NFMS membership. Only two-thirds of member societies applied to the NFMS for funding whilst the Federation was administering grants, so for many societies there were other benefits to membership. Besides, grant administration was a time-consuming process for a small organisation and transferring it to the RAAs has meant that more time has been devoted to advocacy and addressing members' interests. This has been one aspect of a general re-orientation of NFMS activities since the mid 1980s.

The benefits and drawbacks of music competitions continue to arouse discussion. The Competitions Working Party of the British branch of the European String Teachers Association (ESTA) came to the following conclusion on amateur competitions:

> Among 'amateur' competitions, those which cater chiefly for group music-making, whether vocal or instrumental, appear to be enjoyable, often inspiring...

But although the report was supportive of the group side of competitive festivals, it added:

> It is impossible, however, not to have some reservations about the *solo* classes in competitive festivals.[3]

The British Federation of Music Festivals (BFMF) is the national body for competitive festivals in Great Britain (although it has only a small Welsh membership due to the strength of the eisteddfod movement). Whatever the criticisms of some aspects of competitive festivals, the BFMF strongly asserts the educational benefits which stem from the views and comments of professional adjudicators which judge the 300 or so festivals taking place each year. The National Association of Choirs acts on behalf of its members in discussions with the BFMF. Both the British Association of Barbershop Singers and the Ladies Association of British Barbershop Singers organise their own annual competitive conventions.

Some national competitions are organised outside the framework of the music 'umbrellas'. Since 1984, Sainsbury's has sponsored the biennial Choir of the Year competition. This regularly attracts between 250 and 300 entrants from around the United Kingdom and covers the whole range of choral singing from gospel and barbershop to choral societies and children's choirs. The British Federation of Brass Bands (BFBB) does not organise a national competition – that role is undertaken by Boosey and Hawkes Band Festivals Ltd – nor is it responsible for registration of bands (the British Brass Band Registry is owned and managed by Boosey's). Consequently, as an 'umbrella' organisation it exerts relatively little power. This is reflected both in its membership and its inability to levy a reasonable subscription level. Only 19 of the 24 area brass band associations are members of BFBB (and there are other bands active outside of the area associations). Subscriptions for member bands, paid by the area associations, are £2 *per band* – a figure that has remained static since the Federation came into existence in 1969. This compares to the subscriptions levied on individual members of LABBS of around £22 per person per year. The BFBB organised its first conference in 1990 to address some of the issues faced by bands during the 1990s.[4]

If the brass band movement seemed to have particular problems in organising its member societies, there were many issues which were common to most music 'umbrellas'. Except in a few circumstances, 'umbrella' organisations face a range of practical difficulties in organisation and management, for the simple reason that they are national organisations with voluntary national memberships. Inevitably, these problems are greater where funding and staffing are limited. But even where these national organisations are fortunate enough to be run by full-time paid staff, they still tend to rely on volunteer-run, regional structures to provide contact with individual groups. Training initiatives by regional committees of the NFMS exemplify the resulting unevenness of approach: although 2 or 3 regions had achieved much in this area, 12 had been irregular and '6 regions were pretty dead'. The treasurer of the National Association of Choirs complained of a similar problem of 'inactivity' in certain regions. For many of the music 'umbrellas', these problems were exacerbated by the fact that regional structures were outdated or simply not suited to the spread of the existing membership.

Organisations of instrumentalists

There is now a considerable number of nationally organised specialist groups (mainly of instrumentalists) covering a spectrum of musical interests. These cater for amateurs and professionals. Requests for information were sent to 15 such national interest groups in music of which 12 replied. Basic information on membership and date of foundation is given in Table 4.5. In total, the responding organisations recorded a membership of around 19,000. Although some date from before the Second World War, there has been a proliferation of these organisations in recent years. Indeed these musicians' organisations can be put in three groups in relation to the chronology of their dates of foundation: the Incorporated Association of Organists, the Organ Club (whose aims are more 'social' than the IAO), and the Royal School of Church Music were all founded in the mid 1920s. Between 1937 and 1967 recorder players, viola da gamba enthusiasts, harpists, and handbell ringers all formed their own organisations. Between 1979 and 1985 it was the turn of horn players, flautists, trombonists, bass and bagpipe players to form their own societies. Some of the newer groups have followed on from more established interest groups around the world (for instance, the International Horn Society and the North American-based International Trombone Association).

4.5   Selected musicians' organisations: date of foundation and membership

	Date of foundation	Membership
Bagpipe Society	1985	400
Bass Club	1986	140
British Flute Society	1983	1,100
British Horn Society	1979	300
British Trombone Society	1985	650
Incorporated Association of Organists	1927	6,000(a)
National Harmonica League	..	400
Organ Club	1926	700
Royal School of Church Music	1927	7,000(b)
Society of Recorder Players	1937	1,600
UK Harp Association	1964	600
Viola Da Gamba Society of Great Britain	1948	400

(a) In 97 local associations.

(b) Individual members only. The Royal School of Church Music has 8,000 church members.

Most of the organisations keep their membership informed of developments in their particular sphere through journals and magazines. But there are limits to the extent that national interest groups can actually further practical professional/amateur collaboration. Simply being a member of the same interest group does not necessarily further collaboration. However, the more active groups achieve this through running annual festivals or workshops, open to amateur and professional members alike. For the British Trombone Society (BTS):

> the integration of amateurs and professionals is one of our primary aims, and we encourage interest in every kind of music so that traditional barriers are broken down – eg between classical and jazz... The BTS has tended to be run by professionals so far, but as official jobs change hands young amateurs and students are becoming involved. We welcome this. During our fourth year, we staged the 18th International Trombone Workshop...when many of the world's greatest performers, teachers, and academics were on hand for both amateurs and professionals to learn from and meet.[5]

Talking about the annual British Horn Society Festival, the horn player Tony Halstead claimed that the Festival:

> now fulfils an important function. The horn festival can be educational. For example horn players are prone to muscular, mental and physical fatigue... I think the British Horn Society gives the opportunity for people to sit down and discuss their problems.[6]

Another example of shared activity between amateurs and professionals can be found in the Incorporated Association of Organists (IAO). The IAO has 6,000 members in 97 local associations:

> The professionals and amateurs in our association work together in complete harmony (no pun intended!). The IAO Council consists at present of 17 professionals and 15 amateurs plus 12 non-voting past presidents who are all distinguished professionals... Our experience is that the professional organists are unfailingly generous in their help to amateurs and particularly to young learners. This has been a notable feature of National Learn-the-Organ Year 1990 which has encouraged over 1,800 people to register as prospective learners. This ready co-operation is also apparent at our annual congress, attended by nearly 200 delegates. The organisation is done mostly by amateur members, while the performances are given mostly by professionals, but socially all co-exist very happily throughout the week.[7]

Traditional music, song and dance

In England, the largest of the folk dance and song 'umbrella' organisations is the English Folk Dance and Song Society (EFDSS), formed in 1932 by the amalgamation of the Folk Song Society (founded 1898) and the English Folk Dance Society (1911). It lists its principal objectives as being to preserve English folk dances, songs and folk music; to encourage their practice in traditional forms; to expand knowledge of them by classes, demonstrations and festivals; and to promote and encourage research into the development and practice of folk song, dance and music. The EFDSS receives a small grant (£18,172 in 1989/90) from the Sports Council and just over £1,000 from local authorities. A third of its income comes from donations and investments, about a quarter from subscriptions, and it receives some funds from the operation of its London headquarters, Cecil Sharp House, the home of the Vaughan Williams Library, a unique collection of material on English folklore. The EFDSS is still suffering the effects of the row that blew up in the late 1980s largely on the question of whether the Society should or should not sell Cecil Sharp House. Partly because of this row and partly for other reasons individual membership of the Society declined from 10,600 in 1980 to 5,800 in 1990.

The Morris Ring, Morris Federation, Open Morris and Welsh Folk Dance Society are all voluntarily run and financed almost entirely through members' subscriptions. The Morris Ring is exclusively for men's Morris clubs and teams; the Morris Federation started life in 1975 as the Women's Morris Federation, but since its change of name to the Morris Federation (1983), it now actively encourages male, female and mixed sides. A third organisation, Open Morris, dates from

4.6 Folk clubs in England

	1979	1981	1985	1991
Folk song clubs	513	565	423	410
Social dance	430	471	528	486
Ritual dance	361	404	538	714
Total	1,304	1,440	1,489	1,610

Source: English Folk Dance and Song Society, *Folk Directory*.

1979. Open Morris has a more informal, family-based, and less academic approach to morris dancing; it has no restrictions whatever on membership. There is a limited degree of over-lapping between memberships of these various national groupings.[8] Table 4.6 shows the decline in the number of folk song clubs and the increase in the number of folk dance clubs in the 1980s.

4.7 Traditional music, song and dance 'umbrellas'

Group	Date	Group members	Headquarters paid staff Full-time	Part-time	Regular volunteers
English Folk Song and Dance Society	1932	250	6	4	12
The Morris Ring	1934	275(a)	-	-	..
The Morris Federation(b)	1975	258	-	-	6
Open Morris	1979	70	-	-	..
Welsh Folk Dance Society	1949	30	-	-	8
TMSA	1966	50	1	-	6
RSPBA	1930	400	2	-	c200
Royal Scottish Country Dance Society	1923	539(c)	..	..	..

(a) 185 members and 90 associates.

(b) Founded as the Women's Morris Federation.

(c) Includes overseas members.

Since 1987 the Traditional Music and Song Association of Scotland (TMSA) has received a grant from the Scottish Arts Council towards the cost of employing a paid administrator in the post of development officer. The TMSA has a wide-ranging membership and acts as an association of all involved in the traditional arts in Scotland: organisers, performers, festivals and ceilidh-goers. It developed from what was a largely rural association of folk festivals. These rural festivals were usually run by amateurs for amateurs, but the growth of urban festivals whose aims and functions are quite different has brought out some professional/amateur tensions. In addition to its own branch structure, the TMSA has affiliates, and less formal links with a whole range of sub-groups – folk clubs, accordion and fiddle clubs, strathspey and reel societies, and festivals. Aside from its wider promoting role, the Association organises an annual competitive festival.

The Royal Scottish Pipe Band Association (RSPBA) was formed by various Scottish bands in 1930 – the 'Royal' was added in 1980 – has a playing membership of around 400 bands in the UK and, for competition purposes, keeps a registry of the bands' 12,000 members. The annual world championships attract 4-5,000 players and an estimated total audience of 25,000.

The Royal Scottish Country Dance Society has a worldwide membership of over 28,000 people. One important aspect of the Society's work is the organisation of summer schools. These began in 1927 and they currently attract about 1,000 participants each year.

References

1. Ruth Finnegan, *The Hidden Musicians, Music-making in an English town*, Cambridge University Press, 1989, pp.31-2.

2. Jill Ebrey, 'Played in Stoke', mimeo., March 1991.

3. *Music competitions: A report*, ESTA (British branch), 1984.

4. Gary Newborough, 'Brass Bands in the 1990's', conference report for 1990, BFBB, undated.

5. Letter from Anthony Parsons, 4 December 1990.

6. 'Great Bells of Fire', *Classical Music*, 23 March 1991.

7. Letter from Roger Bishton, 7 December 1990.

8. For recent accounts of the organisation of contemporary morris dancing, see *The Evolving Morris*, proceedings of a one-day conference held on 20 October 1990, published by the Morris Ring and the Morris Federation.

5 Drama

The Central Council for Amateur Theatre (CCAT) was established in 1976 when the national amateur theatre organisations agreed to co-operate to pursue common objectives. CCAT meets twice yearly to exchange information and discuss matters of common interest. CCAT has provided a vital function in bringing together nationally based theatre organisations and in enabling them to speak with one voice when required. For example it has partly been through the survey work of the CCAT that the interdependence of the professional and amateur theatre has become more widely appreciated.

The full members of the CCAT are the All-England Theatre Festival, the Civil Service Drama Association, the Drama Association of Wales, the Guild of Drama Adjudicators, the Little Theatre Guild of Great Britain, the National Drama Festivals Association, Radius, and the Scottish Community Drama Association. There are also six associate members of CCAT, of which three are armed forces organisations.

Until its collapse in autumn 1990, the British Theatre Association (BTA) was a member of the CCAT. The BTA (formerly known as the British Drama League) had served both the professional and amateur theatre for more than seventy years, but, although funded for a time by the Arts Council of Great Britain, never attracted sustained public financial support. After going into liquidation the BTA's huge library was split up – the playscripts going to south Wales, under the auspices of the Drama Association of Wales, and the bulk of the archive and reference library going to the National Museum of the Performing Arts, formerly the Theatre Museum, in London's Covent Garden.

The death of the BTA has left a gap in the training and advice services available to amateur drama groups in England, as well as reducing the accessibility of playscripts and other resources for such groups. But the BTA's collapse can also serve to highlight the precarious and inconsistent way in which the organisations servicing amateur drama in the United Kingdom are funded. The CCAT has been heavily dependent on funding from the Carnegie UK Trust. Table 5.1 gives staff, membership and income figures for the Scottish Community Drama Association (SCDA), founded in 1926; the Drama Association of Wales (DAW), which began life in the 1930s as the drama department of the Council of Social Service for Wales; and the Northern Amateur Theatre Association (NATA) which was founded in Northern Ireland in 1979.

Of these three organisations it is the DAW that provides the widest range of services. Its director writes:

> DAW exists to increase public access to drama that is enjoyed and of a high standard. DAW works at the interface between amateur and professional and forges links between them. Services: playscript library, lighting hire, drapes hire, networking and information, small grants, typesetting and printing, training programmes, festivals and competitions and representation.

The Scottish Community Drama Association employs

> two professional advisers for workshops etc. We have five libraries of playscripts sited throughout Scotland. Headquarters will provide information, advice and contacts to any members/groups needing assistance. We run national one act and full-length festivals and playwriting competitions.

The main functions of NATA are to develop a programme of training and workshops to improve skills and raise standards; to help new societies; to promote self-help and co-operation among groups; and to lobby on behalf of the activities of amateur theatre.

In addition to these nationally based service organisations there are three bodies concerned in their different ways with the organisation and adjudication of drama festivals: the All England Theatre Festival, the National Drama Festivals Association, and the Guild of Drama Adjudicators.

5.1 'Umbrella' organisations for amateur drama in Scotland, Wales and Northern Ireland

Name	Membership Groups	Individuals	Full-time staff	Income 1989/90(£s) Total	Public
SCDA	224	733	2	39,763	24,500(a)
DAW	172	70	3	49,896	36,780(b)
NATA	20	6	–	9,923	6,553(c)

Sources of public funding:

(a) Scottish Office Education Department £24,000; Edinburgh District Council £500

(b) Welsh Arts Council £33,280; South East Wales Arts Association £1,000; North Wales Arts Association £1,000; Development Board for Rural Wales £1,500

(c) Arts Council of Northern Ireland £6,553

The objective of the All England Theatre Festival is to encourage amateur drama groups to achieve higher standards of production and performance by the organisation of a countrywide one-act drama festival.

The National Drama Festivals Association was founded in 1964 with 18 member festivals. The Association's *Directory for 1991* gives details of the Association's 47 full members, who between them are organising 36 one-act festivals and 21 festivals for full-length plays in 1991. Of the 47 members, 36 are in England, 7 in Wales, 2 in Northern Ireland, one in the Isle of Man, and one, the Festival of European Anglophone Theatrical Societies, has no fixed abode. One of the Association's objectives is to raise the standard of drama festivals; to this end it helps to organise the British 'All Winners' Invitation Festival, which is held over two weekends and hosted by a different Member Festival each year. Winners of four full-length festivals and six one-act festivals are invited to participate.

The Guild of Drama Adjudicators (GODA) was founded in 1947; its 135 members aim to improve the standards of amateur theatre by providing high-quality adjudications at drama festivals. GODA organises a biennial conference on a theme of importance to the amateur theatre, and a yearly 'entrance conference' at which candidates receive instruction and assessment for membership in the nature and method of adjudication.

LTG and Radius

All these organisations are run by volunteers, as is the Little Theatre Guild of Great Britain (LTG), which was founded in 1946, and which consists of independent amateur theatre groups (65 in 1989/90) which control and, in most cases, own their own theatres. Conferences, workshops and seminars are organised both nationally and regionally. Between them the 61 theatres which supplied information for the year ending 31 August 1990 put on 457 productions, and took approximately £1.5 million at the box office from audiences totalling about 500,000 in that year. Overall the productions played to 76 per cent capacity; the average seating capacity of the theatres controlled by LTG members is 184, with seating capacities ranging in size from 62 at the Barn in Moulton, near Northampton, to 468 at the Grand Theatre, Lancaster. In October 1991 the LTG is involved in a remarkable innovation in British theatrical life – the simultaneous production by 50 of its members of the John Godber play *Happy Families* (see Chapter 13).

Radius, the Religious Drama Society of Great Britain, was formed in 1929 to encourage all drama which throws light on the human condition and to help churches and educational institutions to use such drama for Christian understanding and communication. It runs training courses, holds a large library of religious and other drama, publishes plays and a quarterly magazine. Radius has 800 members (individuals and groups); its London office and library are staffed by a part-time administrative secretary and six volunteers.

NAYT

The last decade has witnessed the remarkable growth of the National Association of Youth Theatres (NAYT). Founded in 1982, and from an organisation with a few dozen members in 1985, the NAYT has grown to a position where there are 350 groups in membership. A Department of Education and Science grant of £15,000 in 1989/90 was increased to £35,000 for each of the two years 1990/91 and 1991/2; NAYT organises conferences, workshops, and training courses, runs a script and resource library, produces a newsletter and other publications, and aims 'to achieve a well-run, well-equipped year-round youth theatre within easy travelling distance of every young person in the UK'. NAYT administers the New Initiatives Fund. The Fund was set up in 1989, and in three years provided financial support for more than 40 innovative youth theatre projects throughout the UK.

Based in Birmingham, the Association employs two full-time members of staff; in addition a full-time fund-raiser was employed from July 1991, and a part-time rural development officer works to strengthen the growth of youth theatre where support is weak or dispersed. In recent years NAYT has built up a computerised database of information about youth theatre in the UK. Appendix C contains facts and figures specially provided from that database for this study.

6 Organisations of craftspeople

The very useful *Arts Address Book*[1] lists dozens of interest groups in different art forms. Many of these groups are national organisations, and some also have a strong international membership. In most cases, they could not be accurately described as either trade unions or as professional bodies. A few are exclusive organisations, or have a membership stratified by experience or ability; they are, for the most part, organisations of enthusiasts, many of whom are highly qualified, and most of whom have a strong commitment to a particular artform and/or to working with particular materials. In most cases no distinction is drawn between those practising at different ends of the professional/amateur continuum. Indeed most of these specialist organisations offer opportunities for amateurs and professionals to learn from each other, even if the opportunities for such learning are not as widespread or as frequent as some of the less experienced members might like.

A short questionnaire was sent to 33 national organisations of craftspeople listed in the *Arts Address Book* from whom 27 replies were received (an 82 per cent response rate).

It can be seen from Table 6.1 that all the organisations of craftspeople have been founded this century, and that between them the 27 organisations listed have more than 40,000 members. These organisations can be looked at in terms of their histories and the economics and popularity of the particular crafts practised by their members. Most of the organisations can be classified into three broad groups.

6.1 National organisations of craftspeople

	Year of foundation	No. of members	Annual subscription UK members, 1990
Association of Guilds of Weavers, Spinners and Dyers	1955	5,376	Various
Basketmakers Association	1975	500	£10
Batik Guild	1986	160	£12
British Artist Blacksmiths Association	c.1978	350	£40 families £15 students/ apprentices
British Doll Artists Association	1979	36	£12
British Origami Society	1967	547	£12 full; £9 students
British Society of Enamellers	1985	76	£30
British Society of Master Glass Painters	1921	395	£22
British Woodcarvers Association	1988	650	£12
Craft Potters Association	1958	760(a)	prof. mem. £46; ass. mem. £17.25
Embroiderers' Guild	1906	11,000(b)	£20; £12.50 (if over 60); £8 students
Guild of Craft Enamellers	1978	230	£16 families; £12 individuals
Guild of Glass Engravers	1975	610	£17 lay members; £30 craft members
Knitting/Crochet Guild	1978	1,200	£12
Lace Guild	1976	9,450	£11
Lace Society	1968(c)	1,250	£4
New Embroidery Group	1968	150	£10
New Scottish Embroidery Group	1981	64	£15
Pipers Guild	1932	280	£5-£12 according to choice
The Quilters' Guild	1979	6,000	£15
62 Group of Textile Artists	1962	60	£40
Scottish Crookmakers Association	1953	140	£2
Scottish Potters' Association	c.1973	200	£20
Society of Italic Handwriting	c.1952	650	£10
Society of Scribes and Illuminators	1921	2,500	£19
Society of Ornamental Turners	1948	300	£15
Thistle Quilters	1981	40	£12

(a) 600 Associates, 160 Fellows.

(b) 3,000 individual, 8,000 in 152 affiliated branches.

(c) As Lace Society of Wales; the Society became a UK-wide organisation in 1976.

Firstly there are those organisations many of whose members are making a living from their work. Examples would be the organisations of enamellers, practitioners of stained glass, potters, blacksmiths and calligraphers; with the exception of the British Society of Enamellers all these organisations are also open to amateurs or part-timers, but in most cases the organisations have more than one category of membership. For example, the Craft (formerly Craftsmen) Potters Association, which was founded in 1958 as a friendly society to sell the work of its members, has not only recently adjusted its name to remove the gender specificity, but is also being re-organised in order to widen the scope of its educational activities and so that it can include many more potters within its membership. It has also revised its membership structure so that it now has three categories of members: Fellows, who have to be selected or invited to achieve that status; Professional Members, a category of membership which is open to all practising potters and pottery workshops on the basis of work shown; and Associate membership, which is open to all with an interest in studio pottery in the UK and overseas.

The constitution of the Guild of Craft Enamellers states that 'the Guild shall comprise Members, Associates, Craftsmen and Fellows, in rising order of achievement'. The secretary of the British Society of Master Glass Painters writes:

> Our membership falls into three categories. Ordinary which is open to anyone with an interest in glass. Associates and Fellows who have their work examined by the Council and are awarded their status for the quality of their work. Associates and Fellows will have their names put forward for any possible commissions.[2]

Election to Fellowship of the Society of Scribes and Illuminators (SSI)

> demands not only technical accomplishment of a high order but also a mature appreciation of the finest historical models and techniques, and a lively adaptation of them for contemporary needs'.[3]

In 1952 the SSI introduced the category of Lay Membership which is open to all those who, by their interest and support, wish to forward the aims of the Society.

Secondly, the textile craft guilds also form a reasonably coherent group. As Alex Bruce and Paul Filmer found in their socio-economic study of craftsmen and women,

> textile work is the most practised set of crafts overall, but mostly undertaken at the part-time and semi-professional levels. As a hobby or handicraft the numbers must make it the most popular activity in the crafts field considered as a whole. Full-timers are mostly weavers and knitters, while other crafts such as quilting, embroidery, fabric printing or lace are mostly carried out at the part-time level or below. Most textile workers are women, for the historical and economic reasons that have combined to make it one of the least rewarded crafts financially.[4]

Between them the Embroiderers' Guild, the Association of Guilds of Weavers, Spinners and Dyers, the Quilters' Guild and the Lace Guild have over 30,000 members. As the report of a seminar on textile crafts in February 1991 put it:

> The constitutions varied: the Embroiderers and the Weavers, Spinners and Dyers had self-supporting, more or less autonomous local branches with various forms of regional structure and a national headquarters. The Lace Guild had an individual membership with many locally formed groups. Each national association had paid administration. The membership was basically amateur. The Embroiderers had some 300 professional members who earned their livelihood by their work, and the Weavers, Spinners and Dyers a smaller number. No-one could make a living out of making lace but some members gained useful commissions which brought in income.

> Most, if not all, guilds tried to prevent themselves from becoming exclusive and keeping away new and inexperienced people. They tried to create a friendly and welcoming atmosphere, organised in their annual exhibitions 'try and see' corners, had beginners equipment for loan or hire, such as lace pillows, and offered occasional free lectures and workshop days for potential newcomers. The three national associations had no stated equal opportunity policies. The Lace Guild had been concerned to help people teaching disabled people and to provide advice on ways to cope with arthritis and other disabilities.[5]

From its foundation in 1979, the Quilters' Guild recognised the value of a regional structure. As membership increased, so the regional organisation spread to cover the whole country. Now there are seventeen regional organisations throughout the UK each administered by a co-ordinator. Although their memberships are composed almost entirely of amateurs, at the national level the textile craft guilds have become professional in their administration. They recognise the importance of this in trying to raise the status of crafts that have certainly suffered from gender stereotyping, despite the fact that 'up until the eighteenth century the majority of embroiderers to kings were men'.[6]

What is perhaps most striking about the organisations of craftspeople listed in Table 6.1 is the growth of these interest groups in the last twenty-five years. 63 per cent of the organisations listed have been founded since 1967. Whilst some of the new organisations are exclusive, in that new members have to be selected by existing members, some of the new groups, as well as many much longer established groups, including, for example, the Society of Ornamental Turners and the Pipers Guild (which fosters the threefold craft of the making, decorating and playing of bamboo pipes) are organised around crafts from which it is extremely hard to derive any substantial income. These organisations could be taken to form a third group of organisations. As the founder of the British Doll Artists Association (BDA) writes:

> Dollmaking is a prime example of the confusion between amateur and professional; BDA is supposed to be for professional artists but in many cases this only indicates one or two sales per year... The purpose was to allow gifted artists to sell a few dolls – mainly to pay for their hobby! No-one expects to make much money.[7]

The British Origami Society was formed by a small group of enthusiasts who wished to share their enjoyment of origami. The Society's secretary writes: 'There are only a couple of professionals in this country – they are members of the society and we don't really make any distinction between them and ordinary members'.[8] Of course, as with all other organisations, people join the British Origami Society partly for social reasons. As the Society's brochure puts it:

> We are keen to give members the chance to meet each other frequently, and two national weekend residential conventions are held each year. Here our members learn new origami designs, exchange ideas and talk long into the night! Folding sessions, informal and

formal discussions, lectures and light-hearted games usually take place at our conventions ,which are attended by a high proportion of the membership.

What is of most significance from the perspective of this study is the extent to which, and the range of ways in which, all these organisations encourage their members, whether professionals or amateurs, part-timers or full-timers, to work together and to learn from each other about matters of aesthetics and technique, and about marketing and selling their work. For example, the textile guilds publish high-quality newsletters and magazines, and also organise lectures, day courses and summer schools. The British Society of Master Glass Painters invites all members to lectures by prominent glass artists. The Thistle Quilters, a small Scottish group, hires professional teachers to give workshops and 'the amateur members are encouraged to share their knowledge with other group members on an organised basis'.[9] The Scottish Potters' Association has 'a quarterly newsletter, 4/6 meetings/ demonstrations per year, with a big get-together for an annual weekend with demonstrators/party/AGM etc'.[10]

As part of the celebrations of its twenty-fifth anniversary, the Craftsmen Potters Association organised a major exhibition, in the catalogue for which Victor Margrie, a potter and founding director of the Crafts Council, wrote:

> The educational commitment of the CPA is considerable, the lecture programme and potters' camps have been of inestimable benefit to the highly motivated amateur. Participation in these events has often been the first insight into the generosity of potters and has provided an opportunity to discuss progress and problems in an atmosphere of dynamic learning that is rarely possible in the local evening class. The willingness of professional potters to give so freely of their time to those with less experience than themselves has been central to the success of the Association in creating a dedicated audience.[11]

Potters are one group of craftspeople who have formed their own autonomous regional organisations as well as having an effective national organisation. Regional groupings like the Southern Ceramics Group, the Midland Potters, the London Potters, and many others can be found throughout the UK; they have no formal links but overlapping membership with the Crafts Potters Association. One principal reason why such groups have been formed is that more and more craftspeople are looking for opportunities to exhibit and sell their work.

Another example of a regional self-help group is the Guild of West Midlands Artists and Craftsmen, which was formed in 1978 by a small group of local craft workers intent upon furthering the appreciation of crafts throughout the West Midlands. The Guild's main purpose is to provide a shop-window for its approximately 70 practising members, mainly through staging crafts fairs. The Guild's Honorary Secretary writes that the Guild prefers to use the terms full-time and part-time to professional and amateur:

> If we do use the term amateur, it would be used in, I hope, a kindly way, meaning the end-product was not yet of a marketable standard. There was once the suggestion that membership should be restricted to full-time craft-workers; this was rejected as the Guild was started by full-timers and this has subsequently proved a wise decision, as we find the full-time members resign when they have enough work to give up craft fairs.[12]

References

1. *Arts Address Book*, Peter Marcan Publications, Third edition, 1989.

2. Letter from Nicola Kantorowicz, 28 December 1990.

3. The Society of Scribes and Illuminators brochure.

4. Alex Bruce and Paul Filmer, *Working in Crafts*, Crafts Council, 1983, p.25.

5. 'Report of the Voluntary Arts Network Seminar on Textile Crafts', 5 February 1991, mimeo.

6. Joanna Banham, 'Subversive Stitch', *Crafts*, No.92, May/June 1988, p.44.

7. Letter from Ann Parker, 28 November 1990.

8. Note from Dave Brill, undated.

9. Letter from Janet Rae, 26 December 1990.

10. Letter from Stuart Whatley, 5 December 1990.

11. Victor Margrie, 'Craftsmen Potters Association', *Studio Ceramics Today*, edited by Emmanuel Cooper and Eileen Lewenstein, Craftsmen Potters Association, 1983.

12. Letter from Derek Fontaine, undated.

7 Visual artists and film societies

According to the results of the Research Services of Great Britain survey conducted for the Arts Council of Great Britain in summer 1991 (see Chapter 3), 3.7 million people claim to draw or paint, almost half of them on a regular basis. But they take up their pencils and brushes with very different aspirations, with varying degrees of artfulness, and at many different levels of experience. The first part of this chapter gives some information about the variety of organisations in the visual arts that either make no distinction between 'professionals' and 'amateurs', or whose activities and concerns span the work of both these categories.

There are many venerable organisations in the visual arts, the oldest of which is the Royal Academy (RA), a self-supporting body of artists and architects who hold loan exhibitions and an annual show of contemporary art. Founded in 1768, it consists of 50 Royal Academicians and 25 Associates. By the end of the nineteenth century the RA was regarded as the home of academic and conservative artists, a reputation that continues to haunt its annual summer show, which is open to both amateurs and professionals. Indeed the RA claims that it does not in any way distinguish between professional and amateur artists. The Secretary of the RA argues that 'art is certainly a discipline, and may be a livelihood... but it seems to me that the quality of the work overrides any qualification or distinction between artists'.[1]

There are a dozen other Royal Academies, Societies and Institutes of artists in Britain. Many of them are highly selective in their membership, but also organise open exhibitions and competitions, which can prove to be of great help to young or relatively unknown artists. Five of the Royal Societies in England, along with four other well-established and exclusive art societies, collaborated to set up the

Federation of British Artists (FBA) in 1960. The FBA runs the Mall Galleries in London, and each of the member societies organises an annual open competition. 'To give confidence and financial support to deserving artists' the FBA administers numerous competitions, with prize money totalling over £100,000 each year.[2] The Society of Scottish Artists, founded in 1891, 'to represent the more adventurous spirits in Scottish Art', has 400 members organised in three categories – ordinary membership, which is open to anyone interested in the visual arts; associate membership, which is for those under the age of 25; and professional membership, to which it is necessary to be both nominated and selected. At its Annual Exhibition the Society shows the work of 200 artists from all over Scotland.

7.1 Selected organisations of visual artists: date of foundation and membership

	Year of foundation	Number of members
National organisations for artists		
National Artists Association	1985	300
Association for Artists and Designers in Wales	1974	300
Artists Collective of Northern Ireland	1981	70
Specialist organisations		
Guild of Aviation Artists	1971	300
Guild of Railway Artists	1979	124
Printmakers Council	1965	500
Society of Botanical Artists	1985	200
Society of Equestrian Artists	1978	375
Slide libraries		
African and Asian Visual Artists' Archive	1988	110
Women Artists Slide Library	1976(a)	800

(a) Open to the public 1982.

Table 7.1 provides an illustrative, rather than comprehensive, list of organisations of visual arts that include both professionals and amateurs. All have been founded in the last thirty years. The national organisations for artists are all concerned to improve the status and economic conditions of all visual artists. In the case of the National Artists Association (NAA) the emphasis is on communication between artists. This is primarily achieved through the annual programme of conferences and meetings.

All these national organisations for artists – though predominantly concerned with the wellbeing of full-time practitioners – have struggled in the attempt to distinguish between professionals and amateurs. The Artists Collective of Northern Ireland reports that 'any discussion about professional status has involved very heated exchanges';[3] and the membership secretary of the NAA wrote that 'the term *professional* caused so many problems in the setting-up stage (1984/85) that we no longer use it in our literature'.[4] The experience of the Association of Artists and Designers in Wales on this point is similar; in its brochure it describes itself as 'open to all artists born, living or working in Wales'. The Association of Scottish Artists, formed in 1989, has yet to get off the ground.

The Printmakers Council is involved in both furthering the appreciation of all forms of printmaking and in supporting the individual printmaker. The five specialist organisations in the table are open to all. For example, the Guild of Railway Artists does not distinguish between professional and amateur artists:

> All artists within the Guild work together and learn from each other through special projects such as our two books combined with touring exhibitions... and members meetings. Instructional and discussion meetings are also held by certain area Groups of the Guild. It is also a policy of the Guild that if any work of art is rejected by a Selection Panel whilst selecting works for exhibition the artist concerned is made aware by either the chairman or one of the Panel Members of the reason for rejection and constructive help and encouragement is given.[5]

Numerous Regional Arts Associations and the Scottish and Welsh Arts Councils have built up slide libraries over the last twenty years. The best recent estimate is that 11,000 visual artists are represented on 37 different slide indexes, and 3,000 on 15 different artists registers. As Susan Jones, the source of these estimates, writes:

A slide index or register is rather like a marriage bureau. It has the potential to bring together artists and 'client' in a mutually beneficial relationship – the sale of work, an exhibition, a commission or paid work.[6]

The African and Asian Visual Artists Archive (AAVAA) and the Women Artists' Slide Library (WASL) are notable examples of self-help among artists, and neither distinguishes between part-timers and full-timers, professionals and amateurs. The co-ordinator of AAVAA writes:

AAVAA does not distinguish between 'professional' or 'amateur' artists. In relation to Black artists, the distinction is hazy and ill-defined, to the point of being worthless. If the term 'professional' relates to an ability to earn a living solely from one's art, then most Black artists would have to be labelled as 'amateur'. However, the term 'amateur' is more often than not used as a term of condescension, rather than to imply or denote something technical.[7]

There are a few regional societies of visual artists, but most of these would tend to define themselves as professionals. Merseyside Contemporary Artists is open to all, but only a few members may exhibit as a right. The Group's organiser, Janine Pinion, defines a professional as somebody who works consistently and develops over a period of time. 'Amateurs' are allowed associate membership of Merseyside Contemporary Artists.

Most visual artists – amateur or professional – are not involved in any of the organisations or groupings mentioned in this chapter so far; or in other specialist organisations for visual artists. Most visual artists work away in isolation or belong to informal groupings. Many more attend various kinds of adult education classes. Over 75,000 are organised in local art clubs and societies. For more information about local art clubs and societies in the UK see Appendix D.

Photography

All 7 study areas had at least one camera club and the majority had several; in total some 20 camera and photography clubs were identified in the 7 case study areas. Most of these were affiliated to a single umbrella body, the Photographic Alliance of Great Britain.

The Photographic Alliance is run entirely by volunteers and is made up of 14 regional federations or associations. Through these regional bodies, around 1,200 photographic societies are affiliated to the Alliance. With an estimated membership of 40 individuals per society, this translates into a total membership of around 47,000. Amongst its services, the Alliance keeps a list of lecturers and panels of judges for competitions which are available to all clubs by agreement with the individual concerned. But as the Alliance specifies, these are not usually professionals; the majority of judges and lecturers are amateurs who give their services free and and are only reimbursed for travelling and other expenses. The Alliance also organises annual print and slide exhibitions and a club championship (sponsored by Minolta).

The club movement only accounts for a small percentage of those active in amateur photography. There are a number of national organisations which individual amateurs can join. The Royal Photographic Society, based in Bath, has an individual membership of around 10,000. Founded in 1853, the Society's promotional literature points out that it is open to everyone – young or old, expert or beginner, amateur or professional, and no distinctions are made between the two. There are, however, different levels of membership. In order to become a Licentiate, an Associate or a Fellow of the Society, applicants have to submit work for assessment by a panel. The Society puts emphasis on the developing links between all levels of membership. Amanda Nevill, the Society's Secretary, writes:

> Within our organisation professionals and amateurs do work together. We have a very comprehensive programme of events which are run not only from Bath, but also from fourteen specialist groups and also fifteen regions within the country.[8]

There are other national organisations for individual photographers which cross the boundary between professional and amateur. The Bureau of Freelance Photographers has a membership of around 10,000. Half are thought to be semi-professional, in that they aim to supplement their main income from photographic work; one quarter are professional; and the remaineder are amateur. As in other parts of the visual arts, the boundaries between professional and amateur practitioners are not easy to draw.

Film

Amateur involvement in film falls into two categories: those individuals and groups active in film and video production; and those societies which meet to exhibit films (film societies). For the former, there are two umbrella groups: the Institute of Amateur Cinematographers (IAC) and Scottish Amateur Movie Makers. The IAC was founded in 1932 and has three part-time paid staff (the size of its group and individual membership are given in Table 3.1). Amongst the services the IAC provides to its members are the use of its extensive film library. It also runs a copyright clearance scheme in conjunction with the British Phonographic Industry and Mechanical-Copyright Protection Society for the use of commercial sound recordings by *bona fide* amateur film-makers; and it organises various national events each year including the IAC International Film Competition and the London Amateur Film Festival.

Film societies are represented at a national level by the British Federation of Film Societies (BFFS). The group membership of the BFFS was 287 in 1990, representing an individual membership of around 55,000. The group membership has declined during the 1980s – it had stood at 545 in 1980 – and this is thought in part to be a consequence of the spread of home video. Nevertheless, film societies continue to play a significant role in film exhibition. This manifests itself in two ways.

Firstly, as with other aspects of the amateur arts, film societies maintain a particular presence in rural areas. As the commercial exhibition industry has become more concentrated, so access in rural areas has become dependent on film societies. The British Film Institute (BFI) 1989/90 annual report notes, 'without these societies, cinema would not be available to many UK communities'. The second dimension relates to the range of films presented. Film societies provide opportunities to see films which simply do not get public screenings, outside the network of regional film theatres and those specialist venues in London and a few other metropolitan centres.

Although a voluntary independent body, the Federation has a close relationship with the Film Society Unit of the BFI. The Unit, which has a full-time staff of 5, was set up in 1982. Its principal contribution to the film society movement is through providing BFI staffing and resources (2 of the staff sit on the Federation's management committee) and also the provision of a grant (£9,000 in 1989/90) towards the running of the BFFS. The Unit itself, closely integrated with the Exhibition and Distribution Division, offers practical advice on the setting up and running of film societies as well as a range of other services.

In 1989, the Unit undertook a survey of its membership to which it got a 50 per cent response rate. In total, members of the Federation screened an estimated 5,206 feature films, attracting an average audience of 85. This is equivalent to a combined audience for film society screenings in excess of 600,000, almost half the annual audience for the network of regional film theatres. Of the three categories of society – school, ordinary and student – student societies have the largest memberships, with an average 674. School and ordinary societies had average memberships of 128 and 152 respectively. Student film societies were also found to be the most active, screening an average of 49 films per season.

References

1. Letter from Piers Rodgers, 19 October 1990.

2. Federation of British Artists, information sheet.

3. Letter from Colin McGookin, 8 October 1990.

4. Letter from Susan Jones, 15 October 1990.

5. Letter from Frank Hodges, 10 October 1990.

6. *Slide Indexes*, Fact Pack 2, AN Publications, 1990.

7. Letter from Eddie Chambers, 24 November 1990.

8. Letter from Amanda Nevill, Secretary, The Royal Photograhpic Society, 6 December 1990.

8 Young Farmers' Clubs, Women's Institutes and Townswomen's Guilds

The arts and crafts feature prominently in the activities of a number of well-established organisations, which have broad social and educational aims.

In 1990 there were 955 clubs in England and Wales belonging to the National Federation of Young Farmers' Clubs (NFYFC); these clubs had a total membership of 36,000, most of whom were between the ages of 15 and 26. Per head of population there are many more YFC members in Wales than in England (for information on YFC activities in Powys see the report on the Powys area case study). Drama and entertainment activities are organised around national competitions; every other year the National Farmers Union Mutual Trophy for drama is competed for by groups from all over the country. There are four rounds of competitions with the Final – for plays no longer than an hour – taking place at the Federation's Annual General Meeting. An entertainments competition is also held in alternate years.

A random sample of six county Federations in England was asked (a) how many of the YFC branches in the County entered for the national drama competition in 1989/90, and (b) how many of the YFC branches in the County entered for the national entertainments competition in 1990/91? The results are shown in Table 8.1.

8.1 YFC branches entering national drama and entertainments competitions

| County | No of YFC branches | Number of branches entering | |
		1989/90 national drama comp.	1990/91 national entertainments comp.
Devon	51	21	23
Herefordshire	18	12	11
Leicestershire	16	4	1
Oxfordshire	16	3	3
East Sussex	12	0	0
Yorkshire	63	21	14

In the case of Herefordshire, the county organiser reported 'approximately 300 members actively taking part'[1] in drama or entertainments. Many members also attend drama workshops throughout the year.

County Federations hold an annual rally which characteristically includes a wide range of visual arts and crafts competitions. In Oxfordshire, where 16 YFCs have a total of 478 members, there were 378 entries for visual arts and crafts competitions at the 1991 County rally. In Herefordshire, where 1,110 members are organised in 18 branches, there were 22 classes of crafts competitions involving 700 members at the 1991 County rally. Among the art and craft competitions at the Devon County rally in 1990 was a competition for a cartoon sketch of the YFC County chairman, and a competition for a 'Novelty Bra, Knickers and Garter from Farm Yard Scrap (for Competitions Chairman)'. Winners from some of the County rallies – though not from Devon's Novelty Bra etc competition – are entered for the national competition finals, the majority of which are held at a competitions weekend in October. In 1991 there were, among other things, national competitions in farm signs, mechanical toys, rustic carpentry and photography.

The NFYFC dates from 1932. The National Federation of Women's Institutes (NFWI) was founded in 1915 and has a membership of 325,000 in approximately 9,100 institutes grouped in 71 federations. The WI movement was built on agriculture and the crafts. The first full-scale exhibition of WI crafts in 1918 was an ambitious affair, and since its foundation the WI has been dedicated to 'the ideal of a national culture as a mosaic of regional diversity'.[2]

In the 1920s music and drama came to be an important part of WI activities and have remained so, although there is probably considerably less WI-based drama than there used to be. Some county federations have a drama festival, and 'Scene 80', an enormous theatrical event on regional themes, and involving over 100,000 people, culminated in four days of drama, music and speech at the Shakespeare Memorial Theatre, Stratford-on-Avon in 1981. The WI has gone in for these major artistic happenings every few years. In 1990 about 200 WI choirs took part in a competitive festival, with Sir David Willcocks adjudicating between the finalists at St John's Church, Smith Square. Most county federations have choirs, although there is no continuing training for choirleaders or conductors. However, a number of 'What no conductor?' days in the mid-1980s produced a small crop of newcomers willing to try their hand at conducting.

Federations and institutes vary considerably in terms of their involvement in the arts. For example, none of the 11 institutes in Telford New Town are involved in any of the performing and visual arts and crafts, nor are any of the 39 branches of the WI in the Brecknock district of Powys. However, hundreds of WI members enrol each year for courses leading to certificates in crafts, photography and drama production. And the WI is fortunate to have its own residential college. Every year about 5,000 WI members take 400 or so two to four day courses in a wide range of subjects at Denman College in Oxfordshire. The annual programme at Denman College has a pronounced bias towards the arts and crafts.

As Piers Dudgeon, the editor of *Village Voices*, the WI's portrait of the first 75 years of its history, writes:

> The life of the institutes has always been a learning process. But nowadays with external adult education courses widely available, and with the success of the organisation's own college, less educational work than before is undertaken in institute meetings. Many of the older members regret this, and recall how effective the instructor demonstrators were, and how much they would look forward to them, not just to learn but to participate... I have tried to show that the original education policy of the Movement was only partly practical, that its other crucial function was cultural – the lectures, the crafts,

the exhibitions, the demonstrations, the village scrapbook competitions, even the country dancing and singing, and village pageants, they all kept people in touch with their rural roots.

In many parts of the WI this policy continues today – the word 'Wales' in the following quote could be substituted for a number of counties in Britain – Mrs Rhiannon Bevan: 'Our policy at the WI is to help people to understand what Wales is all about. We have Welsh culture courses, and courses in the history of Wales. We have a 'Welsh week' every so often, and every year we have a weekend conference gathering when we tend to put on courses about folklore, folk dancing, traditional Welsh cooking, the history of the vernacular, etc'.[3]

The importance of the WI in England and Wales in maintaining a sense of collective cultural inheritance can hardly be overstated. In Scotland and Northern Ireland the equivalent organisations to the WI are the Scottish Women's Rural Institutes (1,138 institutes, 38,000 members) and the Federation of Women's Institutes of Northern Ireland (203 institutes, 10,000 members). Both organise a similar range of arts and craft activities to those promoted by the WI in England and Wales.

Up until 1965 the WI was pledged in its constitution not to institute membership in any place with a population larger than 4,000 – the so-called '4,000 rule'. In 1929, in order to block any moves to form urban WIs, the NFWI took part in deliberations which resulted in the formation of the National Union of Townswomen's Guilds (the NUTG). The NUTG expanded steadily for forty years, so that by the late 1960s there were 2,700 Guilds – 'which meant membership of at least a quarter of a million women'.[4] The beginnings of a new wave of feminism in the late 1960s and 1970s meant that there were suddenly far more organisations appealing directly to women's interests. Membership declined sharply, but has since levelled out at about 120,000 in over 2,000 branches organised in 116 Federations. The arts and crafts activities of TG branches in many ways parallel those of the WI – the occasional 'spectacular' is organised at a national level, like *The Golden Bond*, a dance and mime show specially written to celebrate the NUTG's Golden Jubilee in 1979. In 1989 the NUTG organised a National Drama Festival which had entries from 44 of the Federations, and in 1990 there were 76 entries in a National Music Festival. The former National Secretary of the NUTG writes: 'Most of our guilds are involved with some sort of craft, art, music or drama'[5]

– though it is clear that there is considerably more TG activity in the crafts than in the performing arts. The Honorary Secretary of the Exeter Federation of TGs writes:

> We have 23 Guilds in our Federation and most of them have Arts and Crafts groups. Members work for a big display at the Devon County Show and this year there were 555 entries with 137 Gold, 159 silver, and 165 red stars awarded. 11 of our Guilds have active drama groups... We hold a Playwriting competition for which a cup is awarded every second year.

> 19 Guilds hold Art and Craft classes, when various subjects are taught, either by Guild members who are expert in certain crafts or by professional teachers...

> 13 Guilds have music sections, although some only meet for music appreciation, as they find it difficult to get pianists or conductors. The others entertain outside organisations as well as Guild members taking part in the Federation Carol Service and musical events.

A similar picture emerges from other TG Federations. In the 17 Guilds of the North Staffordshire Federation there are 4 choirs; two of the 20 guilds of the Shropshire and Mid Wales Federation run choirs and approximately 12 others run Arts and Crafts groups, 'which can consist of anything in the Handicraft field, Floral Art, or Drama Groups'. Of the 20 Guilds within the Plymouth and West Devon Federation 13 have an Arts and Crafts section, 14 have a Drama section, and 9 have a Music section.

References

1. Letter from Malcolm Cox, County Organiser, Herefordshire Federation of Young Farmers' Clubs, 12 July 1991.

2. Piers Dudgeon, *Village Voices: A Portrait of Change in England's Green and Pleasant Land 1915-1990*, Pilot Productions for WI Books, 1989, p.55.

3. Piers Dudgeon, *op.cit.*, pp.172-3.

4. Caroline Merz, *After the Vote: the Story of the National Union of Townswomen's Guilds in the Year of its Diamond Jubilee*, Adprint Limited in association with the NUTG, 1988, p.52.

5. Letter from Mrs Rae Campbell-Tanner, 22 March 1991.

6. Information about the activities of Federations of Townswomen's Guilds have been supplied by the Honorary Secretaries of four Federations.

9   National and regional funding bodies

The Scottish and Welsh Arts Councils and the Arts Council of Northern Ireland are far more supportive of the amateur arts than the Arts Council of Great Britain.

The terms of reference that the Council for the Encouragement of Music and the Arts set for itself in 1940 included 'the encouragement of play-acting and music-making by the people themselves'. But its successor body, the Arts Council of Great Britain, has generally resisted direct support of amateur activities, having taken a policy decision to devote the funds at its disposal to support for the professional arts.

The Arts Council has, however, given indirect help to amateurs; for example, for many years substantial funds were channelled through the National Federation of Music Societies to provide professional 'stiffening' of amateur orchestras or to enable amateur orchestras or choral societies to engage professional conductors or soloists. Much of this responsibility was devolved to the Regional Arts Associations in the mid-1980s as a result of the *The Glory of the Garden* strategy. The Arts Council also provided grants to brass bands for them to commission works by professional composers. The Secretary- General of the Arts Council writes:

> Although it can't be quantified, the work in recent years of the dance and music animateurs supported by the Arts Council and Regional Arts Associations has also had a significant impact on amateur activity, as has the network of arts centres, which are now, of course, mainly funded at a regional rather than national level... Finally, it is

not possible to identify how much financial support benefits amateur arts activity via the Council's support of the RAAs, animateurs and clients, etc, though I can say, for example, that much of the £50,037 grant to the Notting Hill Carnival Bands in 1989/90 and some of the commissions for Asian music groups will be primarily directed to work with amateurs. Similarly, grants to some of the London and regional orchestras may include an element for their amateur choruses, but it is impossible to quantify this.[1]

In its Three-Year Plan 1989/90-1991/92 the Scottish Arts Council pointed out that 'although the Council's financial support for the arts is restricted to professional arts activities, the Council operates a number of programmes designed to assist amateur groups to have access to professional assistance of a high standard'. These include financial support to amateur drama groups, community organisations and youth groups 'towards the costs of engaging a professional theatre practitioner whose skills are seen as being of central importance to the realisation of a specific project'. Similarly, funds are provided to enable amateur, youth or community dance groups to engage a professional choreographer or work with the group on a specific project. In 1991/2 a limited fund is available to subsidise performances by amateur opera societies of infrequently performed operas; one of the conditions of this scheme is that 'professional artistic personnel must be employed' The Council's subsidies for amateur choral and orchestral societies are channelled via the National Federation of Music Societies.

The Scottish Arts Council also gives grants to a number of national organisations, including the Scottish National Association of Youth Theatre (£2,500 in 1990/91), the Traditional Music and Song Association of Scotland (£13,220 in 1990/91), the Scottish Poetry Library (£31,250 in 1990/91), An Comunn Gaidhealach (£22,800 in 1990/91), which mounts a large competitve annual festival, as well as a wide range of other initiatives in support of the Gaelic language; and the National Gaelic Arts Project (£50,080 in 1990/91) which has also facilitated the formation and development of numerous arts activities in the Gaelic speaking parts of Scotland. The Scottish Arts Council has also published *Helping the Arts* – a very useful directory of assistance for the amateur arts in Scotland.[2]

Amateur arts traditions are peculiarly strong in Wales, and the Welsh Arts Council (WAC) has a long tradition of support for the amateur artist. In 1991/92:

- £140,000, which amounts to 37 per cent of the WAC budget for dance, is being devoted to community dance projects.
- £108,000 is being spent on amateur music-making through the Welsh Amateur Music Federation.
- The Drama Association for Wales is receiving nearly £47,000; and the National Youth Theatre of Wales £8,500; additional amounts are offered for training.
- Guilds, craft groups and societies may apply for project grants; the department's newsletter provides a link between the amateur and professional craftsperson.
- In the visual arts, support for amateurs comes through artists in residence and some community arts schemes, and through Gweled, a society which was formed in 1984, and which aims to establish a living tradition in the visual arts that is an integral part of the cultural tradition of Wales.

Like the other Arts Councils, the Welsh Arts Council also does a a great deal to encourage and promote contemporary indigenous writing; WAC points out that in literature it is often well nigh impossible to express the division between the lowly paid 'professional' and the highly paid 'amateur'.

In 1990, in responding to the Government's request for a Corporate Plan, the Arts Council of Northern Ireland (ACNI) set out systematically the policies and strategies that underlly its operations. The document stated that

> the Council encourages participation in the arts by non-professionals through support for amateur arts, federations, community arts groups and programmes, youth dance and drama schemes, archival and promotional programmes for traditional music.[3]

ACNI sees its main role in supporting the amateur arts as providing professional leadership, and, in many cases, augmenting the level of arts funding that is provided by local authorities for locally based amateur and community arts activities.

ACNI has developed a particularly strong network of youth drama centres – there are 13 designated centres, run by people who have a high-powered induction and training, and who receive a support service provided by an officer of the Arts Council. In 1990 ACNI completed the first year of a parallel youth dance scheme, based on the creation of a number of youth dance centres. In 1989/90 ACNI spent a total of £60,000 on its youth drama and dance schemes, and a further £29,900 on community drama and drama training.

ACNI also provides finance towards professional support for choral societies, since

> professional training and conducting can result in the creation of 'instruments' of high quality provided there is competitive auditioning to ensure good voices.
>
> In the field of instrumental music and singing, the Council supports masterclasses that may be attended by professionals or by talented amateurs. Amateur chorus training is an important part of the work of the locally based opera company which otherwise is completely professional in every other respect[4]

ACNI spent £13,500 on amateur/participatory musical activities in 1989/90.

'Traditional Arts' – including traditional music, dancing, mumming, story-telling and crafts – are also strongly supported by the Arts Council of Northern Ireland (£66,400 in 1989/90). The 'traditional arts' are rooted in community life. Their practitioners, though frequently highly skilled, remain in the community with other occupations, though a few may make a living from their musical or craft skills; archival records play a vital role in conserving and transmitting traditions and styles.

The Crafts Council finds the term amateur 'unhelpful'. The National Strategy for Crafts document includes a section on 'status' which argues that

> the distinction between professional and amateur is especially troublesome in the crafts. This is largely because in craft (unlike disciplines such as the performing arts) the two categories have a tendency to merge. It is quite common for amateur makers to sell some of their work, while some professional makers actually sell little, or do full-time jobs outside the realm of making.

The document asks whether there is a valid distinction between professional and amateur craftspeople? In its Royal Charter and in a policy statement on 'The Crafts Council and Craft Education' no distinction is drawn between professionals and amateurs; rather the Council's mission is expressed in terms of advancing and encouraging 'the creation and conservation of works of fine craftsmanship', 'the promotion of the work of craftsmen', and 'the education of the public generally in the understanding and appreciation of fine craftsmanship'.

As with other art forms, the amateur/professional continuum in the crafts is certainly not straightforward or one-dimensional. As the Strategy for Crafts document points out, some craftspeople are pleased to be described as amateur, 'because the term implies that their activity gives them pleasure. Also it must not be suggested that specific exhibitions be confined to one category or the other; if the work is relevant to the exhibition, the classification of the maker is a triviality'. The Director of the Crafts Council explains that each Crafts Council grant benefits a different group of craftspeople as well as benefitting the general public in different ways. For example, in 1989/90 the Crafts Council awarded grants totalling £25,000 to the organisers of a Textile Arts Festival: these grants were for

> exhibitions and towards the whole event which also included workshops for interested members of the public (amateur craftspeople if you will). The grant to Gateshead [£14,000 towards the Gateshead Garden Festival] was to encourage the public to enjoy the crafts.[5]

In sum, whilst most Crafts Council expenditure directly assists those professionally trained and seeking to make a living from their work, those craftspeople lacking the qualifications, talent or confidence to work professionally can also benefit very considerably from the Crafts Council's work.

Regional Arts Associations/Boards

The Welsh Regional Arts Associations have generally given more support to the amateur arts than have their English counterparts. The North Wales Arts Association supports the amateur arts across the art forms, including projects undertaken in both English and Welsh.

Before their translation into Regional Arts Boards, the English Regional Arts Associations (RAAs) did not, for the most part, fund work which was entirely amateur, but concentrated their help to the amateur arts by supporting many kinds of professional/amateur collaboration. The Director of Eastern Arts writes:

> In the main, our brief is to support professional work, but we do aim to enrich amateur experience and practice through making possible collaborations of amateur organisations with professional artists.[6]

West Midlands Arts supported

> both financially and otherwise a range of amateur arts organisations in the region for artistic activities which involve them engaging professional artists.[7]

At East Midlands Arts a distinction was drawn between, firstly, amateurs

> as individuals or groups who seek to emulate professionals but do so essentially for their own enjoyment and entertainment and are not, therefore, seeking to develop a career or derive an income from such activity;

and, secondly,

> those groups and individuals who are seeking to attain professional status (to build a career and derive an income from such activity) but lack the experience, resources and skills to do so. However, these individuals and groups may still engage in unpaid arts activity.

Nigel Wallis of East Midlands Arts writes:

> Limits on our resources mean that our input into amateur arts activity should be focussed on professional input into developing and improving practice. Therefore, by necessity if nothing else, we find ourselves working within the second definition.

He listed numerous ways in which East Midlands Arts supported work by or for 'amateur' artists who are seeking to attain professional status. These included:

- The Literature Department offering three bursaries each year to support developing and unpublished writers.

- The Film, Video and Broadcasting Department giving priority to the development of film makers, script writers and others who are starting out in their careers.

- The Combined Arts Department through funding workshops and arts centres.

- The funding of the Artists at Your Service Scheme (a scheme for placing artists in an education or community context), animateur appointments and writers attachments.

- The Drama Department's funding of Directors' fees for Youth Theatre activity and a number of other projects.[8]

It can be seen from this list that there are a wide range of ways in which professional/amateur collaboration can be fostered, and has been supported by Regional Arts Associations. Inevitably RAAs have promoted and supported such collaborations with differing degrees of enthusiasm and effectiveness, and different levels of practical and financial support. For many years the Southern Arts Amateur Theatre Scheme (budget £5,000 in 1989/90) has provided funding for amateur and community groups to employ a professional director, producer or playwright to work on a project outside the group's usual range of activities. Preference has been given to projects requiring professional skills because of the adventurous nature, or scale, of the production, or because of the need for special training.

For more than a decade, and as a core feature of its dance development work, Greater London Arts has been supporting a selection of youth dance groups, including the organisation of a 'One Night Only' Youth Dance Event every December. But in November 1990 the Head of Marketing for Greater London Arts wrote:

> As demand for funding far exceeds the money available in the professional sector, we are somewhat loath to develop amateur arts provision unless resources are forthcoming.[9]

For 1991/2 Greater London Arts cut its Amateur Music Performance Fund, through which in 1990/1 30 orchestras, choirs and groups had received £60,500. The Amateur Music Performance Fund was set up following the devolution of responsibility for funding

NFMS groups from the Arts Council to the Regional Arts Associations in 1985.

Russell Jones, the administrator of the NFMS, has calculated that whereas NFMS member societies were receiving £414,000 from Arts Council funds in 1984/5, funds available from the English Regional Arts Associations for promotions by amateur music societies in 1991/2 amounted to about £371,000.[10] Thus it would appear that devolution of funding responsibilities has resulted in a considerable drop in real terms in these forms of support for professional/amateur collaborations. And the available funds are spread more thinly. Many Regional Arts Associations have broadened out their support for professional/amateur collaborations in music to encompass, for example, non-European cultures; some jazz and folk music; and some staged opera and music theatre.

It has already been argued in this report that a distinction can usually be drawn between community arts and amateur arts in terms of where the impetus to organise the arts activity came from. Did it come primarily from a group of people getting together to practise and enjoy the arts, or did it come from somebody – perhaps a community artist, community worker or adult educator – who is paid to take initiatives? Given that distinction, some RAAs have given much greater priority to encouraging community arts than to supporting the amateur arts. In a *Community Arts Review* published in June 1990, Cliodhna Mulhern, then assistant director responsible for planning for North West Arts, wrote:

> What is clear is that amateurs receive much poorer service from NWA than do 'community' projects. The latter are considered to be desirable in that they increase access and somehow reflect NWA's policy, the former do not enjoy this status. It would seem that the convenient labelling of activity into 'amateur' or 'community' has distracted us from the need to define the principles upon which we support any activity. Amateur arts activity constitutes a considerable proportion of the cultural life of the region. It is often the only arts activity available locally. Those active in the amateur movement are skilled, experienced and fiercely committed. They constitute an invaluable resource to the region particularly where rural arts development is concerned. Since the early '70s they have been perceived as unfashionable and their treatment within NWA seems to corroborate that.

Why amateur activity has suffered a lesser status may be explained by the prevailing notion that amateurs are middle-class (and therefore not a priority), cliquish (therefore not accessible) and unadventurous. In fairness we should acknowledge that if this be the case with some amateur organisations, it is also sometimes the case with community projects and often the case with professional arts organisations.

Cliodhna Mulhern went on to recommend that

we bring amateur activity from the periphery of our work and adopt organisational guidelines for developing work in the Amateur and Community sector. Those guidelines might prioritise, for example:

- innovatory work (new art, new partnerships, new approaches)
- initiatives which have open access (ie not a closed shop)
- initiatives which actively encourage wider participation
- skill sharing
- equipment sharing
- developing networks.[11]

Northern Arts has helped to establish a network of Local Arts Development Agencies (LADAs) partly to encourage

a wide range of project work that others might define as amateur. We would define it as work of quality. The LADA concept encourages participation in the arts alongside enjoyment of professional arts.

Certainly the range and quality of products coming from recently funded projects bears out the correctness of our stance.

Folkworks, the regional agency for folk music in the North, has utilised local people known for their musical skills by giving them a platform in other communities. The respect which has been given to them is a credit to their performance quality not their definition as amateur. Similarly with crafts making projects run for Asian women in Middlesbrough, work has been created that has allowed esteem to grow alongside confidence. Removing that work from the context of the community in which it is made without reference leads to inaccurate presumptions and unnecessary comparisons. The work in context is excellent.

The development of brass band music in the North has always been seen in the context of the making of music in the community. The quality of Northern Arts support for that is based upon a comparison of like with like.

It is not insignificant that crafts has proved to be such a consistently good example of our work in this area. The quality of work both technically and aesthetically has proved conclusively that a high level of residual skills and aesthetic sensitivity lies in all groups, whether they practice full-time or part-time. This was proved with the enormously successful community group and individual project called 'Hookey Matters'. Here the quality of the hooked mats (a traditional form of craft in the North) proved the value of trusting in the integrity of work produced in the context of the home.

A sign of Northern Arts confidence in the judgement of quality in context, or 'better art for more people', is the progress we are making in the devolution of funds to the LADAs. Local definition of what is good is, for us, far better than any artificial definition of amateur and professional.[12]

Whether or not they share Northern Arts' 'confidence in the judgement of quality in context', a priority for the new Regional Arts Boards should surely be to develop a clear set of policies and programmes for encouraging and supporting active participation in the arts, and to develop more systematic and sophisticated ways of evaluating those policies and programmes.

References

1. Letter from Anthony Everitt, Secretary-General of the Arts Council, 21 November 1990.

2. *Helping the Arts*, Scottish Arts Council, second edition, 1990.

3. *Objectives and Strategies*, Arts Council of Northern Ireland, 1990, p.5.

4. Letter from J. Kenneth Jamison, Director of the Arts Council of Northern Ireland, 6 November 1990.

5. Letter from Tony Ford, Director of the Crafts Council, 12 April 1991.

6. Letter from Andrew Milne, Director of Eastern Arts, 27 November 1990.

7. Letter from Janet Sisson, Training officer of West Midlands Arts, 19 December 1990.

8. Nigel Wallis, 'The Nature and Extent of Amateur Arts Activity in the UK', mimeo, 8 November 1990.

9. Letter from Robert M. Gordon Clark, Head of Marketing, Greater London Arts, 5 November 1990.

10. Russell Jones, 'Voluntary Music is Suffering Too', in *National Campaign for the Arts Newsletter*, No.21, Spring 1991.

11. Cliodhna Mulhern, *Community Arts Review*, North West Arts, June 1990.

12. Letter from Laurie Short, Planning and Development Officer, Northern Arts, 25 July 1991.

10 Local authority support for the amateur arts

PSI sent letters to a sample of 100 local authorities in the UK, stratified by type of authority (72 in England, 11 in Scotland, 8 in Wales and 9 in Northern Ireland) requesting lists of grants and guarantees offered by the authority in 1989/90 and 1990/91. The authorities were also asked to send full details of the help given to amateur organisations through rent reductions, publicity, loans of equipment, scripts and music, and any other help in kind. After one reminder letter, 53 replies were received (38 English, 8 Scottish, 5 Welsh and 2 from Northern Ireland). Unless otherwise stated the quotations in this chapter are taken directly from the replies to this survey.

I. Direct financial support
England and Wales
Channelling help through local arts councils and local arts associations is one approach taken by local authorities to assisting the amateur arts. 25 out of the 33 London boroughs have an arts council.[1] For example, Waltham Forest Arts Council received a grant of £14,750 in 1990/1 and also received £21,000 of staffing support from within the budget of the Libraries and Arts Department of the London Borough of Waltham Forest.

Outside London local arts councils and arts associations are also widespread. 8 out of the 16 shire districts in England and one of the 6 metropolitan districts responding to the survey mentioned local arts councils. If respondents to the survey are representative of authorities in England as a whole, this would suggest a total of some 180 local arts councils and arts associations in receipt of local authority funds in England. (This estimate is probably on the high side since responses to the survey tended to come disproportionately from larger authorities and from authorities with specialist arts officers. In turn such authorities are more likely to have assisted the initiative of setting up a local arts council or association.) And whilst closely associated with the development of local amateur arts groups, many local arts councils (such as that in Exeter) fund both amateur and professional bodies. One survey of local arts councils undertaken in 1987 showed that more than two-thirds of responding arts councils (42 out of 69) promoted both 'amateur and professional events'.[2]

In inner city areas in particular, the request for information about support for amateur arts groups presented problems for many local authority officers. In Islington:

> The most obvious one is the definition of 'amateur'. The other is that we have not in the past kept monitoring records which identify support to amateur activities in any consistent way. The problem is compounded in Islington by the fact that we support activities that could be described as amateur in several different ways – through revenue support; through small grants (approximately £20,000 a year) to community organisations which can themselves be either amateur or professional for activities which can involve amateur or professional artists, or both; and finally through assistance to community organisations staging events, which can range from full-scale co-promotion, to provision of technical equipment and support, all of which is hard to quantify.

> The easy answer is to tell you that in the current year we gave revenue support of £14,580 to the Tower Theatre, which is an amateur company with its own building (but due to be cut to £4,500 in 1991/92) and development grants to two classical music organisations, the Haydn Orchestra and Islington Choral Society. The minute one moves away from these traditional European amateur activities however the difficulties mentioned above begin to surface.

The London Borough of Lambeth gives very little assistance in kind to support amateur groups, but in 1990/1 gave over £550,000 in grants to local arts groups, most of them community arts groups, community or arts centres or resource centres rather than traditional amateur arts groups. Lambeth Council is proud of the Borough's multi-racial characteristics and promotes positive action to overcome racial discrimination. Many of the grants go to groups consisting largely of ethnic minorities.

The City of Wakefield Metropolitan District Council has two arts development officers who support the amateur and community arts through (a) the Wakefield District Festival, an annual event whose planning group represents all council departments and a variety of voluntary agencies and community groups; and (b) Wakefield District Arts, a local arts council whose function is to ensure a fair distribution of the money which the District Council makes available to assist individuals and organisations wishing to pursue, promote or develop some form of creative activity.

A generational difference between amateur arts and community arts comes through in some local authority policies. The City of York

> has a policy of encouraging community arts development which often means supporting professional artists and animateurs who work with community groups. This is different from the old-style amateur arts organisation which was and is a free association of individuals interested in a particular art form aiming to produce something that emulates the performances and styles of professional companies and artists.

Figures on amateur arts spending from *Leisure and Recreation Statistics 1990-91 Estimates*[3] suggest that, on average, the shire districts in England spend at least four times as much, per head of population, as the shire counties. 'Other than where an amateur organisation is considered of strategic importance', it is Cornwall County Council's policy 'to fund the professional input into amateur organisations only'. Lancashire County Council gives no grant aid to support amateur arts organisations. In contrast, Norfolk County Council's grants to amateur groups are made from two committees at arm's length from the County Council: the Norfolk Association for the Advancement of Music and the Norfolk Drama Committee. Between them, these two arm's length bodies received £12,500 from the County Council in 1990/1. In addition, the Maddermarket Theatre ('amateur players but with professional director and administrator running the theatre') received £5,500 from Norfolk County Council. In Hampshire, grants to amateur arts organisations are available through five separate budgets.

10.1 Local authority financial support for amateur arts in England and Wales, 1990/1

£s

	PSI survey of grants to amateur arts	CIPFA estimates
London boroughs		
Croydon	31,896	36,630
Waltham Forest	65,160	54,200
Metropolitan districts		
Newcastle-upon-Tyne	45,819	66,712
English shire counties		
Cambridgeshire	10,000	–
Humberside	17,211	262,000
Lancashire	–	–
Norfolk	19,300	17,375
Warwickshire	11,175	7,044
English shire districts		
Fenland	200	–
Peterborough	65,770	10,770
Slough	7,150	–
Thurrock	12,950	–
Harlow	14,500	21,040
Wealden	2,200	–
Maidstone	7,940	10,500
York	6,301	24,630
W Oxfordshire	4,260	–
S Shropshire	4,300	–
Rugby	11,600	4,260
Stratford-upon-Avon	3,047	–
Welsh counties		
Clwyd	11,500	490
Powys	14,200	–
Welsh districts		
Rhuddlan	835	–
Ynys Mon	5,415	250

In Wales, responding district authorities put in about three times as much to the amateur arts as the county councils. But how much in total are local authorities putting in to the amateur arts? In the case of 24 authorities in England and Wales, it is possible to compare the findings of the PSI survey of local authority financial support for the amateur arts with the figures printed in the CIPFA *Leisure and Recreation Estimates*.

It should be emphasised that the CIPFA figures are estimates and the PSI survey figures were also collected before the end of the financial year in question, and so may not be final figures. It can be seen that there are very considerable discrepancies between the two sets of figures.

Some of the discrepancies can be fully or partially explained. The PSI figures for Waltham Forest, Peterborough, Thurrock, South Shropshire and Rugby include grants to a local arts council or arts association. In the case of the CIPFA figures it would appear that these grants are included under the heading 'grants to arts funding bodies' rather than under 'grants and contributions to amateur arts organisations and activities'. The County Arts Officer for Humberside is confident that whoever filled in the CIPFA return for that county included some hefty grants to professional organisations under the heading of grants and contributions to amateur arts.

Again CIPFA has a separate heading for grants and contributions to arts festivals. Some of these have wholly or largely voluntary administrations but a largely or wholly professional programme. In other cases – for example the Royal National Eisteddfod of Wales – the core administration is professional but all the participants are amateur. So whereas, for example, in the case of Ynys Mon (the Isle of Anglesey Borough Council), grants of £3,400 are included in the PSI figures, in the CIPFA figures this sum is included under 'arts festivals'.

The CIPFA data are useful only as the broadest guide to local authority spending on the arts in general and the amateur arts in particular. Grossing up figures for non-responding authorities (the 1990/1 CIPFA figures had a response rate of 72 per cent), it can be estimated that local authorities in England and Wales contributed £3.5 million to the amateur arts out of a total expenditure of £300 million on the arts and museums. The figure of £3.5 million is a conservative estimate. As has been noted above, it excludes some grants to local arts councils and some grants to festivals and eistedfoddau. It also probably excludes much support to the amateur arts through education departments, as opposed to leisure and recreation departments.

Scotland

The pattern of spending by local authorities on the amateur arts in Scotland is not dissimilar to the pattern in England. The Orkney Islands Council seems exceptional. There are 19,500 people living on the Orkneys, but in 1990/1 the Islands Council contributed £18,630 in grants and contributions to the amateur arts – almost £1 per head. This figure excludes £23,000 offered to the St Magnus Festival, which has a mixed amateur and professional programme. It also excludes a guarantee against loss of £3,000 to the Orkney Folk Festival.

Of the regional councils, Lothian Regional Council gave grants totalling £102,560 to 15 different amateur arts and community arts events and organisations (and a further £65,280 to Edinburgh's Theatre Workshop). However the other regional council in our sample, Dumfries and Galloway, reported that its education committee considered that support for local arts organisations is primarily a matter for the attention of district councils.

The four district councils that supplied figures on grants to amateur arts organisations were contributing an average of 8 pence per head of their resident populations to those organisations; this compares to 5 pence per head on the amateur arts by the non-metropolitan districts in England.

Northern Ireland

Of the 9 district councils in Northern Ireland which we approached, only two replied. Both Fermanagh District Council and Lisburn Borough Council fund substantial arts centres, which among other things provide a base for many local amateur arts groups. Between them, these two authorities (total population 147,800) contributed about £15,000 in grants to amateur arts organisations in 1990/1, about 10 pence per head of population.

II. Indirect support

In addition to direct financial support to the amateur arts, assistance is often provided in kind. 16 of the responding authorities in England and Wales (37 per cent) mentioned one or more forms of indirect support given by local authorities to the amateur arts. The most frequently mentioned forms of indirect support were as follows:

• reduced hire costs or free use of venues (theatres/rehearsal spaces/meeting rooms) (mentioned by 9 authorities)

- assistance with publicity/marketing (9)
- access to equipment banks or free loans of equipment (6)
- free exhibition space (4)

Use of schools

The contribution which local education authorities make towards the amateur arts and crafts is two-fold: access to school premises and the provision of arts-related adult education. One indication of the significance of maintained schools premises for amateur arts activities comes from a survey of shared and extended use of schools in England in 1983 by the Department of Education and Science. An analysis of user-type by organised groups (excluding school use out of hours, youth service and adult/further education) showed music, art, drama, literary and other cultural groups to be 'common regular users of schools'. Groups in this category accounted for 15 per cent of regular use of primary and secondary schools. Only sports users exceeded this group (20 per cent of primary and 44 per cent of secondary schools). Cultural groups also accounted for 4 per cent of occasional primary and 12 per cent of occasional secondary school usage.[4]

The NFMS findings and the case studies confirmed the popularity of maintained schools for meetings and rehearsals in preference to other venues. The NFMS survey revealed that one third of choirs and 43 per cent of orchestras regularly rehearsed in local education authority (LEA) schools. The case study findings also revealed a significant reliance on LEA premises.

References

1. See *Directory of Borough Arts Contacts*, London Research Centre, May 1990.

2. Terry Bristow and David Lee, *The Restless Arts: Problems and Possibilities*, National Association of Local Arts Councils, 1988.

3. Chartered Institute of Public Finance and Accountancy, *Leisure and Recreation Statistics 1990/91 Estimates*, CIPFA, 1990.

4. Department of Education and Science, Statistical Bulletin 2/85, *Survey of Shared and Extended Use of Schools in 1983*, January 1985.

11 Adult education and the amateur arts

In 1979, the Advisory Council for Adult and Continuing Education, the Arts Council of Great Britain, the British Film Institute and the Crafts Council collaborated to commission an enquiry into 'the provision of adult education in the arts, crafts, and film', and invited the author of the enquiry report 'to recommend ways to improve working relationships between artists, arts administrators, and adult educators in order to enhance and enlarge this provision'.[1] The report of the enquiry was published in 1981; Geoffrey Adkins, its author, listed numerous examples of co-operation between arts organisations and adult education agencies, and produced four pages of recommendations. But he noted in his introduction that 'the conduct of the survey was clouded by the recent accumulation of public financial cuts. Local authority adult education courses have been reduced in number, shortened in length, fees have risen, and in a few places there have been periods when almost all adult education provision has been suspended.'[2]

In the mid-1980s Cherry Ann Knott completed a research project on the teaching and learning of twenty-four crafts disciplines in adult education in seven areas of England and Wales. The picture that emerged was one of great diversity – with great variations between the perceptions of students and tutors, as well as in the resources available for crafts classes in different parts of the United Kingdom. The research was conducted between June 1984 and January 1986, and the author observed that provision for the crafts in adult education was diminishing, with reductions in the number of subjects and in the resources allocated to them.[3]

The most recent England-wide survey of courses undertaken at adult education centres was conducted by the Department of Education and Science in collaboration with the National Institute of Adult and Continuing Education (NIACE). The survey included only LEA-run courses; it excluded courses provided by the Workers' Educational Association and those courses run by University Extra-Mural Departments. Nor did the survey cover the range of residential adult education courses offered by many education authorities.

Just under 30,000 arts and crafts courses were recorded by 80 of the 97 local education authorities (see Table 3.11). Using the average enrolments figure recorded for courses of all types, arts and crafts enrolments exceeded 0.5 million in 1985/6. This figure is likely to underestimate the extent of activity in England. First, no attempt was made to gross up for the 17 local education authorities who did not respond to the survey. Furthermore, dance classes were excluded from the above analysis; the categories used by the DES included 'dance' under the heading 'sport and physical education'. A survey by the Dance Research Unit of dance provision in Surrey showed that the formal adult education system was the main provider of dance classes, accounting for 59 per cent of all lessons in 1983.[4]

The 1990 review, *Education for Adults*, by Her Majesty's Inspectorate, provides further evidence of the extent of adult part-time education. In 1987/8 there was a total of 3.4 million enrolments in all subjects – including 1.6 million people studying part-time in adult education centres, 1.1 million adults over the age of 25 in higher and further education institutions, 0.5 million signed on for courses provided by 'responsible bodies' including University Extra-Mural Departments and the Workers' Educational Association, and 0.2 million enrolled for courses at adult residential colleges. Most of these latter enrolments are at 36 'short-term' colleges in the UK which offer courses only a few days long, principally in the arts, humanities and craft subjects.[5] Of 1,266 courses and study tours in Great Britain listed in the 1990/1 guide to residential study breaks published by the National Institute of Adult Continuing Education (NIACE), 107 were painting courses, 89 singing and other music-making, 47 literature (including poetry) and drama, 35 photography and 30 creative writing courses, including writing for radio and television.[6] Some of these residential colleges are subsidised by local education authorities and in other ways; others depend largely or entirely on income from fees for their survival. Among the latter group is the Benslow Music Trust, formerly the Rural Music Schools Association, which puts on about 80 short courses each year for adult amateur musicians.

When questioned in 1990 by the British Market Research Bureau, 17 per cent of the British population aged 17 or over said that they were engaged in informal learning, which can be defined as 'any learning which is not primarily structured by a formal educational institution'.[7]

Of these 10 per cent mentioned the handicrafts, 10 per cent musical instruments, 5 per cent photography, and 2 per cent drama, theatre, or dance, as the subjects that they were learning informally. This gives figures of approximately 750,000 British adults learning crafts informally, 750,000 learning to play a musical instrument, about 375,000 photography, and 150,000 adults studying/learning one of the theatre arts outside a formal educational institution, that is either teaching themselves or learning at work, at home, with friends or in a club.

While informal learning is obviously important, and while largely self-financing initiatives like the Open College of the Arts, which was founded in 1986, and which has about 3,500 students, about 300 tutors and about 120 tutorial centres are offering new opportunities for students to explore their potential as artists in different media, the basic framework of adult education, built up over many decades, has come under increasing pressure arising from the government's approach to public expenditure in general and to local government finance in particular.

The Inner London Education Authority (ILEA), which was abolished by the government with effect from April 1990, had a particularly proud record of adult education. In Inner London in 1986/7 there were 224,000 student enrolments in adult education, or, as was stated in 1988, 'with under 5 per cent of the country's population, ILEA provides almost 14 per cent of the local authority provision of adult education in England and Wales'.[8] The ILEA also kept its fees low. In 1987/8 the average hourly fee for non-vocational courses was 39p compared with 77p per hour for non-vocational adult courses provided by the English 'shire' counties.[9]

Increasing fees and decreasing public provision have become the norm for adult education in many parts of the UK. In many London boroughs both adult education and grants to voluntary organisations have been cut. A recent survey of 18 adult and community education institutions in Inner London produced 14 replies. The main findings were as follows:

> Respondents were asked to compare their budget for 90/91 with that for 89/90. One reported it was bigger, 6 the same and 7 smaller. 2 boroughs reported vacancies unfilled, while one of the independent institutions was hit by the loss of a borough grant.

Respondents were also asked to compare their budget for the year 91/92 with that for 90/91: 'One reported an increase, 4 the same and 9 smaller'.

> The staffing implications of cuts of this scale are major. Over a 4 year period (89/90 to 92/93), no service or institution expected an increase in full-time staff, 3 were hoping to stay the same, and 11 were reducing. For part-time staff the figures were one increasing, 2 the same and 7 less. The steepest cuts in full-time staff were from 80 to '40-50', 73 to 40 (this figure was pre-poll-tax-capping) and 80-30. Two of these institutions were cutting part-time budgets by 50 per cent and 38 per cent. The third was trying to keep up the part-time budget by cutting full-time staff, but acknowledged that 'It is difficult to see how far one can go shedding full-time staff to maintain part-time teaching hours'. Three other boroughs (including one not returning the questionnaire) were expecting redundancies and unfilled vacancies.[10]

A wider survey, *The Poll Tax and Adult Learners*, conducted by NIACE found that 29 per cent of 95 local education authorities responding to the survey reported reductions in the proposed adult education budget either in 1990/1 or 1991/2:

> Half of these reported that cuts were due directly to the introduction of the community charge itself; a further quarter because of charge 'capping'.

Among the short-term decisions taken in the face of budget cuts were:
- one month's delay in starting autumn programme
- cancellation of the prospectus for the whole authority programme
- closure of colleges and main site buildings

- major fee rises
- cuts in class offers
- staff redundancies.

> The most dramatic, and well publicised, impact of the Community-charge capping affected Barnsley and Haringey. In Barnsley all evening and day classes for adults have been cut, except for day-time basic education classes; in Haringey a 50 per cent reduction in the adult education budget has led the authority to close an adult education centre, halve provision, and prioritise offers to basic education and provision for adults with special needs. Manchester has made cuts to avoid charge-capping which have the effect of reducing provision for adult education by some 30 per cent.[11]

Although the amateur arts are largely practised outside the long-established system of non-vocational adult education in Britain there is a considerable interdependence between the amateur arts and adult education – not least because many people transfer skills developed in one context to working in another context. The substantial recent reductions in adult education provision, taken with the further pronounced bias against, and threats to, liberal adult education expressed in the 1991 White Paper, *Education and Training for the 21st Century* must be considered as deeply disturbing to those concerned with the links between adult education and the arts.

References

1. Geoffrey Adkins, *The Arts and Adult Education*, Advisory Council for Adult and Continuing Education, 1981, p.iv.

2. Geoffrey Adkins, *op.cit.*, p.3.

3. Cherry Ann Knott, *'I Can't Wait for Wednesday'*, Crafts Council, 1987.

4. *Provision for Participation in Dance and Movement Activities in the County of Surrey*, Report by the Dance Research Unit of the University of Surrey, 1984.

5. Her Majesty's Inspectorate, Department of Education and Science, *Education for Adults*, 1991, pp.2-6.

6. *Time to Learn*, National Institute of Adult Continuing Education, 1990.

7. Naomi Sargant, *Learning and 'leisure'*, NIACE, 1991, p.58.

8. Alan Tuckett, *The Jewel in the Crown, Adult Education in Inner London*, ILEA, 1988, p.10.

9. Alan Tuckett, *op.cit.*, p.42.

10. John Payne, 'Adult Education in Inner London', *Adults Learning*, September 1991.

11. *The Poll Tax and Adult Learners*, NIACE, 1990, p.1.

12 Professional/amateur collaboration in music

A quick glance at the findings of the case studies reveals that, of all the art forms, music offers the greatest opportunities for professional/amateur collaboration. But it has already been noted that the music world is far from homogeneous; there are many musics and the opportunities for collaboration between amateur and professional vary between each.

If Ruth Finnegan's seven 'musical worlds',[1] classical music, brass band, folk, music theatre, jazz, country and western, and rock and pop are adopted as a framework, two in particular – classical music and music theatre – offer the greatest opportunities for formal collaboration between amateur and professional. The Musicians' Union recognises this fact:

> The amateur musician is not normally seen as a hindrance to the profession, the fact that there exists a large number of amateur musicians is welcomed by this Union... The Union has actively encouraged amateur/professional cooperation in the orchestral sphere, we have a special rates structure for professionals performing with amateur orchestras, amateur choirs, in choral societies and for musicians performing with amateur opera companies. The Union actively encourages the engagement of professional musicians to accompany amateur operatic society productions by providing a small grant to those societies who fill the criteria for funding.
>
> We enjoy a harmonious relationship with the... National Federation of Music Societies... Following a decision by Greater London Arts... to withdraw funding from a number of amateur organisations

throughout London, the Union actively assisted the NFMS in their representations.[2]

Neil Hoyle, Chief Executive of the Incorporated Society of Musicians (ISM), offered some generally positive views about the contribution of amateurs to the music profession describing them as:

> On balance, an undoubted benefit. Voluntary promoters (music clubs, choirs, singers, orchestras and instrumentalists) provide a lot of employment for professionals: this is particularly valuable for younger career musicians, who need experience as well as money. The number of opportunities may be smaller at present, and fees may have fallen in real terms; but this is as much a result of the general economic climate as anything else. Amateur musicians also commission and perform works by professional composers: without their contribution, it is unlikely that much large-scale choral music would be written, still less heard. Amateur musicians also make up a significant proportion of audiences for professionals, and are important consumers for the music industry. They become a real hindrance only when their work is of a low quality and they are at the same time the only providers of music to a community: this can damage appreciation of proper professional standards and of music itself.[3]

The National Federation of Music Societies (NFMS) agreed to provide PSI with access to its mailing list to allow a full survey of its membership to be undertaken. The structure of the survey reflected the different types of society in membership. Separate questionnaires were constructed for choirs, orchestras and music societies (or music clubs).

1,240 questionnaires were distributed (762 to choral societies, 202 to orchestras and 276 to music societies). The principal function of music societies can be described as arranging and promoting concerts.

The response to the survey was good. Usable questionnaires were returned by 441 choirs, 157 promoting societies and 120 orchestras. Further details of the survey are given in Appendix B; the following paragraphs concentrate on aspects of professional/amateur collaboration.

Choirs and orchestras
Many choirs have developed an active two-way relationship with the professional music sector. They engage orchestras and ensembles

(across a range of professional standards) to accompany them; and some choirs are themselves engaged by professional orchestras in the performance, and occasional recording, of works from the choral repertoire. Of responding choirs, 19 had undertaken a total of 30 recording sessions. Only 14 per cent of choirs undertook promotions with full-time professional orchestras; accompanied performances were most frequently undertaken with *ad hoc* orchestras (330 concerts). In all, own promotions involving some professional orchestral input – full-time, *ad hoc* and semi-professional orchestras – accounted for 44 per cent of all promotions.

12.1 Regular professional input for rehearsals: choirs and orchestras(a)

	Number of groups	Percentages
Choirs		
Chorusmaster	61	14
Chorusmaster and pianist	266	60
Pianist only	27	6
Other	15	3
None	72	16
Total	441	100
Professional sessions	23,393	
Orchestras		
Conductor	32	27
Conductor and leader	52	43
Leader only	2	2
Conductor, leader & other	13	10
None	21	18
Total	120	100
Professional sessions	13,987	

(a) Base = 441 choirs and 120 orchestras.

The role that amateur music plays as a creator of employment for professional musicians has traditionally been central to the rationale for centrally-funded support for the amateur. Choirs and orchestras were asked whether they regularly engaged, on a fee basis, professional tutors (conductors, chorusmasters, pianists, leaders, etc). Only 16 per cent of choirs and 18 per cent of orchestras did *not* regularly engage any professionals for rehearsals. A majority of choirs and orchestras engaged two professionals, chorusmaster and pianist (60 per cent of choirs) or conductor and leader (43 per cent of orchestras). On this basis, it is possible to estimate the number of professional sessions generated by rehearsing alone [the sum of (annual rehearsals x professionals employed per session)].

12.2 Choirs and orchestras: total expenditure on professional artists

£ thousands

	Choirs	Orchestras	Total
Chorusmaster/conductor/ accompanist/leader	487.5	159.5	647.0
Soloists	557.9	92.6	650.5
Engagements of ensembles/ professional stiffening	1,203.2	198.1	1,401.3
Total professional spending	2,248.7	450.1	2,698.8
Grossed up estimates of professional spending	3,922	735	4,657

Responding orchestras and choirs generated a total of 37,380 'professional sessions' from rehearsals alone during the 1989/90 season (grossing up gives a combined estimate of 63,655 professional sessions per year; 40,800 for choirs and 22,855 for orchestras). Average spending on chorusmasters and/or pianists was £1,240 per choir per year and accounted for 12 per cent of responding choirs' combined turnover. For orchestras, 83 per cent incurred expenditure on conductors and/or leaders and average spending was £1,595 per annum (18 per cent of turnover). Expenditure on professionals was identified in two additional categories: engagements of accompanying orchestras/ensembles or professional stiffening of orchestras, and spending on soloists.

Music promoting societies
The principal function of music clubs and societies is the promotion of concerts, often, though not always featuring chamber music

repertoire. They act as a facilitating mechanism for the promotion of professional artists and ensembles. Whilst the statistics collected as part of this survey cannot show it – the historical data inevitably deals only with 'births' rather than 'deaths' – it is a widely held view that the current network of societies is far less extensive than that which existed 25 years ago.

Nonetheless, music clubs still constitute a significant element of the voluntary sector's total contribution to professional music. Only one of the responding music societies recorded no expenditure under the heading of professional engagements. Total recorded spending under this heading was £581,000 in 1989/90, an average of £3,725 per society (the equivalent grossed up figure for all societies was exactly £1 million).

So NFMS member organisations – orchestras, choirs and music societies – spent an estimated £5.7 million on professional engagements in 1989/90; the combined expenditure of the Bournemouth Symphony Orchestra and Sinfonietta, the City of Birmingham Symphony Orchestra, Hallé and Northern Sinfonia, on full-time players, extra players, guest artists and conductors was £6.7 million in 1987/8.[4]

Education and training

Finances aside, the amateur music sector performs a significant role as an arena for informal training for aspirant professionals. Ruth Finnegan argues that 'professional music feeds directly on local amateur activities and would be impossible to sustain without them'.[5] This aspect of professional/amateur collaboration manifests itself in various ways. The notion that all professional musicians were amateurs once has much truth to it. So, in spite of the growth of youth orchestras, the amateur sector still plays an important role in providing players with experience under performance conditions before, during and after their years of professional training. This is especially true of conductors and concert soloists.

Some specific examples of this informal training will illustrate the point. Referring to a project in which Wagner's *The Ring* was played in its entirety, under workshop conditions, with a young professional cast and amateur orchestra, Music Camp's Bob Montgomery explained 'many of the professional singers who sang it have subsequently sung their roles at the Royal Opera House, and for

instance, in the current truncated *Ring*'.[6] The late Harold Gray, a
former conductor of the City of Birmingham Symphony Orchestra,
developed his conducting skills working with amateur choirs.[7] A
more recent example is the young conductor Mark Wigglesworth,
winner of the 1989 Kondrashin Competition. In reviewing his career
to date, Michael John White wrote:

> How are young conductors encouraged to develop? It is no secret that
> learning is done on the job. As Wigglesworth admits: 'If a pianist
> came to an orchestra to play a concerto with the same lack of
> experience as a young conductor, it wouldn't be tolerated.'[8]

Wigglesworth's only work outside amateur and youth orchestras
was through a group of professionals which he started himself. There
are limits to what can be achieved through conductors directing, or
soloists playing with, amateur ensembles ('it teaches you the music
but not the psychology of professional musicians'). Nevertheless, and
as with the other performing arts, the amateur movement provides an
arena for informal training which is often simply not available within
the professional environment. There are few professional conductors
who have not at some point in there careers stood in front of an amateur
orchestra.

Another area of collaboration between amateur and professional
is to be found in the competitive music festival. The British Federation
of Music Festivals lays stress on the significant professional input into
competitive music festivals through the payment of professional
adjudicators to comment on the merits of individual performances.
The adjudicators are engaged as professional tutors. Assuming that the
competitive festivals in the case study areas were typical of festivals
across the country, some £1 million might be generated in
adjudicators' fees.

Extolling the benefits of the amateur sector as a generator of
professional work has its limitations. Although it is a condition of
music societies in receipt of RAA funding that they should pay the
minimum rates recommended by either the Musicians' Union (MU)
or the Incorporated Society of Musicians, such agreements can, in
practice, be difficult to police. Consequently, included within
'professional payments', particularly for orchestral stiffening, are
likely to be not insignificant amounts of funds given over either at
below the union rate or to non-union players, and even sometimes to

established groups of amateurs. This aspect of the amateur movement was a source of anxiety for the MU:

> There is concern about amateurs displacing work opportunities for professionals; often amateur groups, ensembles or orchestras are used as 'amateurs', that is an organisation, or they as individuals may receive a payment as reimbursement for so-called expenses. These 'expenses' can sometimes be of a reasonable amount but not the correct professional rates.[9]

The concern that the activities of amateur musicians 'displace' work which otherwise would be taken up by professionals is almost certainly misplaced. It seems likely that a whole different set of considerations and value judgements are employed by the audience for an amateur performance than for a professional one.

Empirical studies and more subjective observations of the amateur classical music world point to the fact that the audience for amateur music performances – and probably other elements of the amateur performing arts – are made up quite substantially of 'friends and relatives' or others known to the performers taking part. Ruth Finnegan makes this point in her detailed account of the workings of the Sherwood Choir in Milton Keynes.

> 'Publicity' was seen as an essential prelude to a concert, something which helped to define it as a 'proper' public performance. How far this in itself sold tickets or brought in the audience was less clear; indeed some doubted whether anyone ever came to a concert just from having seen a poster. Most probably depended on the informal efforts of the choir itself... Friends and relations of the performers always made up a large proportion of the audience.[10]

A recent survey of audiences for concerts given by a number of choirs at the South Bank Centre concert halls confirms that a large proportion of the audience for amateur music-making is made up of friends and relatives. The survey, undertaken jointly by the National Federation of Music Societies and Greater London Arts, was carried out as part of the Office of Arts and Libraries' Arts Marketing Scheme. The survey was spread over 10 concerts and four types of choir – old-established choirs, choirs with a long South Bank association, chamber choirs and choirs with a strong community following.[11]

Amateur opera, operetta and musical comedy combine the worlds of amateur dramatics and music. The case studies reveal that these societies were frequently larger than most other amateur organisations in financial terms and many pay substantial sums for the engagement of musical directors and accompanying professional players. When amateur performances are undertaken in Theatrical Management Association (TMA) venues, the TMA/MU agreement means that musical comedy, operatic and light opera societies either have to engage a *bona fide* amateur orchestra or a band made up of MU musicians at the appropriate MU rate. For other venues, a different set of MU minima apply; but the sheer scale and diversity of amateur activity in this field make it much harder for the MU to enforce its minimum rates for the employment of professional musicians. In such cases, pit musicians' fees are, in practice, likely to vary considerably.

There are two main forms of professional/amateur collaboration in brass band music. First, many musical directors are paid professionals. Secondly, some brass bands commission new work from more or less established composers, and public funds are available for this purpose.

Jazz, rock and pop

The structured nature of amateur classical music – the process of learning set works – is largely an educative process which requires professional tuition in the preparation of a set repertoire. This provides one type of opportunity for professional involvement by conductors and music directors. A second type of opportunity derived from the facilitating role which professionals provide – as soloists, accompanists or for 'stiffening' – is in performance. These forms of collaboration simply do not exist in jazz, rock and pop. Non-professional rock and pop bands have established members which stay together to be successful – and are not augmented for performance. Furthermore, the individuality which forms an integral part of many bands extends to their learning and performing much of their own composed material. Ruth Finnegan found that although some individuals had benefitted from school instrumental tuition, most bands were self-taught. This is not universal however. The establishment of the Lewisham Academy of Music is one example of the provision of tuition in a variety of contemporary forms and styles, financed mainly from public funds.

Of course, the distinctions between amateurs and professionals are even less clear in jazz, pop and rock. Chris Hodgkin at Jazz Services felt that whilst the division between 'amateur' and 'professional' was more defined in the classical world, this was not the case in jazz. What exists is a grey area of paid performing musicians who were in effect amateur, not necessarily of the highest quality nor adhering to Musicians' Union rates and conditions. Ruth Finnegan described jazz musicians in Milton Keynes as being 'practically all... towards the amateur end of the "amateur/professional" continuum in the sense both of relying on other means than jazz for their income and in their view of musical activity as basically enjoyment rather than job'.[12] Likewise, rock and pop bands were 'amateur' in that most had other employment besides playing, few were organised for money-making, did not have managers and invested their own money in performing. But although bands did play for free, they frequently received fees for their services, even if the net financial benefit was actually found to be small. On this basis, they would fail one test of amateur status.

But the on-the-job training element apparent in the classical music sector does have its parallels in rock, pop and jazz. Groups would form and re-form but they invariably started out as non-earning until they moved further along the amateur/professional continuum, and payment for services became expected. Successful bands would continue and some might ultimately become fully professional.

References

1. Ruth Finnegan, *The Hidden Musicians, Music-making in an English town*, Cambridge University Press, 1989, p.31.

2. Letter from Dennis Scard, General Secretary, Musicians' Union, 30 July 1991.

3. Letter from Neil Hoyle, Chief Executive, Incorporated Society of Musicians, 31 July 1991.

4. *Cultural Trends 4: 1989*, PSI, 1989.

5. Ruth Finnegan, *op.cit.*, p.17.

6. Letter from R.W. Montgomery, 22 January 1991.

7. Harold Gray, obituary, *The Independent*, 2 April 1991.

8. 'Conduct Becoming', *The Independent on Sunday*, 10 March 1991.

9. Letter from Dennis Scard, General Secretary, Musicians' Union, 30 July 1991.

10. Ruth Finnegan, *op.cit.*, p.248.

11. Office of Arts and Libraries, *Encouraging the Others*, HMSO, 1990.

12. Ruth Finnegan, *op.cit.*, p.87.

13 Professional/amateur collaboration in drama

The Cork report, the Arts Council of Great Britain's enquiry into professional theatre in England,[1] placed amateur theatre as part of the 'Wider Theatre of Tomorrow?' Thus the Arts Council acknowledged that the amateur theatre has an existence, and a possible future, even if, by implication, the amateur theatre was denied much of a past. But, more positively, the Cork report acknowledged that 'amateur theatre complements professional theatre'.[2] The report went on to refer to some of the ways that amateurs and professionals collaborate: for example, in amateur groups using professional directors, in community plays, in a variety of other participatory projects, and in the involvement of professional theatre-workers in youth theatre.

In the decades following the Second War, opposition to professional/amateur collaboration in the theatre came from the actors union, Equity. Equity now appears to have a somewhat more flexible attitude to such collaboration. Its policy has been clearly stated by Peter Finch, the Union's Assistant Secretary:

> We... recognise that amateur theatre can be a source of employment for some of our members, particularly Directors, Designers, Fight Directors and Choreographers.

> Our long-standing policy has been to raise no objection to the engagement of professional artists in *bona fide* amateur companies, although we would not normally agree to amateur involvement in professional theatre companies.

Occasionally, people without any professional experience, who could be classed as 'amateurs', are engaged as 'supernumeraries' in theatre companies, in a 'spear-carrying', 'filling-the-stage' capacity. This would normally be with the agreement of the Broadcasting, Entertainment and Cinematograph Technicians' Union, the old NATTKE/BETA.

There have also been a number of occasions when our Council has agreed to the participation of amateur performers, usually people living locally, in certain large-scale productions, mounted by theatre companies and which would not otherwise be possible, without their involvement. Various productions of Coward's *Cavalcade*, *Mystery Plays* and other large-scale, 'pageant-type' productions spring to mind.[3]

One important aspect of professional/amateur collaboration is in the shared use of buildings, and the many ways in which professional, technical, publicity, box office and front of house staff collaborate with amateur groups. In its survey of professional/amateur co-operation in the theatre, the Central Council for Amateur Theatre (CCAT) discovered that 170 out of 179 professional theatres surveyed provided facilities for amateur organisations, the great majority of them receiving rental payments from the amateur groups, though in the case of 56 of the 179 theatres (31 per cent) there were also arrangements for sharing box office income. In the case of 117 of the theatres, facilities were provided for amateur theatre for more than five weeks in every year. In most cases (151 out of 179) there was a great deal of collaboration between the amateur groups and the technical staff of the professional theatre on the handling of the technical aspects of the show.[4] The Arts Council has produced figures that show that at the 34 repertory theatre companies in England subsidised by the Council there were 192 weeks of amateur performances in 1989/90. For example, at the Northcott Theatre, Exeter that year there were visits from 3 student societies and 2 local amateur societies presenting 6 productions over 7 weeks. The attendances were 13,900, and the rental paid by the companies concerned represented 4 per cent of the Northcott's total income in 1989/90. At the New Victoria Theatre, Newcastle-under-Lyme, in 1990/91 there were 8 performances by amateurs in the main theatre; a total of 4,275 seats were sold, an average of 88 per cent of the seats available. At His Majesty's, a major receiving theatre in Aberdeen, four different amateur dramatic and lyric companies put on 22 performances between them in 1990/91 to audiences totalling 14,847.

In the PSI study of arts centres in the United Kingdom it was found that in 1985/6 there were 3,550 performances of 1,070 amateur drama productions at 242 arts centres; 90 per cent of these arts centres have professional staff. In the same year there were 7,500 professional drama performances at arts centres.[5]

But probably the most substantial and significant area of development of professional/amateur collaboration in drama in the last ten years has been found in the community play movement. Community productions were pioneered by Ann Jellicoe and the Colway Theatre Trust; characteristically, community plays take the form of specially commissioned plays which involve hundreds of members of local communities under the direction of professional directors, designers and musicians, and occasionally, as in the case of the York Mystery Plays, using professional actors. Among the well-established writers who have been involved in community plays have been Howard Barker, Nick Darke, David Edgar, John Godber, Steve Gooch, Adrian Henri, Fay Weldon and Arnold Wesker. As one writer has expressed it:

> It is a form of theatre which has appealed right across the spectrum of society: from the inner city to the rural community, from the suburbs to the leafy village hall and to HM prisons. The subject matter has diversified but always with a vital statement to make – whether the celebration of a community's history or in addressing itself to the social problems that beset a particular society.[6]

Ann Jellicoe has shared her unique experience in her book *Community Plays*.[7] Support from the Carnegie UK Trust has been important in assisting a number of local plays. In recent years Carnegie has offered sums totalling £127,000 to support more than two dozen community plays. The Trust's conditions of grant required that the story had to include the social history and traditions of the local area and that the aims must include encouraging the continuation of arts activity in the locality after the play has been performed.[8]

Under the Fish and Over the Water by Peter Terson was performed at St Laurence School, Bradford-on-Avon between 26 November and 8 December 1990. In addition to the writer, the play involved a professional production team of six. Of this production Jonathan Croall wrote:

> Like most of its predecessors, the Bradford play involves huge numbers of people. Apart from a cast of 160, aged 4-70, many of whom have never acted before, some four hundred have helped – either backstage, front of house, or in one of the myriad of committees set up to fund-raise, seek sponsorship, handle publicity and public relations, or do research. In addition, some 3,500 people saw the play during its two-week run.

> The research committee, comprising twenty volunteers, played a crucial part during the writing of the play. They provided Peter Terson with possible ideas and, once he had chosen his story, travelled far afield, following leads, researching and checking to ensure the detail was authentic. They also acted as readers for, and critics of, the various drafts...

> Staff at St Laurence are clear about the beneficial effects of the play for the school... Headteacher James Wetz says: 'Unless your school is involved with the community, you might as well shut up shop. The play has brought people together more than any other initiative has. It's also changed relationships and attitudes between staff and children.'[9]

There has been a good deal of follow-up activity to the Bradford-on-Avon community play. Jim Mason, a former deputy head of a London secondary school, whose organisation All Change Arts has been involved in a number of community plays, is not only concerned with the importance of follow-up activity, and the danger of what he calls the 'circus leaves town phenomenon', but also points to the difference between the writer's approach to community plays and what he regards as a more educational and enabling approach in which local people are helped to find their own voice and to devise their own scripts: 'If people feel that they have been given the words to say, they can easily feel empowered, but they are powerless' says Mason.[10] Richard Hayhow and Elisabeth Katis (both formerly of the Worcester Arts Workshop) are currently evaluating a number of community plays and their report should throw light on the dynamic and longer-term impact of these examples of 'cultural empowerment'.

All community plays are partnerships between professionals and the people. The forms and nature of that partnership can be very different. What is important is that any professional/amateur collaboration is based on genuinely mutual co-operation, with clear benefits to both the amateurs and the professionals. The interface between amateurs and professionals working in the theatre is broadening all the time, but the danger that some of the amateurs in professional/amateur theatre collaborations may be reduced to the status of moving wallpaper needs to be remembered. One adult educator, involved in a community play, said recently that one of the main things that she had learned from the experience was 'just how awful theatre people are'.

In spring 1990, the Central Council for Amateur Theatre (CCAT) set up a working party to investigate the possibilities for further collaboration between amateurs and professionals in the theatre. The working party (which is being chaired by Roger Fox of the Drama Association of Wales) decided to concentrate its efforts in three areas: (a) building-based theatre resources, (b) professional touring promotion by the amateur theatre and other community groups, and (c) new writing for the theatre.

The working party is studying in detail three contrasting examples of professional theatres where use of the theatre by amateurs is substantial, limited, and non-existent respectively – the aim being to identify ways in which greater co-operation between the amateur groups and the building-based professionals can be encouraged.

Secondly, conscious that a great deal of promotion of professional touring companies is undertaken on an entirely or largely voluntary basis, the working party plans to publish a guidebook, with examples of good practice and guidelines which are being devised to help both the amateur/voluntary promoters and the touring companies.

Thirdly, and perhaps most ambitiously, the working party is looking at the feasibility of establishing a permanent new writing archive, so that scripts that have been performed perhaps only once – and that are unlikely to be published – are readily available for further productions. It would be part of the purpose of those organising such an archive, which would serve as a resource for all branches of the theatre, to try to ensure that many more producers and directors are made more aware of the availability of a great variety of new writing for the theatre. The working party, whose work will continue at least through 1992, will, no doubt, be recommending how such an archive should be funded.

As this report goes to press, preparations are well-advanced for a decidedly original and daring form of professional/amateur collaboration in the theatre. With sponsorship from British Telecom, 50 theatre companies – 49 throughout Great Britain and one in Israel – all members of the Little Theatre Guild, are launching, more or less simultaneously, a new play by John Godber. BT describes this initiative as 'the world's largest ever opening season'.[11] The play, *Happy Families*, has its first night on 12 October 1991 and the British Telecom sponsorship enabled the 50 directors and two actors from each company to get together with the writer and members of the Hull Truck theatre company, with which Godber has worked for many years, for a weekend master class at the BT training school at Stone in Staffordshire. BT is also making its marketing expertise available to all the theatres involved, and the signs are that the partnership between the Little Theatre Guild and BT should prove to be of great mutual benefit. BT intends to run the sponsorship every two years.

References

1. *Theatre is for All, Report of the Enquiry into Professional Theatre in England*, Arts Council of Great Britain, 1986.

2. *Ibid.*, p.32.

3. Letter from Peter Finch, 21 June 1991.

4. *Amateur Theatre in Great Britain*, Central Council for Amateur Theatre, 1989.

5. Robert Hutchison and Susan Forrester, *Arts Centres in the United Kingdom*, Policy Studies Institute, 1987.

6. Charles Vance (ed.), *Amateur Theatre Yearbook 1989/90*, Platform Publications, 1989, p.219.

7. Ann Jellicoe, *Community Plays, How to put them on*, Methuen, 1987.

8. The Carnegie United Kingdom Trust, *Seventy-seventh Annual Report*, 1990, pp.26-27.

9. Jonathan Croall, unpublished review, December 1990.

10. Conversation with Jim Mason, 10 April 1991.

11. 'BT Amateur Theatre Sponsorship', BT media information sheet, 22 April 1991.

14 The Royal National Eisteddfod of Wales

The Royal National Eisteddfod of Wales (RNE) is probably the largest amateur arts event in Europe. Its overriding purpose is to promote the Welsh language and Welsh culture.

The first recorded Eisteddfod took place in the 12th century as a competition for poets and musicians. The RNE now takes place during the first full week in August and has been organised annually on similar lines since 1880.

The RNE is organised by 20 paid full-time staff working with about 1,000 volunteers each year. The location for the RNE changes every year alternately in the north and south of Wales. Planned several years ahead, the trend has been for a local authority to invite the Eisteddfod to be set up in its area. As the report *Wales: The Arts of the Possible* puts it:

> The Eisteddfod is unique. It is not just that it is an annual celebration of the oldest living language in Northern Europe; nor that it is a major arts festival boasting the largest, portable theatre in Britain, and one of the largest arts and crafts exhibitions in the country. Its strength derives from the base of popular local support, and that it serves to introduce many people for the first time to the joys of the arts. It is a truly amateur festival, organised in a highly professional way, that leaves behind, not just a lasting impression, but an array of spin-off activity.

> Its structure is complex but proven. It involves the Court, Elected Council and a Local Executive Committee to look after logistical arrangements for the Eisteddfod location. There are three structures in place at any one time, dealing with the Eisteddfod recently finished

and the next two in line. As many as 1,000 people in each location are involved in the planning; 5,000-7,000 people compete in 250 events; 150,000 visitors throng the Eisteddfod field.[1]

The RNE is mainly competitive. Among the 245 competitions held at the Eisteddfod at Mold in 1991, 73 were in music (including 4 in pop music), 45 in art and craft, 34 in literature, 22 for learners of Welsh, 14 in elocution, 14 in drama, 13 for Cerdd Dant (singing to harp accompaniment), 12 in science, 9 in folk dancing and 9 in first aid (which would be needed by anybody who attempted to attend all the competitions). There is, in addition, a full programme of exhibitions, lectures and discussions on almost every aspect of Welsh life, together with a large number of amateur and professional evening concerts and plays. A very active 'fringe' element has grown around the 'official' programme, featuring pop, rock, revue, folk and poetry sessions.

The RNE has 2,100 individual members each of whom pays a £4 subscription. The RNE's financial year is the calendar year. In 1990, the total income for the RNE was £1.8 million of which £320,000 came from central government through the Welsh Office, £210,000 came from the box office, £124,000 from the appeal fund (each year dozens of fund-raising committees are established), £284,000 from commercial sponsorship, £217,000 from local authorities, and £156,000 from site rentals.

Table 14.1 gives information about the total attendances at the RNE for the years 1984-89 inclusive, together with a breakdown of the percentage of the total attendances coming each year from each area. Over 90 per cent of those attending come from the Principality and about 5 per cent of the entire population of Wales attends the RNE each year (the *pro rata* equivalent of more than 2 million people attending an annual week-long competitive festival of the amateur arts in England).

While 21 per cent of the total population of Wales lives in the strongly Welsh-speaking counties of Gwynedd and Dyfed, between 41 per cent and 66 per cent of the total number of attenders at the RNE come each year from these two counties.

Organisationally the RNE sits at the top of a pyramid which also includes county and local (town and village) eisteddfodau, many of which can be seen in part as preparatory to the RNE.

14.1 Attendances at the Royal National Eisteddfod of Wales(a)

		1984 Lampeter Dyfed	1985 Rhyl Clwyd	1986 Fishguard Dyfed	1987 Portmadoc Gwynedd	1988 Newport Gwent	1989 Llanrwst Gwynedd
Total attendance	(000s)	153	144	126	163	148	163
Percentage attending from each area:							
Welsh counties(b)							
Gwynedd	(241)	17	36	22	52	23	45
Clwyd	(411)	8	30	6	10	6	15
Powys	(117)	4	3	3	2	2	2
Dyfed	(353)	48	10	42	14	18	11
West Glamorgan	(363	5	4	4	3	4	2
Mid Glamorgan	(538)	4	4	5	3	8	5
South Glamorgan	(404)	6	7	11	9	18	8
Gwent	(447)	2	1	1	1	15	–
Rest of Britain		5	6	5	5	5	8
Overseas		2	1	4	2	1	2

Source: Royal National Eisteddfod of Wales

(a) Based on approximately 840 interviews each year

(b) The figures in brackets are the population of each Welsh county in thousands.

The fate and fortunes of the RNE are directly tied to those of the Welsh language. As more people come to realise that language is part of belonging, personality and roots, more and more people are turning to Welsh as a second language. Emyr Jenkins, Director of the RNE, says that 'the only education area that is growing is probably education through the medium of Welsh. But the death of older people and the migration into Wales means that the loss of Welsh-language speakers is still greater than the gains.'[2]

To maintain the standards of work in different art forms the RNE attaches importance to the processes of criticism and adjudication, which are an integral part of each competition. The tradition in Wales is that every competitor in the written competitions competes under a pseudonym – and many people enter the competitions to receive the adjudications and criticism as much as out of any desire or expectation to win.

In a questionnaire-response Emyr Jenkins listed three challenges facing the RNE in the 1990s:

1. Adopting and developing a long-established cultural festival to meet the expectations of the 1990s.

2. Preserving the financial viability and developing alternative sources of income.

3. Ensuring the continued flow of volunteers to maintain the voluntary structure of the organisation.

The report *Wales: The Arts of the Possible* summarises the problems facing the RNE as follows:

> It will always be difficult to attract and involve 'outsiders' in a festival whose nature is designed to be inward-looking, notwithstanding the residue of cultural activity that the Eisteddfod leaves behind. In the end, it must be hoped that the teaching of Welsh as a core subject in secondary schools will go a long way towards developing a wider audience for the future.[3]

References

1. Institute of Welsh Affairs, *Wales: The Arts of the Possible*, Volume 2, May 1990, p.72.

2. Conversation with Emyr Jenkins, 17 January 1991.

3. Institute of Welsh Affairs, *op.cit*, p.74.

15 Creative writing

In a country that has produced Chaucer, Shakespeare and Dickens, literature has a strong claim to being judged *the* national art form. Reading and writing tend to be solitary activities though poetry groups and writing groups of various kinds are to be found in most towns and cities in the UK.

In April 1991 the Poetry Society, which was founded in 1909, had 3,243 individual members in the UK and Ireland, 306 overseas members and 29 affiliated poetry groups (10 in London, 19 in the rest of the UK). The Federation of Worker Writers and Community Publishers (FWWCP), which was founded in 1976, now has over 50 group in membership; with the help of an Arts Council grant the FWWCP currently employs a development worker, based in Brighton, who is helping new groups to form all over the UK.

The sixth edition of the *Directory of Writers' Circles*[1] lists about 420 writers' circles and similar groups in the UK and Eire. Some of these groups are based at adult education institutes, but the majority are free-standing 'independent' groups of writers. And the list is certainly not complete. In Scotland 25 writers groups belong to the Scottish Association of Writers which was founded in the late 1960s. Many members of these groups will have had work published, but many will not. Very few are in a position to write full-time.

In the last ten years hundreds of thousands of adults in the UK have written novels, short stories or poetry – only a tiny percentage of which has been published either in book form, in non-specialist magazines or in one of the hundreds of little magazines or community publications that are based in all parts of the UK. The 1991 edition of the *Small Press Yearbook* lists approximately 400 'small presses' which operate 'on the fringes of – sometimes way outside –

mainstream publishing'.[2] About a quarter of these small presses publish poetry, and about 40 publish fiction.

There are dozens of literary competitions in the UK – most of them of recent origin. The organisers of twelve of the poetry competitions listed in the *Guide to Literary Prizes, Grants and Awards in Britain and Ireland*[3] were asked by PSI to send a few basic facts about their competition. The responses are summarised in Table 15.1.

15.1 Selected poetry competitions

	First year of competition	First prize	Entry charge per person 1991	No. of entries 1990
Rosemary Arthur Award	1989	(a)	£5(a)	107
Arvon Foundation	1980	£5,000	£3.50	15,000(b)
Bridport Arts Centre Creative Writing Competition (poetry section)	1980(c)	£1,000	£3	5,520
City of Cardiff International Poetry Competition	1986	£1,000	£3	2,000
London Writers Competition (poetry section)	1977	£450	£2	902
Poetry Society National Poetry Competition	1978	£2,000	£4	14,000
Ver Poets Open Competition	1973(d)	£500	£2	800
Mary and Alfred Wilkins Memorial Poetry Competition	1986	£100	£1	300

(a) For 40 poems, the winner receives £100, a suitably inscribed carriage clock and the complete funding of a perfectly bound book of his or her work.

(b) 1989 figure.

(c) As a national competition.

(d) As the Michael Johnson Memorial Poetry Competition, 1973-83. Restarted under present name in 1985.

In one year in the early 1980s there were 32,000 entries for the Poetry Society's competition, which is for an unpublished poem of less than 40 lines by anyone over 16 who lives, works or studies in the UK or the Republic of Ireland. The competition has given a leg-up to such poets as Carol Ann Duffy and Tony Harrison (1983 and 1980 winners respectively).

The Arvon Foundation Poetry Competition is biennial. Prize money totals £10,000. As with the Poetry Society competition, there have been more than 30,000 entries in at least one year. *The Observer* newspaper always publishes the first six winning poems, and Arvon publishes an anthology of all winning poems and those selected for special commendation.

The Bridport Arts Centre Creative Writing Competition started on a local basis about 20 years ago, but was launched on a national basis in 1980. There are two categories: poetry and short stories with a first prize of £1,000 in each category, and numerous supplementary prizes. 5,520 poems and 4,437 short stories were entered for the 1990 competition. The competitions secretary writes:

> It took us a few years to become recognised as a major competition, but we now have many an honourable mention in various literary publications, and I think we can claim to enjoy the respect of much of the literary world. We are still rather young to claim the discovery of any *major* talents as our successes have hardly had time to develop into big names, but a win with us does help now, and in the past few years some of our winners have been able to get their work accepted and, hopefully, will become better known as time goes on. Amongst these are Atima Srivastava (recently sold her first novel, and has had a short play on Channel 4), David S. McKenzie (just had his first novel published), Deborah Randall (has had at least two anthologies published since her win with us). A recent development of some significance is that a leading London literary agent has agreed to read the principal winning stories in future competitions.[4]

Although the vast majority of those who write poetry, short stories and novels probably never enter competitions, literary competitions provide one index of just how widespread is the practice of creative writing. The quarterly *Poetry Review*, published by the Poetry Society, receives 'about 5,000 submissions, or more than 30,000 poems each year'.[5]

Plays[6]

The urge to write plays seems no less powerful than that to write poetry. BBC Radio, which broadcast 217 original single plays in 1990 receives 10-13,000 playscripts each year. A similar number of playscripts was received annually by BBC Television's drama script unit until the unit was closed in June 1991. In addition the BBC receives 4-5,000 light entertainment scripts each year.

The Royal National Theatre received 750 unsolicited playscripts in 1990 and a further 314 had arrived in the first six months of 1991. The Royal Shakespeare Company receives 4-500 unsolicited playscripts each year. It puts on between three and seven new plays each year, but in the last 13 years only 2 of the new plays put on have been unsolicited.

The Royal Court Theatre receives about 2,000 unsolicited playscripts each year – including plays for its young playwright scheme. The Hampstead Theatre Club, which puts on 6-7 productions a year (nearly all new plays) receives about 1,200 playscripts a year, most of them unsolicited; but it is pretty rare for an unsolicited play to be put on at the Hampstead Theatre Club.

Outside London, the Traverse Theatre in Edinburgh receives plays from all over the world – about 240 of them a year. It puts on 10 plays a year – on average one of the new plays each year comes through the unsolicited system. The Nottingham Playhouse put on 4 'premieres' in its main theatre between September 1990 and July 1991, as well as 7 plays written in the last 3 years. The theatre receives about 200 plays a year.

Most of these theatres have teams of readers who provide reports and comments on the plays submitted. But the odds are very heavily stacked against an 'unknown' writer getting a play put on in one of the principal subsidised theatres – even those specialising in new work. Building-based theatre companies funded by the Arts Council put on far fewer new plays each year in the second half of the 1980s than in the previous fifteen years. Somebody setting out to get a play performed professionally might be well advised to write for radio first. But, also, the Arts Council does have several theatre writing schemes and awards to assist playwrights. And amateur drama companies should be increasingly encouraged and supported to put on new plays.

Novels and short stories

It is every bit as hard to get a first novel published as it is to get a first play performed. The 1991 recession made things worse for new novelists and their publishers. Dan Franklin, Publishing Director of Martin Secker and Warburg, says:

> Things are bad at the moment, and there's no question that the thing
> which is suffering most in the current recession is hardback fiction.
> It's suffering *very very* badly indeed. Sales have dropped even for
> the big names, but down at the bottom, with the unknown first-time
> novelists, they've dropped almost to invisibility.[7]

But manuscripts of unsolicited novels and short stories continue
to pour into the publishers. Both Jonathan Cape Ltd and William
Heinemann Ltd, two of the best known names in fiction publishing,
receive about 50 unsolicited letters or manuscripts each week from
'unknown' fiction writers.[8] Heinemann no longer look at unsolicited
manuscripts. The literary agents Sheil Land Associates receive 10
unsolicited manuscripts each week. Of the many thousands of fiction
manuscripts submitted to agents and publishers each year, only a tiny
percentage get published. In 1990, 190 first-time novelists were
published in the UK.

The situation for short-story writers is just as difficult. A tiny
number of publishers – and a limited number of magazines – publish
short stories. Yet it is probable that hundreds of thousands of short
stories are written by adults each year. As we have seen above, a
competition run by a small arts centre in Dorset attracted more than
4,000 short stories in 1990.

Of course much of the work submitted to publishers is unoriginal,
uninspiring, unimaginative, badly written or worse. Giles Gordon, an
experienced literary agent, says that publishers are desperate for good
books: 'It is the greyness of so many of the manuscripts that is
depressing'.[9] Given that, the work of the Arvon Foundation, which
brings together established writers (particularly poets) in week-long
residencies with less established writers, can be seen to have a vital
role in raising standards and aspirations. Such an 'apprenticeship
model' is perhaps widely applicable in the arts.

Impressed as he is with 'the sheer amount of creative writing going
on up and down the country, much more than people recognise',
Alastair Niven, Literature Director of the Arts Council of Great Britain
is keen to stress that reading is at least as important as writing:

> of course you can nurture talent but I personally would place the
> emphasis on reading – get people excited about a book, get them to
> express a reaction. A lot of people read books but only for relaxation.
> We should also read to extend our awareness and enlarge our
> sensitivity.

Creative writing is very important but people will do it if they want to. And if they don't read they'll probably end up as very poor writers. There's no substitute for reading rather a lot.[10]

References

1. Jill Dick (ed.) *The Directory of Writers' Circles*, Laurence Pollinger, sixth edition, n.d.

2. *Small Press Yearbook 1991*, Small Press Group of Britain.

3. Published by the Book Trust and Society of Authors, sixth edition, 1990.

4. Letter from Margaret Chapman Andrews, 25 May 1991.

5. *Writers' and Artists' Yearbook 1991*, A. and C. Black, p.257.

6. The information in this section is drawn from phone conversations in July 1991 with Alan Drury (BBC), Giles Croft (RNT), Ben Jancovich (RSC), Mel Kenyon (Royal Court Theatre), Anna Koutelieri (Hampstead Theatre), Ruth McKenzie (Nottingham Playhouse) and Jean Ellis (Traverse Theatre).

7. Kevin Jackson, 'Grub Street revisited', *The Independent*, 9 August 1991.

8. Phone conversations with Lisa Glass and Marion Steel, August 1991.

9. Phone conversation with Giles Gordon, 24 July 1991.

10. Quoted in Violet Hughes, *Literature Belongs to Everyone*, Arts Council, 1991, p.61.

16 Conclusions and recommendations

This chapter has three sections. In the first section estimates are given of the number of adults in the UK involved in the amateur arts and crafts. Secondly, the principal reasons for attaching importance to the amateur arts are laid out. Finally some recommendations to policy makers and arts funding bodies are presented.

The size of the amateur arts sector

The seven case study areas covered 2.2 per cent of the population of the UK. However, they were selected to cover as many countries and regions of the UK as possible and to include a mixture of urban, suburban and rural areas. Although Northern Ireland and some English regions were not represented in the selection of case study areas, overall the seven areas can be taken to be reasonably representative of the UK as a whole.

Table 16.1 gives estimates for the number of members of 'formal' amateur groups in the case study areas. The number of participants involved in each area has been grossed up to account for non-responding organisations. Those amateur groups where the members are not directly involved in creative participation – film societies and music promoting groups – have been excluded from this part of the analysis. University-based groups have also been excluded from the grossing up process since they largely cater for students who are not resident locally. The total number of participants is then expressed as a percentage of the resident population aged 16 and over.

There is a problem with possible double-counting of individual participants. Many participants in the amateur arts are highly active in their fields and some of the most committed spend time in more than one group. So in areas where there is more than one drama society, choir or orchestra, it seems likely that some sharing of membership will exist. (Indeed some people are active in more than one art form.) It has been beyond the scope of this study to take account of overlapping memberships in the statistical analysis. But any double-counting may compensate for the inevitable failure to identify every single amateur arts organisation in the study areas; whilst individuals may be double-counted, organisations have not been.

16.1 Membership of amateur arts groups in the case study areas, 1989/90(a)

	Performing groups	Non-perf. groups	Membership as a percentage of resident popn, 16 and over:			Popn per square km
			Perf.	Non-perf.	Total	
Aberdeen	2,460	455	1.5	0.3	1.7	1,142
Exeter	1,690	195	2.1	0.2	2.3	2,331
Lewisham	800	350	0.4	0.2	0.6	6,528
Powys	1,945	390	2.1	0.4	2.5	23
Stoke/Newcastle	2,815	760	1.0	0.3	1.2	1,202
Teignbridge	1,375	530	1.6	0.6	2.2	164
Telford	1,035	250	1.0	0.2	1.2	468
Total	12,120	2,930	1.2	0.3	1.5	..

Source: Case study findings; *Population Trends 64*, Summer 1991; *Regional Trends 26 1991 Edition*, HMSO, 1991.

(a) 'Formal' groups only. Figures have been grossed-up within the various art form categories to allow for non-responding societies. The membership of university-based societies has been excluded from the figures; 'non-performing groups' excludes all music promoting societies, film societies, carnivals and festivals.

It can be seen from the table that in the predominantly urban areas a smaller percentage of the adult population tend to belong to 'formal' amateur arts organisations than is the case in the less densely populated areas (Teignbridge and Powys). Powys recorded the highest participation rate, with 2.5 per cent involved in amateur arts groups, more than double the figures for Telford New Town and Stoke/Newcastle. In five of the seven areas, the level of membership of formal amateur arts groups works out at between 1.2 and 2.3 per cent of the adult population. Even after excluding student-based groups, Exeter and Aberdeen recorded a comparatively high proportion of the adult population involved in amateur arts groups (2.3 per cent and 1.7 per cent respectively). Both are important regional centres, and both case studies produced evidence that they act as a focus of arts activity within their own travel-to-work areas. One Exeter choral group attracted participants not just from Devon, but also from adjacent counties.

The clustering of participation rates recorded in the case study areas permits some confidence in our ability to extrapolate from the seven areas for participation rates in the United Kingdom as a whole. We estimate that within the United Kingdom as a whole, 625,000 people are members of active local amateur performing arts organisations, and that a further 150,000 people are members of local amateur groups covering the visual arts and crafts (including photography), creative writing, and amateur cine and video. These figures include students, but exclude members of film societies and music promoting groups, and those involved in the arts in women's institutes, townswomen's guilds, and young farmers' clubs. Of the total of 775,000 (1.7 per cent of the adult population including students) involved in 'formal' amateur arts groups, approximately 425,500 (52 per cent) belong to groups affiliated to one of the 28 national 'umbrella' organisations (excluding 'other groups') listed in Table 3.1. (This calculation includes the assumption that half of the 46,000 members of youth theatres, youth orchestras and young choirs affiliated to their appropriate national organisations are aged sixteen and over). Although, as has been seen in Chapter 3, amateur groups not affiliated to any national organisation considerably outnumber those belonging to an 'umbrella' organisation, groups affiliated to 'umbrella' bodies tend to be more established, larger and have higher profiles in the locality than many 'non-umbrella' groups.

The survey of participation amongst the general population carried out in Ipswich (1986) found that 81 per cent of those claiming to be involved in amateur arts and crafts activities in the previous year, had been involved in the four weeks prior to interview.[1] So information from the *General Household Survey* (GHS), which covers participation in the four weeks before interview, is likely to give a fairly accurate picture of the number of individuals involved in amateur music and drama *on a regular basis.* 4 per cent of the adult population aged 16 and over were involved in amateur music and drama according to the 1986 survey. Applying this percentage to the population of Great Britain aged 16 and over gives an estimate of 1.76 million participants. Of these, 625,000 are involved in 'formal' amateur arts groups, and the remainder in church choirs (which have not been included in this study) and a great variety of informal groups (including pop and rock groups), as well as in playing and practising music at home. Participants in adult education classes are explicitly excluded from the 1.76 million figure arrived at by the GHS. The most recent (1985/6) survey of local authority education classes indicated that there were an estimated 600,000 enrolments for arts and crafts classes in England alone in that year. These figures exclude dance classes.

The other figures from the *General Household Survey* printed in Chapter 3 – those for participation in dance and the textile arts (knitting, dressmaking and needlework) – although useful, do not necessarily identify those actively engaged in the amateur arts. And the GHS provides no information about involvement in the visual arts and non-textile crafts. But the GHS figures indicate that over 12 million people each year undertake some dressmaking, needlework or knitting, and the survey conducted by Research Services of Great Britain for the Arts Council of Great Britain in 1991 found that 5 million people claim to be actively involved in working with textiles (but not as full-time professionals), 3 million of them on a regular basis. From the same survey it can also be estimated that 3.7 million people regularly practise photography and 1.8 million are regularly involved in painting and drawing. Only a small minority of these practitioners belong to a 'formal' amateur arts group.[2]

Performing arts: performances and attendances
The membership of the National Operatic and Dramatic Association (NODA) is made up largely of operatic and musical comedy societies. According to NODA, approximately one third of their membership is accounted for by drama rather than opera societies. The findings from the 5 English case studies reveal that in England only 19 per cent of adult drama societies are affiliated to a national 'umbrella' organisation. Extrapolating from the 5 English areas surveyed, there are 2,020 drama societies unaffiliated to national organisations in England (estimates for Scottish and Welsh non-umbrella drama societies have been provided by the respective 'umbrella' organisations). In total the PSI estimate is that there were 3,575 adult

drama societies in the UK in 1990 (Table 16.2). This excludes youth theatres, and drama organised by women's institutes, townwomen's guilds and young farmers' clubs.

16.2 Drama societies in the UK

	Groups
Little Theatre Guild of Great Britain	65
National Operatic and Dramatic Association	665
Drama Association of Wales	170
Scottish Community Drama Association	225
Northern Amateur Theatre Association	20
Radius	215
'Non-umbrella' drama societies	
England	2,020
Wales	60
Scotland	75
Northern Ireland	60
Total 'non-umbrella'	2,215
Total estimated adult drama societies	3,575

NODA's membership of operatic societies, estimated to account for some two-thirds of all societies affiliated to NODA (around 1,300 societies), makes up the largest part of the amateur opera movement in the UK. For the seven areas combined, however, 34 per cent of all opera companies were outside the national 'umbrellas'. On this basis it can be estimated that there are 1,970 amateur opera companies in the UK.

For these two categories of performing arts group, amateur dramatic societies and operatic groups, sufficient information was provided by the responding societies in the case study regions to provide a basis for estimating the total number of performances and attendances at the national level.

Between them the 65 members of the Little Theatre Guild of Great Britain gave an estimated 3,350 performances in 1989/90 to a total audience of just under half-a-million. PSI estimates are that the remaining 3,510 drama societies in the UK gave an average of 12.6

performances each to an average audience of 151 per performance. Excluding performances by members of the Little Theatre Guild of Great Britain, this produces a total of 44,226 performances played to audiences totalling 6.7 million. Adding in the activities of Little Theatre Guild members produces the figures given in Table 16.3.

Grossing up results from the case studies produces a figure for attendances of just over 4.7 million, at 18,500 performances of musicals, opera and light opera. In total, operatic and dramatic societies gave about 66,000 performances in 1989/90, watched by an audience of about 11.9 million. This audience total is larger than the total audiences at London's West End Theatre in 1990.

16.3 Drama groups and operatic societies: estimated performances and attendances, 1989/90

	Drama	Opera	Total
Groups	3,575	1,975	5,550
Performances	47,576	18,500	66,076
Attendances (millions)	7.2	4.7	11.9

The surveys of choirs and orchestras affiliated to the National Federation of Music Societies show that they undertook 4,350 performances in 1989/90, attracting a total audience of around 1.1 million. The figures on performances and attendances for other choirs and orchestras have not been sufficiently reliable to justify an overall estimate of performances of, and attendances at, all amateur choral and orchestral concerts.

The importance of the amateur arts

The number of people in the arts who make a living from the activity from which they would like to make a living appears to be very few. In all the arts and crafts there are tens (if not hundreds) of thousands of people who earn something from their art or craft activity each year, but not enough to support themselves or their families. Within the financial and time constraints within which they operate, many of these artists and craftspeople have a thoroughly professional, that is disciplined and dedicated, approach to their work. It is a basic argument of this report that amateurs need not have lower standards than professionals and that the pursuit of excellence should be encouraged in all sectors of society.

The importance of the arts, whether practised by amateurs or professionals, can be put in five main ways. These are:

(1) The social importance of the arts – as ways of bringing people together, increasing understanding between people from different backgrounds, and encouraging a variety of forms of collaborative action; for many people, the processes of taking part in the arts are as important as the end products.

(2) The recreational importance of the arts – as ways of refreshing the human body and spirit and giving pleasure to individuals and groups.

(3) As forms of personal development. Most people go through life without realising a fraction of their talents, including their artistic talents. Practising the arts with any seriousness involves developing skills and techniques; and the arts demand the exercise of the imagination and provide ways of developing self-confidence.

(4) The psychological importance of the arts – for those with or without religious belief the arts are a way in which people can express their deepest values, and affirm or explore their identity. Partly because they are frequently practised at home, the amateur arts are often a more integral part of everyday life for many people than the professional arts.

(5) The economic importance of the arts – about which much has been written in recent years.

While the economic and recreational aspects of the arts are important, the social and psychological importance of the arts, and their significance for personal development, are worth underlining in these dehumanising times. In fast-changing technocratic, and increasingly multicultural, societies the importance of cultural identity, of social awareness, and of the unique value of the individual personality – all aspects of life which can be illuminated and explored through artistic endeavour and expression – can hardly be overstated. And the arts have this social and psychological importance whether practised by professionals or amateurs, full-timers or part-timers.

The professional and amateur arts are, and should be seen as, intertwined and interdependent.   Professional theatres generate income by being let to amateur companies; professional conductors, musicians, directors, actors and singers have gained invaluable experience by working with amateur choirs, orchestras and drama groups – indeed it is usually not just the amateurs who benefit from the many forms of professional/ amateur collaboration. And tens of thousands of 'part-time professionals' in all the main art forms earn much of their living by teaching the arts.

All professional artists begin either as children, as students or as adult amateur artists. More generally, as Peter Cox has argued, greater public recognition needs to be given to the contribution that the amateur arts make to:
- the quality, variety and cultural diversity of the arts provision in the country;
- the provision of arts entertainment where little or none other exists;
- the early training of future professionals and the employment of professionals artists;
- audience-building for professional events;
- the support of the arts industries;
- the preservation of traditional art-forms, both indigenous ones and those brought in by immigrant populations;
- individual and community well-being.[3]

There are as many kinds of amateur artists as there are of human beings. But arguably the crucial distinction in the arts is not between the 'amateur arts' and the 'professional arts', but between the 'lively arts' and the 'deadly arts'. The distinction draws heavily on Peter Brook's lecture on the 'The Deadly Theatre'.[4]

The 'lively arts' are those practised in a skilful way by people with energy and imagination. At best, the outcome is work that is technically accomplished, challenging and perhaps daring, emotionally profound, probably aware of tradition but nonetheless original, perhaps intellectually exciting and certainly generous in spirit. The 'deadly arts' are hackneyed, cliché-ridden, mean in spirit, unimaginative, emotionally shallow, tired, self-satisfied, safe and usually (just to compound the misery) technically unaccomplished. The amateur arts have no monopoly on the 'deadly arts', though much amateur work (and indeed much professional work) is pretty deadly, and many amateur groups are too set in their ways.

However, underpinning the policy recommendations that follow is a belief that a great deal more can and should be done to enhance artistic standards in the amateur arts and to encourage more people to develop their potential as artists. In general, the more people develop their artistic skills, the more likely they are to enjoy their artistic activities.

Policy issues and recommendations

1. Because of their cultural, social and psychological importance, and because of the interdependence of the professional and amateur arts, consideration of how best to support the amateur arts should be a major component of the National Arts Strategy, not a fringe issue.

2. The main national and regional funding bodies for the arts and crafts in the UK need to join with other agencies (the youth service, adult education agencies, local authorities) to develop and implement a coherent set of policies for supporting and evaluating programmes that involve people in practising the arts. These should include policies to encourage more school-leavers to continue to practise the arts once they leave school, and policies to develop higher standards of teaching and animation and to stimulate more adventurous and challenging work across the range of the participatory arts (community arts, adult education, youth arts, amateur arts).

3. The nationally-organised service organisations (referred to in this report as 'umbrella' organisations) provide an administrative framework through which amateur arts activity can be further developed. The partnership between the Little Theatre Guild and British Telecom is a good example of how an outward-looking 'national' organisation and an enlightened sponsor can work together to enhance the amateur arts both artistically and organisationally. In some cases the 'umbrella' organisations already receive regular financial support from the appropriate Arts Council to help provide the training, advice and other services that they offer. But the Arts Council of Great Britain has not been as helpful in this respect as the other three national Arts Councils in the UK. In particular in partnership with the Central Council for Amateur Theatre, the ACGB should encourage, and support

financially, the establishment of a Drama Association of England to fulfil in England the functions undertaken by the Drama Association of Wales in the Principality.

4. Many of the arts activities of ethnic minorities override and render insignificant any distinction between amateurs and professionals. Many of the assumptions of ethnic minorities' cultures differ from those of the indigenous British, but arts activities are of vital social and psychological importance to the lives of ethnic minorities. At the same time, the potential of Asian, Afro-Caribbean, East European, and other cultures to enrich the culture of the UK has yet to be fully realised. Although in recent years there has been some increase in awareness of the cultural contribution and needs of ethnic minorities, arts funding bodies and the national arts service organisations (including the Voluntary Arts Network) need to introduce or develop clear policies for enhancing cultural diversity and need to monitor and publicise their programmes for implementing such policies.

5. The development of many kinds of collaboration between professionals and amateurs was one of the most encouraging aspects of the arts in Britain in the 1980s. There is nothing straightforward about most such collaborations; indeed they usually demand considerable sensitivity and subtlety of approach. But, at best, they are an excellent way of sharing experience and raising the aspirations of those involved. Further supporting and evaluating such collaborations – and developing guidelines as to how they can work most effectively – should be one of the principal tasks of the new Regional Arts Boards.

6. Financial support and support in kind from local authorities is important to thousands of amateur arts groups. These forms of support continue to be eroded by the ever-increasing pressures on local government finance and the introduction of local management of schools. Because of their educational and recreational benefits, local authorities need to help provide equality of access to the amateur arts for all sections of society. Local government support for the arts – including the amateur arts – needs to be more carefully monitored and good practice among local authorities that give appropriate and consistent support to the amateur arts needs to be widely publicised.

7. British education grows increasingly utilitarian with diminishing importance attached to the education of the imagination and the emotions. Arts activities, both in and out of school, are under threat from the current changes in the curriculum and management of education. A full and independent study of the arts in primary and secondary education is needed to analyse, monitor and report on what is happening; a study is also needed to evaluate the longer-term benefits of encouraging active participation in the arts at a young age. At the same time, the principal arts funding bodies need to be consistent and resolute in advocating the importance of the arts in education.

8. Liberal adult education is under severe threat both from the attrition in local government expenditure and from the proposals contained in the White Paper *Education and Training for the 21st Century*. Adult education classes have been a route taken by hundreds of thousands of people to practise and develop their artistic skills. In an affluent society like Britain, there should be no question that those who wish to engage in arts and crafts, either as beginners or as more experienced practitioners, and who wish to develop their skills and knowledge, should have the opportunity to do so. A new study of the arts in adult education is needed. This could compare provision, and the nature and extent of partnerships between arts organisations and adult education agencies, in the early 1990s with those in the late 1970s when the last comprehensive study of the subject was made.[5]

References

1. John Myerscough, *The Economic Importance of the Arts in Ipswich*, PSI, 1988, p.112.

2. *RSGB Omnibus Arts Survey*, Report on a Survey on Arts and Cultural Activities in Great Britain, Prepared by Research Services of Great Britain Ltd for the Arts Council of Great Britain, 1991.

3. Peter Cox, 'The Amateur Arts within a National Arts Strategy', mimeo, May 1991.

4. Peter Brook, *The Empty Space*, Penguin, 1972.

5. Geoffrey Adkins, *The Arts and Adult Education*, Advisory Council for Adult and Continuing Education, 1981.

Area studies – introduction

For each of the seven areas selected for the case studies, lists of amateur arts groups were drawn up and consistently revised during the course of the study. The help of local authority officers, librarians, local arts organisations, journalists, and others has been invaluable in this process. In our postal questionnaire surveys of groups in the selected areas we were concerned to concentrate on those groups that were run by volunteers for volunteers. All adult education classes have been excluded (unless the class also has an active artistic life outside the adult education framework); youth groups were excluded unless the majority of those participating were 16 and over and the group was organised largely outside the framework of the professional youth service. Arts projects whose existence depends heavily on the work of paid community artists or community workers have also been excluded. These exclusions were made partly to make a very wide-ranging research project a little less unmanageable and partly to distinguish amateur arts from other types of participatory arts activity (see Chapter 2). However, as can be seen, the case study reports do include some information about, and discussion of, adult education and youth arts provision, as well as community arts.

In some cases active groups have been identified at a late stage in the research. These have been included in the number of groups identified although in a few cases the groups were not sent a questionnaire.

The amateur arts world is in a constant state of flux. There are no definitive lists of amateur arts groups. Even local arts officers or journalists specialising in the arts on the local radio and in the local press are not always in a position to say whether, for example, a local amateur drama group is still operating. Groups constantly form and sometimes split; their officers change; sometimes groups go dormant for prolonged periods; sometimes they revive unexpectedly.

However, as these studies show, many amateur arts organisations have had long lives and have survived many vicissitudes. Unless otherwise stated quotations in the text are taken from questionnaires returned by amateur arts groups.

1   Aberdeen

With a resident population of 215,300, Aberdeen is Scotland's third largest city and the administrative centre of the north east of Scotland. The City has a long and distinguished history, but, in recent years, the traditional industries of inshore and deep-sea fishing, granite quarrying, and engineering have to some extent been overtaken by developments associated with the exploitation of North Sea oil. In 1981, the oil industry in Aberdeen employed 33,000 workers and by 1986 this figure had increased to over 44,000. The pattern of expansion has subsided somewhat since the mid-1980s, but in 1991 the sector was estimated to account for 30 per cent of all employment in the City. The oil industry is one of the principal factors explaining Grampian region's position as having the third highest GDP per head in the UK.[1] Outside the oil sector, employment in primary, construction and manufacturing industries is comparatively small, with more than half of the City's total workforce in non-oil service industries (77,000). Central and local government administration in the City generates around 20,000 jobs.

Although the oil industry has brought additional wealth to Aberdeen, it has also brought a range of problems which inevitably accompany a large influx of transient workers. The sudden increase in the demand for housing brought about exceptional inflation in the property market. In the period from the early 1970s up to 1984 prices increased from below the UK average to 25 per cent above the average.

Cultural traditions
The geographical isolation of Aberdeen – which is some 125 miles from Edinburgh – has helped to ensure the survival of a strong local and regional culture. Aberdeen's famous granite has given the cityscape a highly individual character. In his recent report on the participatory and performing arts in Aberdeen, Malcolm Rennie

remarked that Aberdeen and the North East had a cultural identity more akin to the Scandinavian countries than parts of Great Britain.

> [The city has] a folk tradition that reaches back over the generations and exists not only in song, verse and music but in the very way in which resident Aberdonians relate to each other. The native speech and vocabulary are extraordinarily rich in dialect words and regional phrases...
>
> The traditional and folk art of the North East is a huge, precious and living cultural asset which... is at the core of cultural life in the area.[2]

Superimposed upon these traditional cultural practices are the influences of the more recent past. The City has gained a strong reputation in the field of the visual arts. The establishment of the Aberdeen Artists Society in 1885 proved to be particularly significant. The Society played a vital part in the establishment of Aberdeen's art gallery. The Grays School of Art and the Peacock Printmakers enhance this reputation. The church has had a marked influence on creative activities within the City, and, in combination with the University, has ensured that choral music has remained an important part of the cultural life of the city. The University's origins lie in two separate foundations – the College of St Mary founded by William Elphinstone, Bishop of Aberdeen (1505), and Marischal College founded by George Keith (1593). The two foundations were reconstituted in 1860 as the University of Aberdeen.

The Lichtenfels Report on drama provision in Aberdeen and the Grampian region describes the city's theatrical history as 'remarkable'.[3] The first recorded play performance dates from 1440; Shakespeare brought his company to the city in 1601 at the special request of James VI; and Shaw's *Candida* was premiered in 1904. But the absence of a resident professional company has not served to lessen the significance of participation in drama. Far from it. As will be discussed in more detail later, Aberdeen has built up a thriving network of amateur and community theatre.

Arts organisations and institutions

One of Aberdeen's cultural strengths lies in its museums and galleries. The District Council runs four museums, of which the Art Gallery consistently attracts one of the ten highest recorded attendances for municipal museums and galleries in the UK. The Art Gallery was opened in 1885 under the auspices of the Aberdeen Artists Society. At the turn of the century, Alexander Macdonald bequeathed to the city his own collection. The Town Council took over responsibility for the Gallery in 1907.

The city's performing arts establishments are receiving venues. In spite of its size, Aberdeen has neither a producing theatre nor an art film cinema, and the lack of the former has tended to dominate discussions about arts provision within the City. Aberdeen is home to a small-scale touring company, the Invisible Bouncers. The principal receiving venues are the Music Hall and His Majesty's Theatre (HMT). Both were refurbished during the 1980s. The HMT, opened in 1906, was notable for being the first theatre to be built entirely of granite. The theatre receives funding as part of the Scottish Arts Council (SAC)/City of Aberdeen District Council Stage One Scheme. In 1989/90, 10 productions and 79 performances were given under the scheme with combined SAC/District Council funding of £157,700. The Music Hall, the main venue for large-scale classical concerts, has a seating capacity of 1,287 and is run by the District Council. The Royal Scottish Orchestra, Scottish Ballet, Scottish Opera, the Scottish Chamber Orchestra all make regular trips to Aberdeen. The Scottish Ensemble is one of a number of smaller groups and ensembles which perform in the Cowdray Hall, adjacent to the Art Gallery in Schoolhill.

There is a range of smaller venues capable of holding performing arts events. The Aberdeen Arts Centre dates from 1963, making it one of the first generation of British arts centres. The Arts Centre acts as a venue for small-scale touring and amateur product and is run directly by Aberdeen District Council. Aberdeen Arts Centre Association receives a small annual grant from the SAC. It has some rooms for workshop and club meetings and also holds regular exhibitions by local artists. The Arts Centre acts as the base for the Aberdeen Arts Carnival. The District Council also operates the Beach Ballroom, a multi-purpose venue. The Northern College of Education has a small auditorium, although it is located some distance from the city centre on the college campus and is currently without a performing license.

Amateur arts activities

In the view of Ian McKenzie Smith, the City Arts Officer 'the geographical insularity of Aberdeen has led to a highly developed amateur structure'.[4] A total of 46 amateur arts organisations were identified in Aberdeen. Excluding groups run by the University Music Department (which were covered by a single questionnaire), and those groups which fell outside the definition of amateur used for the purposes of this report, usable replies were received from 40 groups, a response rate of 87 per cent. Table AB1 breaks down identified organisations and responses by category. Two outstanding features of the amateur arts in the City are the extensive involvement of the University in the field of music and the activities of the amateur dramatic and operatic societies.

AB1 Aberdeen responses to questionnaire

	Number identified	Number responded
Performing groups		
Drama	6	4
Light operatic	7	6
Choirs(a)	9	8
Brass bands(a)	4	3
Orchestras(a)	1	1
Folk and country dancing	7	6
Non-performing groups		
Painting and drawing	2	2
Crafts	2	2
Camera clubs/photography	3	3
Writing/poetry groups	2	2
Music promoting	3	3

(a) Excludes groups administered by University Music Department.

It is widely acknowledged that the University plays a central role in music provision, for both amateur and professional alike.[4] The University promotes free lunchtime recitals in the Elphinstone Hall and evening concerts at the Mitchell Hall – 33 were given in 1989/90 – by both student groups and professional artists. The Music Department runs a variety of ensembles including a symphony orchestra, choral society, chamber choir, wind band and a string ensemble (King's College Chapel has its own choir). But members of the Department-run groups, estimated to number some 220 performers, are not simply limited to the student population. The Department also encourages the participation of non-student members. As well as providing the necessary practical opportunities for full-time music students, Roger Williams, the Head of Music, felt that the Department made two other equally important contributions to the community:

> by promoting professional concerts by visiting groups and enlarging opportunities for participatory arts [and] stimulation of more ambitious events than any other single organisation could mount, both artistically and financially.

In addition to the Music Department's direct contribution to promoting non-professional music, there is at least one student-run madrigal choir in receipt of a small grant from the Students Representative Council (SRC). From the end of the academic year

AB2   University arts groups: membership, 1989/90

	Number of members	Date of foundation
Performing groups		
Gilbert and Sullivan Society	70	1976
University Madrigal Society	25	1987
Royal Scottish Country Dancing Society	109	1949
Treading the Boards	60	1989
Bare Necessities	90	1987
University Music Department groups	225	..
Total performing	579	
Photographic Society	102	1976
Fine Arts Society	76	1990
Total fine arts	178	
Total	757	

AB3 Aberdeen amateur performing groups: membership, performances and attendances, 1989/90

Type of organisation	Number responding	Total member-ship	Total perform-ances	Average attendance per perf.
Drama	4	192	29	92
Light operatic(a)	6	353	35	333
Choirs	8	1,286	54	110
Brass bands/wind bands/ orchestra	4	215	49	..
University Music Department groups	na	225	43	101

(a) One society had formed during 1990 and had not, at the time of the survey, undertaken any performances.

1991/2, the Music Department will no longer teach undergraduate degree courses, but it will offer a one-year MA in Music and maintain its role as a promoter of concerts. Seven other university societies returned questionnaires and information on their date of foundation and memberships are given in table AB2. Table AB3 gives details of the membership, attendances and performances by drama and opera groups, choirs and bands in the City.

Apart from the groups organised through the University Music Department, there was one wind band, North East Wind, and 3 free-standing bands – UDI Brass, Aberdeen City Band and Bon Accord Silver Band, which consisted of an 'A' and 'B' band. The oldest of all the responding music groups was UDI Brass, established in 1908; the band rehearsed at Marconi UDI's office canteen. All of the bands were affiliated to their respective 'umbrella' organisations: the brass and silver bands were members of the Scottish Area Brass Band Association and North East Wind was a member of the British Association of Symphonic Bands and Wind Ensembles. Although none of the responding bands engaged professionals for performance or rehearsals (Table AB4), they all received some local authority financial assistance, either through paid engagements or small grants.

AB4 Aberdeen amateur performing groups: professional input into rehearsals and performances(a)

	Number responding	Groups with some professional input into rehearsals	into performances
Drama	4	1	–
Light operatic	6	2	3
Choirs	8	5	2
Brass bands/wind bands/ orchestra	4	–	–

(a) 'Professionals' may be directors, conductors, singers or musicians; they include tutors.

The various investigations into drama provision in the city have all commented on the quality and commitment of amateur dramatic societies. The Lichtenfels report remarks that

[Aberdeen's] characteristic traits of isolation, caution and self-reliance led to the development of a unique tradition of exceptionally high quality amateur work to supply the need for straight theatre...

[The] various strands in Aberdeen theatrical life... are accompanied by a steady counterpoint consisting of the high level and varied output of non-professional work.[6]

Whilst the nature of amateur activity has undoubtedly altered since the Lichtenfels Report was written 13 years ago, Aberdeen still has a large number of active amateur dramatic and operatic societies, including some which have only just been formed. Two of the responding societies had only been in existence since the beginning of 1990, and although this suggested a healthy state of affairs, the acting musical director of Limelight Theatre Group felt that the existence of more and more companies meant problems in terms of 'competing for audiences in the city'. At the same time, some groups have died. The ACE (Aberdeen College of Education) Theatre Group was disbanded following the closure of the Drama Department at the College. Of the 13 independent amateur dramatic and operatic societies identified, 10 returned the questionnaire. A high proportion

(70 per cent) of respondents were members of either the Scottish Community Drama Association (SCDA) or the National Operatic and Dramatic Association (NODA). Unlike the corresponding societies in Exeter, the University Gilbert and Sullivan Society and student theatre company ('Bare Necessities') were both members of NODA and SCDA respectively.

AB5 Aberdeen amateur performing groups: number of performances at each type of venue, 1989/90

Type of organisation	School (LEA)	Coll./ univ.	Theatre/ arts centre	Comm. centre	Church	Park	Other
Drama	–	6	18	–	–	–	8
Choirs	–	5	5	21	12	2	9
Orchestra	–	1	1	–	–	–	–
Light operatic	–	–	29	–	–	–	–
University Music Department	–	43	–	–	–	–	–

Table AB5 gives details of venues for performances and rehearsals by type of performing group. One member spoke for many of the drama societies in her criticism of the lack of suitable performance spaces in the city. For the drama groups, with their smaller memberships, the option of hiring the HMT was not financially viable and consequently the Arts Centre, in spite of its structural limitations, was the only acceptable venue for amateur drama. But as Paula Gibson, the Aberdeen secretary of the local SCDA branch, explained, a virtual doubling in hiring fees for the Arts Centre had caused financial problems for a number of local drama groups.[7]

Four of the larger societies use His Majesty's Theatre for at least part of their annual season – the Aberdeen Opera Company, the Lyric Musical Society, Limelight and Attic Theatre. Only two of these groups responded to the survey. However, according to His Majesty's, between 31 March 1990 and 1 April 1991, the four companies gave a total of 22 performances at the theatre, generating attendances of 14,847 and a combined box office of £76,296. The average ticket yield for the four productions was £5.13. Aberdeen

Opera Company was the oldest and largest of the responding dramatic and operatic societies with 90 members. 6 of the 10 respondents assessed artistic quality as being very important to the life of their society. One opinion which seemed to sum up the views of many of the societies came from the newly established Phoenix Theatre:

> Two principal motives are to give our audience the highest quality of amateur performance and to give enjoyment to ourselves and members – these are not divisible in that the greatest enjoyment will only be achieved by giving the best.

AB6 Aberdeen performing groups, sources of income, 1989/90

	Opera/operetta/musicals(a)		Choirs(b)	
	(£s)	Percentages	(£s)	Percentages
Box office	32,575	72	2,623	26
Subscriptions	2,356	5	2,276	22
Business sponsorship	4,205	9	927	9
Fund raising	2,565	6	1,577	15
Other earned	3,309	7	1,493	15
Local arts council	–	–	644	6
Scottish Arts Council	–	–	600	6
Total	45,010	100	10,140	100

(a) Figures relating to 5 societies, of which 4 were members of NODA and had a combined income of £41,220.

(b) Figures relating to 5 societies, of which 1 was a member of an 'umbrella' organisation but which accounted for 60 per cent of total income.

As Table AB6 shows, none of the responding operatic societies received any funding from public sources. And although financial issues were considered central to the running of a successful company, it was sponsorship that was specifically mentioned as a possible solution to higher theatre costs and possible deficits. Four of the operatic and dramatic companies received income from business sponsorship (to a total value of £4,205). At least one company received business support of a more traditional kind. The Exel Theatre Group is a BP subsidised society set up in 1980 to 'provide entertainment to Exel club members and families in the form of a Christmas pantomime and summer show'. Four of the five choirs which provided details of their finances were not affiliated to the NFMS. However, the Aberdeen Bach Choir – which was affiliated to the NFMS – accounted for the bulk of the choirs' combined incomes.

As well as groups practising local cultural traditions, Aberdeen provides a good example of the spread of cultural activities from other parts of the world. The city has a barbershop choir, an American Kilk Kickers Dance Group and the Tepsichore Folk Dancers, who specialise in traditional Balkan dancing. All these groups had been established over the last ten years. Just as recent, if a little more local, are the Bon Accord Cloggies, a group specialising in clog dancing from the North of England.

Aberdeen has a long history of involvement with children's theatre, which although strictly outside the scope of this study, is worthy of mention. A municipally-funded theatre for children was set up by the then Education Committee in 1939. An off-shoot of the children's theatre, the Longacre Players, was established in 1963 as an education authority-funded youth group, whose members are aged between 16 and 20.

The strength of Aberdeen's heritage in the field of the visual arts is based on a few groups rather than a large number of active societies. The Aberdeen Artists Society illustrated clearly the difficulty of strictly adhering to the labels of 'amateur' and 'professional', particularly in the field of the visual arts. The Society uses separate categories for professionals (86 members) and others (57 members), and prices its subscriptions accordingly. Indeed, the President felt uncertain as to whether it was valid to include the Society, with its large professional membership and professional aspirations, within a survey of the amateur arts. Although the society met 10 times between September 1989 and August 1990, its principal aim is the organising of an annual exhibition 'to foster an interest in art'. Around three-quarters of the Society's income is generated from business sponsorship and in 1989/90 it received no direct public funding. Access to the Art Gallery is provided free of charge by the District Council. Table AB7 gives details of the activities of the arts and crafts societies. Only 2 of the 7 visual arts and crafts bodies did not engage professional tutors and one craft group, with over 100 members, spent around £800 on professional tuition alone.

AB7 Aberdeen visual arts and crafts groups

	Number responding	Groups with paid tutors	Total members	Number of exhibitions held 1989/90
Painting and drawing	2	1	133	2
Crafts	2	2	155	2
Camera clubs	3	2	237	3

Arts festivals

Aberdeen has become home to a variety of festivals; in the five months between June to October only September is 'festival-free'. Virtually all feature some aspect of professional/amateur collaboration. Only two of the festivals identified were run entirely by volunteers. The annual competitive play festival organised by the Aberdeen branch of the Scottish Community Drama Association caters for local members of the SCDA and provides an annual focus for amateur dramatics in the City. The Festival is held at the Arts Centre and attracts on average between 10 and 14 entries from 7 or 8 drama societies in the City. The Aberdeen and North East of Scotland Competitive Music Festival is a typical example of the 300 competitive festivals in membership of the British Federation of Music Festivals. In 1990, festival performances attracted around 1,800 paid admissions, although around one half of the festival's income is from entrance fees; adjudicators' fees totalled £3,921.

The Aberdeen Arts Carnival is a mixture of arts performances and workshops centred around, and organised by, Aberdeen Arts Centre Association, on behalf of the District Council, with a grant from the Scottish Arts Council. The Arts Carnival has two distinct elements to it: a series of daytime art, dance, music and drama workshops which are professionally tutored and aimed mainly at children; and lunchtime and evening performances featuring both amateur and professional groups.

In 1991, Giz Giz, the Gallery Players, Studio Theatre Group and the female barbershop chorus, Sweet Adelines International, were amongst the amateur groups featured in the evening performances. The Arts Carnival is also the platform for performances by the Texaco

Theatre Summer School, a five week full-time theatre experience to give young people opportunities to rehearse and perform a show, to work together and learn theatre skills.

Preceding the Arts Carnival in the annual calendar is the Bon Accord Arts Festival, which runs for one week in June. The Festival was originally inspired by the ending of a serious outbreak of typhoid during the 1960s, and has been running ever since. Unlike the Arts Carnival, there is no workshop element to the festival, which aims to provide between 3 and 5 indoor and outdoor performances per day. The Bon Accord Festival is run as a District Council promotion, although most events are organised with little, if any, volunteer assistance; performances involve both amateur and professional groups and have a strong local flavour.

There are two large independent festivals with full-time administrations: the Aberdeen Alternative Festival and the Aberdeen International Youth Festival. The Alternative Festival celebrates the 'culture of Scotland alongside the best of music and entertainment from around the world'. The Festival receives funding from the District Council, SAC and the Aberdeen Tourist Board as well as various corporate sponsors, but it is dominated by professional product, professionally administered. There are a number of workshop events and a community programme ('Native', which in 1990 included dancing by the Gainsborough Dancing Club), but only one event, a fiddlers' rally featuring over 100 performers from strathspey and reel societies, stands out as a major example of amateur participation in the Alternative Festival. The Aberdeen International Youth Festival is also administered by a full-time professional administration, but caters exclusively for non-professional groups under the age of 23.

Adult education

Since the 1930s, community arts activity has been fostered by the City Education Department's development of school-based youth clubs. The youth clubs' programmes of activities have tended to feature a range of arts-based activities. The Education Department opened Aberdeen's first community centre at Powis in 1941; by 1958 the city had a further 13 similar centres operating. Aberdeen's network of community centres, now the responsibility of Grampian Regional Council, continue to play a significant role in the provision of adult and youth arts education. There are now some 24 community education centres of which 10 are integrated with primary and senior schools. The remainder are free-standing centres, and most are staffed. This accounts for only one half of the Regional Council's provision for community and adult education in the city. The community education centres are supplemented by classes organised through the network of Further Education Centres around the City.

AB8 Aberdeen arts-related adult education classes, 1990/91

	At Community Education Centres		At Further Education Centres	
	Classes	Participants	Classes	Participants
Performing arts				
Total	15	439	6	87
of which dance classes	8	268	1	12
Visual arts/crafts				
Total	14	152	..	806
of which painting/drawing	6	54	33	461
Writers' clubs	1	8	–	–

Table AB8 gives figures for adult education classes and participants at these two types of centre. The dance classes at community education centres cover ballet, contemporary, old time, ballroom, Latin and Scottish country dancing. There were 264 enrolments for crafts classes at the two types of centre.

With the exception of a writers' workshop run by the University, the two other strands of adult education provision in Aberdeen, the Workers Education Association (WEA) and courses run by the University's Centre for Continuing Education, do not include any participatory arts classes.

Public funding for the amateur arts

The City of Aberdeen District Council makes limited contributions to the direct funding of the amateur arts through the Arts and Recreation [Arts] Sub-Committee and the Arts and Recreation [Art Gallery and

Museums] Sub-Committee, which channel grant-aid to community initiatives, amateur groups and smaller festivals. In 1990/1, more than half of the latter budget of £22,000 was allocated to the Peacock Printmakers. Of the 13 groups or projects receiving funds from the Arts and Recreation budget that year, only 3 groups – North East Wind, the Scottish Community Drama Association and the Aberdeen & North East of Scotland Music Festival Association – fell within the definition of free-standing amateur groups. By November 1990, all 13 groups had been allocated funds of £52,125 out of a total budget of £67,500, of which the 3 amateur groups had received £1,888. But if this direct commitment to the amateur sector seems modest, it does not represent the totality of assistance through the City Council. The City Arts Department also engages resident and visiting bands (some of which are of amateur status) to play in the various parks and other venues around Aberdeen; and it covers the costs of amateur groups engaged in the Bon Accord Festival; income generated in ticket sales is then kept by societies involved. Other support is in kind: the provision of the Art Gallery for the Artists Society's annual exhibition is one example. Furthermore, the Department operates an extensive equipment loan scheme.

The City Arts Department has recently been assessing ways of fostering the arts within the City. The City's Arts and Recreation Committee gives full recognition to the role of amateur arts:

> However, the arts are more than a spectator activity. The opportunities for participation in the arts must encompass the possibility for everyone both to express themselves creatively in whatever medium they feel appropriate to their life and experience, and to attain in that medium as high a level of proficiency as they can.

> Given the support and encouragement of a skilled practitioner some means of artistic expression require only basic resources to offer an individual the opportunity to participate actively in the arts....

> Major resources and collective activities are best provided for at a local level to ensure their accessibility to as many people as possible. The City of Aberdeen is committed to offering locally-based opportunities for participation in the arts.[8]

It remains to be seen whether, and to what extent, the commitment to ensuring full arts participation in the City will be backed up by the financial commitments that the practical execution of such an objective requires.

Conclusion

Amateur arts in Aberdeen embrace a range of styles and cultural traditions – local, regional, national and international. Whilst the City has a long tradition in the amateur arts, there is no shortage of new groups. Geographically isolated, and with little in the way of resident professional performing arts, Aberdeen provides a good example of the way in which a variety of authorities – university, district council, regional council – assist the amateur by indirect rather than direct means, through the provision of venues, help with publicity and in other ways. However, there is a legitimate concern over the steadily increasing costs of much amateur arts activity and acknowledgement of the shortage of suitable performance spaces.

References

1. *Regional Trends 25*, HMSO, 1990.

2. Malcolm Rennie, *Sleeping Beauty: A Report on the Performing and Participatory Arts in the City of Aberdeen*, December 1990.

3. Peter Lichtenfels and Anthony Phillips, *Professional Drama Provision in the City of Aberdeen and Grampian Region*, Scottish Arts Council, 1978.

4. Conversation with Ian McKenzie Smith, City Arts Officer, Aberdeen District Council, 22 October 1990.

5. 'Report by the National Association of University Music Staff to the Music Working Party of the Arts Sub-Committee of the University Grants Committee', May 1988.

6. Peter Lichtenfels and Anthony Phillips, *op.cit.*, p.3.

7. Conversation with Paula Gibson, 23 July 1991.

8. 'The Arts in Aberdeen', paras. 5.12 to 5.14, City of Aberdeen Arts and Recreation Committee, Draft 3 1991.

2 Exeter

The City of Exeter has a population of 102,300. It is located in the south eastern corner of the county and, although it is half the size of its western neighbour Plymouth, it is still recognised as the County town of Devon. The City dates from Roman times when it became the centre for administration for the whole of Devon and Cornwall. The City benefits from good road and rail links with the rest of the country and this has been one factor in the development of a range of tertiary sector industries, particularly retailing, distribution and tourism. These three industries account for the largest proportion of employment in the City. According to a recent economic strategy document prepared by the City Council, employment in the service sector made up 85.1 per cent of all employment. Manufacturing industry, which is concentrated predominantly on two sites, Marsh Barton and Sowton, accounted for just under 9 per cent of all employment.[1]

As well as being close to both Dartmoor and Exmoor National Parks, Exeter is a tourist centre in its own right and boasts various museums, a gallery, and numerous buildings of historical significance. Of these, the Cathedral, an example of Gothic architecture located in a largely undisturbed part of the City, is outstanding. In parallel with developments in many other British cities, the riverside basin area is currently being developed as a tourist centre. Located on the eastern edge of the City is the campus of Exeter University.

In 1989, the consultancy Practical Arts was commissioned by a consortium of Devon-based local authorities and South West Arts to undertake a survey and suggest a strategy for the development of arts in the County.[2] South Devon's cultural strengths are to a great extent associated with its long traditions in the fields of the visual arts and crafts.

Main arts venues and institutions

The 1990/91 *Museums Yearbook* lists 7 museums within the city boundaries. Five of these are branches of the City Council's museums service. There is one major independent museum, the Maritime Museum, which has an international collection of historic ships and boats and attracted some 90,000 visitors in 1990. Wyvern Barracks houses the seventh museum, that of the Devonshire and Dorset Regiment. Apart from the exhibition space which forms part of the Royal Albert Memorial Museum, the City also has a publicly-funded gallery, the Spacex Gallery, located in a building owned by the City Council. Although this primarily functions as an exhibition space, the two upper floors of the Spacex Gallery are in use as studios.

Financial partnerships between the City Council, County Council and South West Arts characterise the funding of Exeter's arts venues; the Spacex and the two principal performing arts venues, the Exeter and Devon Arts Centre and the Northcott Theatre, receive funding from all three bodies. Located on the university campus and dating from 1967, the Northcott is an Arts Council-funded producing theatre which puts on a varied programme of professionally produced plays, films and amateur and student productions. The Exeter and Devon Arts Centre is a more recent development, the result of a joint initiative by the City Council and County Council in the early 1980s. The Centre offers performances across the full range of art forms as well as acting as a resource for a variety of arts-related adult education classes.

Although Exeter now has its arts centre, it still lacks a purpose-built concert venue. Performances of chamber music and orchestral and choral concerts take place in an assortment of locations around the City. A regular series of concerts by the Bournemouth Symphony and Sinfonietta (promoted by the Western Orchestral Society) take place at the University, as well as part of a series of chamber music concerts promoted by the University itself. The Great Hall also hosts pop and rock concerts organised by the University Guild of Students. Otherwise, large-scale classical music performances, amateur and professional, tend to take place in the Cathedral or churches, although at least one amateur orchestra performs regularly at the Plaza Leisure Centre.

Some chamber music concerts are put on at the Barnfield Theatre, a 303-seat venue located close to the city centre. However the venue is more usually regarded as the principal venue for amateur dramatic and operatic productions in the City. It is housed in a council-owned building, which the council converted to a theatre in 1972 and subsequently leased to the Exeter Little Theatre Company. The University's School of Education, located away from the main campus, also has a small 100-seat theatre which shows a variety of student productions as well as the work of some small-scale companies.

Amateur arts organisations

64 amateur groups were identified in Exeter, of which 39 replied, giving a response rate of 61 per cent. Table EX1 breaks down respondents into their respective categories. Part of the explanation for the high number of active groups lies in the many University-based arts societies. It has already been noted how, from surveys of the general population undertaken at the national level, students are particularly active participants in amateur music and drama and the wider arts. The University has comparatively small drama and music

EX1 Exeter: responses to questionnaire

	Number identified	Number responded
Performing groups		
Drama	10	7
Light operatic	6	5
Choirs	13	7
Brass bands	1	1
Orchestras/wind bands	5	4
Folk and country dancing	11	6
Non-performing groups		
Art/craft	5	2
Camera clubs/photography	2	2
Film	2	–
Writing groups	1	1
Music promoting	2	2
Other	6	2

departments. Nevertheless the 17 University societies attract many active participants and, to a large extent, the City and University worlds flourish as separate entities. Both have their discrete sets of societies and groups. Adjusting for non-respondents, an estimated 1,668 out of a student population of 5,000 were involved in Guild-affiliated arts societies. Table EX2 lists responding societies and their memberships. One Guild-affiliated society which did not respond to the survey was Campus Bands. They aimed to assist student bands through the provision of venues for rehearsals and promoting performances.

EX2 University societies: membership(a)

	Number of members
Performing groups	
Student theatre	150
Stage musical	40
Gilbert and Sullivan	45
Choral Society	200
Orchestra	100
Total performing	535
Music society	110
Photographic society	110
Art group	30
Total membership	785

(a) Non-responding societies included Campus Bands, Cinsoc, Folk, University Singers, Wind orchestra, Film makers and 2 dance societies.

In common with the other case study areas, the analysis of amateur groups excluded all those functioning as an immediate result of initiatives taken by community workers and community artists. However where a group had started life as a community-initiative, but had subsequently established itself as a free-standing society, this fell legitimately within our sample. One example of this is the Exwick Community Drama Group. The group was originally set up by the Wren Trust in 1987 as part of a wider scheme to organise the biggest local pageant in Exeter. Exwick Community Drama Group became a free-standing organisation in 1989; in the 1990/1 season it presented two productions, a Christmas pantomime and a summer charity production as part of the Exeter Festival. The group maintains its links with the Wren Trust which continues to provide support-in-kind (props and musical instruments) for productions. Furthermore, a professional director from the Trust is hired for rehearsals and to devise a basic script, which is then embellished with contributions from members of the group. In 1989/90 the group received a small grant from the Exeter Arts Council.

Exeter-based societies benefit heavily from the existence of two theatres in the City. Access to performing or rehearsing venues was not mentioned by any of the responding societies as being a special problem for them, whilst two were in the fortunate position of owning their own clubhouse/rehearsal venue. The responding drama societies gave over 66 per cent of their performances in theatres or arts centres whilst light opera companies gave 74 per cent of their performances in this type of venue. Choral performances, as elsewhere, were largely given in churches (Table EX3).

EX3 Exeter: choirs, orchestras, dramatic and operatic societies: rehearsals and performances by venue, 1989/90

	Total	School LEA	School Indep.	Univ.	Arts centre/ theatre	Comm. centre	Church	Other
Drama	131	–	–	15	86	10	20	–
Choirs	47	–	–	3	1	5	35	3
Orchestras	15	–	–	5	3	–	5	2
Light operatic	43	–	–	–	32	11	–	–
Rehearsals (percentages)	100	13	21	25	–	13	12	17

As with the other University-based societies, the student drama, musical theatre and Gilbert and Sullivan societies all benefit from access to free rehearsal spaces at the University. However they had to pay the standard fee for the use of the Northcott Theatre for performances. In 1989/90, the Northcott Theatre was host to 6 productions by 5 non-professional societies (3 student and 2 amateur). These productions lasted some 7 weeks, making up 13 per cent of the Northcott's entire season, and generated attendances of 13,900 and box office receipts of £75,814. The average ticket yield for amateur performances at the Northcott was £5.45. This compares to an average ticket yield for professional home-based performances of £5.33. In total, the rental paid by amateur societies amounted to 4 per cent of the Northcott's income.[3]

As lessees of the Barnfield Theatre, Exeter Little Theatre Company (ELTC) is responsible for maintaining its interior and technical equipment; the City Council is responsible for the theatre's structure and external maintenance. The Barnfield has only one paid member of staff, Mrs Margaret Denman, who works half-time as the theatre manager. The theatre has its own bar, staffed when necessary by volunteers from the ELTC. All other staffing for performances is undertaken by the hiring societies. The ELTC accounts for about 25 per cent of the Barnfield's total performances, including a two-week,'money-spinning', Christmas pantomime. The rest of the time, the theatre is used by other societies, dance school shows, the Devon and Exeter Competitive Festival, and some of the University-promoted subscription concerts. Margaret Denman believes that audiences for the ELTC were not as good as they had been when the Company was established in 1954, partly as a result of the growth of professional theatre (and particularly pantomimes) in Exeter and Plymouth. But there had also been a growth in the number of dramatic and operatic societies based in the City in recent years.

The Barnfield clearly provides one of the focal points for amateur activity in the city. However, the ELTC felt that it faced a dilemma in how to fund the necessary renovation of the theatre's interior and technical facilities. In the 1989/90 financial year, the company had already spent in excess of £20,000 on the renovation of rehearsal facilities at its club headquarters. It is not surprising that the fact that ELTC owned its own premises was considered to be a stabilising influence on the company in that 'it holds the company together'.[4]

The amount of professional input into amateur dramatic and operatic production in Exeter is limited. Three of the musical comedy societies regularly engage pianists for rehearsals and, as has been noted above, the Exwick Community Drama Group engage a paid director. But apart from these examples, only the Exeter Amateur Operatic Society (EAOS), recorded any major expenditure on professionals, spending more than £1,600 on professional tuition – a professional director – and an estimated £5,500 on Musicians' Union payments to the pit band in 1989/90. The EAOS is one of the amateur groups which hires out the Northcott Theatre. Its youth section, Quest, gives performances at the Barnfield Theatre. According to Eric Luffman, the Society's Honorary Treasurer, 'it is becoming increasingly difficult for our main performances at the Northcott to be self-financing. The increase in the cost of production for the larger amateur companies may force up the true price which needs to be charged to a point at which our audiences may not continue to support us in such numbers as in the past'. The Society was already financing the loss on its Northcott performances by donations and income from investments.

The artistic aspirations of amateur companies performing in Exeter are high. 9 of the 12 dramatic and operatic societies (75 per cent) claimed that the achievement of artistic quality was very important to the life of the group.

EX4 Performing arts groups: sources of income, 1989/90(a)

| | Opera/operetta | | Drama | |
	(£s)	Percentages	(£s)	Percentages
Box office	52,657	91	43,578	82
Subscriptions	1,054	2	1,836	3
Business sponsorship	382	1	3,400	6
Fund raising	1,556	3	820	2
Other earned income	2,434	4	3,110	6
Local arts council	–		527	1
Total(b)	58,083	100	53,271	100

(a) 5 operatic societies and 7 dance societies.

(b) Of the 12 drama/opera societies only 3 were members of NODA, but they accounted for £56,745 of the societies' combined income (58 per cent of the total).

Table EX4 gives details of dramatic and operatic societies' sources of income. With the exception of the Exwick Community Drama Group, and a number of small grants from the University Guild of

Students to the student societies, non-professional drama activity in the City was found to be effectively self-financing. The other responding dramatic and operatic societies were funded entirely through a combination of subscriptions, box office income, some sponsorship and other earned income. Dramatic and operatic societies in the City cover a range of sizes. The two smallest societies generated an annual income of just under £2,000, and the majority of societies turned over less than £10,000. But two companies, both members of the National Operatic and Dramatic Association, earned in excess of £25,000 in 1989/90.

EX5 Exeter amateur performing groups: membership, performances and attendances, 1989/90

Type of organisation	Number responding	Total member-ship	Total perform-ances	Average attendance per perf.
Drama	7	436	131	154
Light operatic	5	336	43	303
Choirs	7	506	47	262
Brass bands/orchestras	5	283	17	356
Total	24	1,561	238	217

Table EX5 summarises the basic details of the principal performing groups based in Exeter. Two factors in particular separate out music societies from dramatic societies. Firstly, the level of direct amateur/professional collaboration is much more significant in the musical life of the city; and, secondly, public funding for music is limited, for drama it is almost non-existent. Those amateur choirs and orchestras which gave details of their finances received more in the way of public funding. Two choirs and one orchestra were in receipt of public contributions totalling £2,050.

Table EX6 shows that compared to the responding drama societies, it was the musical comedy societies, choirs and orchestras based in the City which had a much higher level of professional input for both rehearsals and performances. This says something about the opportunities for professional/amateur collaboration in music-making and it also highlights a structural feature of the public funding system

EX6 Exeter amateur performing groups: professional input into rehearsals and performances(a)

Type of organisation	Number responding	Groups with some professional input into rehearsals	into performances
Drama	7	2	–
Light operatic	5	3	2
Choirs	7	4	5
Brass bands	1	–	–
Orchestras	4	3	2

(a) 'Professionals' may be directors, conductors, singers or musicians; they include tutors.

for amateur activities in England which is biased more towards music than the other arts.

In terms of size, the range of music groups mirrors that of amateur dramatic and operatic societies. There are a number of smaller groups, mainly choirs, sometimes organised on an informal basis, and one or two much larger societies which generate substantial annual incomes. Four of the City's societies were members of the National Federation of Music Societies and these tend to account for the majority of income. Of course size is not everything. One choir with only 24 members described itself as a 'high powered chamber choir... [with] at least 6 people travelling from the other side of the county for rehearsals... regular attendance is expected and... a waiting list of people wanting to join is kept'. 75 per cent of the responding music groups claimed that achievement of artistic quality was 'very important' to the group, the remainder claiming that it was 'important'.

In terms of their active memberships, the two largest music groups are the Exeter Musical Society (EMS) and the Exeter University Choral Society. The former is a long-established choral society (1929) which engages either an *ad hoc* professional orchestra or the Bournemouth Sinfonietta for performances which require orchestral accompaniment. Like many NFMS-affiliated choral societies, the EMS engages a professional conductor and a pianist for rehearsals. All performances are undertaken in the Cathedral. The EMS also ran an amateur orchestra, but since 1989 this has operated as a separate Society. Not all the music societies saw performing as the ultimate aim. The Exeter Rehearsal Orchestra had started out in 1960 as the Devon Federation of Women's Institutes Orchestra, but had become an independent organisation in 1990. As the name implies, the group did not give public performances but aimed simply to 'enable enthusiastic amateurs of all ages to play music from the classical repertoire'.

Exeter British Rail Band has been in existence since 1944 and currently its membership ranges in age from 9 to 84 years. Although the band recorded no professional input for either rehearsals or performances in 1989/90, it did incur substantial expenditure, financed by means of a loan, on the purchase of new instruments.

The organised world of folk music and dance is a third easily identifiable sector of amateur performing arts in Exeter. All but one of the six responding folk dance groups were members of one of the national 'umbrella' bodies. At least two of the responding dance groups did not actually perform publicly but simply met to dance, or as one group explained 'to enjoy ourselves in a social activity'. When asked to give details of the age range of its membership, one club described it as being 'thirtysomething'.

The Exeter Folk Club is a promoting rather than a performing group with around 45 members. The Club engages 'local, national and international artists' of both professional and non-professional standing. Engagements of professional artists are paid for out of admission fees whereas admission is free on those occasions when club or local singers are performing.

The variety of student-based arts activity occurs in a largely uncoordinated fashion. This is in spite of the efforts of a Guild Arts Committee which is charged both with booking a limited number of professional (and often fringe) arts groups for performances on the University campus, as well as promoting and co-ordinating arts-related Guild societies. The Committee has been particularly successful at promoting one-off events for any student to participate in. Since 1987, a termly Cabaret has been organised at the Arts Centre, incorporating some 25 acts and playing to around 200 people. But even this example of city-university interaction ends up by being attended by a largely student audience.[5]

Festivals

Exeter has two festivals. The Devon and Exeter Competitive Festival is a volunteer-run competitive music festival affiliated to the British Federation of Music Festivals. It started in the 1920s and runs for two weeks in March and February of each year. Apart from the payment of adjudicators, the festival is run entirely by more than 20 volunteers.

The annual Exeter Festival is funded and administered by the City Council, through the Chief Executive's Office. The Festival takes place over a three-week period in June. The Practical Arts report on arts in the County – commissioned by a consortium of Devon local authorities – made a number of criticisms about the 'elitist image' the Festival had acquired through its concentration on classical music concerts.[6] However increasingly the Festival is attempting to combine more mainstream promotions with community-linked involvement. Lesley Bardrick, the Festival Administrator, explained that the festival 'falls into three categories i) main events ii) events programmed through the Exeter and Devon Arts Centre iii) community events... the 1991 Festival will feature approximately 70 community events... organised by individual groups or individuals concerned, and run by them. The Festival Office co-ordinates these events into the Festival brochure thereby giving them the advantage of wide publicity... beyond that, these events receive no further help from us – they simply use the festival as a means of self-promotion which in turn enhances the flavour of the Festival'.[7]

Adult education provision

Adult education in the City is the preserve of five different organisations: the County Council, Workers Education Association, University of Exeter Centre for Continuing Education, Exeter College and Exeter and Devon Arts Centre. Courses on offer were advertised in a single brochure and whilst the 5 bodies try to organise complementary classes rather than duplicate existing classes, there is no formal attempt to allocate fields between the different bodies. The Arts Centre takes a lead role in arts-related adult education. The current director of the Arts Centre, John Struthers, attaches considerable emphasis to the Centre's role as a resource for the local community (although its responsibilities stretch well beyond the city boundary). The most recent version of the Arts Centre's Policy Document lists engaging 'people in creative participation to meet their own needs' as one of the six principal policy aims. In addition to directly promoting a number of classes, the Arts Centre offers individual tutors the opportunity to advertise privately for students, charge them, and pay an 'at cost' rent for using the Arts Centre. This approach is justified on the basis that it allows a degree of flexibility in the provision of classes which might attract only a few participants. At the start of the 1990 term, the Arts Centre was advertising an average of 10 classes per weekday run by private tutors, although not all of these would fall within even a particularly generous interpretation of the word 'arts'. The Arts Centre also houses the Exeter Darkroom, managed by Fair Exchange South West. As well as offering facilities to members (membership is open to anyone), the Darkroom provides tuition and runs a number of workshops and courses.

According to Amanda Statham, Adult Education Co-ordinator for East Devon, County Council-run courses are geared towards the visual arts/crafts rather than the performing arts, where the Arts Centre is particularly strong. In 1990, the County Council organised 9 performing arts classes of varying length – 1 singing, 1 drama, 3 music workshops and 4 dance classes. By contrast, there were 23 painting and drawing classes, 4 of which were 3 hour/3 term classes catering for the 'serious' painter. Participants in the various art classes were encouraged to organise their own exhibitions on Library premises or other central locations, although these were not organised by the tutors. With an average of 16 participants per visual arts class, the courses had higher enrolment levels than many other classes. The County Council also ran 25 classes in crafts and pottery, 4 in photography and 2 in creative writing.[8]

The Department of Continuing Education and Adult Education at the University of Exeter offers a variety of classes in music and arts appreciation but, in 1990/1, only one participatory course (on women and video, run in conjunction with the Arts Centre), was advertised. Exeter College, on the other hand, offered a full range of creative classes, 17 of which involved some arts participation. These included access to the college orchestra, choral society and big band.

Public funding for the amateur arts

Exeter City Council provides an annual grant to the Exeter Arts Council(EAC), which is responsible for distributing grants to both professional and amateur clients with a turnover of less than £10,000. Funding for professional arts organisations with a turnover in excess of £10,000 is directed through the City Council. The running of EAC is completely dependent on volunteers and the full membership of the Arts Council – 6 members – includes city councillors as well as others involved in the arts in Exeter. Only one member of the Arts Council, Hilary McGowan (Assistant Director of Leisure and Tourism with responsibility for Museums and Arts), attends in a formal capacity. In 1990/91, grants and guarantees offered totalled £7,651. A significant part of this went towards funding individuals and small professional groups; only £3,000 went to amateur groups identified during the course of the study. The public sector contribution in terms of venues is covered elsewhere in this report, although it is worth adding that the City's libraries are from time to time used for exhibitions by amateur artists' groups.

Conclusion

Of the case study areas, Exeter comes closest to the classic example of amateur artistic activity in an English City. It has a number of large performing groups which have long histories and are well-established in the City, but the setting up of smaller groups in recent years is a feature of Exeter as it is elsewhere. The two groups of amateur artists in Exeter – the locals and the students – tend to function quite separately, which is in stark contrast to the situation in Aberdeen. The establishment of the Arts Centre has added a new dimension to arts participation, mainly through courses and workshops. Direct local authority financial contributions to the amateur arts are small but there is a better range of arts buildings – the Northcott Theatre, the Arts Centre, the University and the Barnfield Theatre – than in many similar places. That said, there is still no purpose-built concert venue and music-making outside the University is confined largely to ecclesiastical venues across the City.

References

1. 'Exeter City Council Economic Development Strategy', undated.
2. *A Strategy for the Arts in Devon: A Discussion Document prepared by Practical Arts*, undated.

3. Letters from John W. Clarke, Administrator, Northcott Theatre, 6 December 1990 and 16 August 1991; Arts Council of Great Britain.

4. Conversation with Margaret Denman, 20 December 1991.

5. Conversation with Chas Early, Chair of the Guild of Students Arts Committee, 26 November 1990.

6. *A Strategy for the Arts in Devon*, *op.cit.*, p.28.

7. Letter from Lesley Bardrick, Festival Administrator, 1 February 1991.

8. Conversation with Amanda Statham, Adult Education Co-ordinator, East Devon Area, 26 November 1990.

3   The London Borough of Lewisham

The London Borough of Lewisham is located in the south eastern part of the capital, bordered by the Thames to the North, Greenwich to the East, Bromley to the South and Southwark to the West. It has a total population of 228,900. Figures estimated on the basis of the Labour Force Survey and the 1981 Census indicate that for the period 1986-1988, ethnic minorities accounted for 18.5 per cent of the total resident population.[1]

The Borough was born out of the Local Government Act of 1963, which brought together the former metropolitan boroughs of Deptford and Lewisham in a single authority from 1965. Deptford, in the north of the borough, was originally a fishing village which grew to become a major shipbuilding centre after Henry VIII established a Royal Dockyard in 1513. Despite the post-war decline in the docks Deptford is still the location for much of what is left of Lewisham's indigenous industrial employment. The southern part of today's Borough had all but succumbed to London's growing residential sprawl by the time of the Second World War. Towards the east of the borough, the boundary bisects Blackheath High Street, where the large Victorian houses and village setting, bring about a quite different atmosphere.

But of all the case study areas, Lewisham posed the most difficult problems. In Lewisham it was harder to identify the 'sense of place' that could be found in the other study areas.

Main arts venues and institutions

The Borough has a number of multi-purpose arts venues, the largest of which is the Lewisham Theatre. Dating from the early 1930s, it has a capacity of 850 and is located in Catford, in the south of the borough. It is funded and managed by the Borough Council. The venue provides a range of arts and light entertainment, and is one of the few buildings suitable for use by the borough's larger performing amateur groups. The Broadway Studio, a 102-seat venue was opened in 1987, converted from a public hall. Located close to Deptford High Street is the Albany Empire, a purpose built arts centre which acts as host to a variety of professional and community groups. Until 1991 it was funded jointly by Lewisham Council and Greenwich Council, Greater London Arts (GLA) and the London Boroughs' Grants Unit. Greenwich withdrew its funding in March 1991; GLA and Lewisham ended their funding in June 1991; and the London Boroughs' Grants Unit awarded only a six-months grant for 1991/2. The building is still open for use by its resident projects, who retain their funding. The Great Hall at Goldsmiths' College occasionally hosts concerts, and just outside the borough, in Greenwich, are the Blackheath Concert Halls which originate from the late nineteenth century. After a long period of inactivity, the larger of the two halls is soon to be renovated. Lewisham has one principal museum, the Horniman Museum which houses collections that 'illustrate the world we live in' – cultures, arts, crafts, the natural environment, and music. Until 1986 the Horniman was funded by the GLC. On the abolition of the GLC, responsibility was transferred to the Inner London Education Authority and, since that body's demise in April 1990, the Museums and Galleries Commission has been given responsibility for the Horniman's funding. The museum now has independent charitable status. The role of Goldsmiths' College, the Blackheath Conservatoire of Music and the Arts and the Lewisham Academy of Music will be addressed later.

Amateur arts activities
Two principal sources of information were used to compile a list of active amateur arts organisations: the useful, if dated, *Lewisham Arts Directory* and the Lewisham section of GLA's Greater London Arts Audit. These were supplemented by information from the principal national 'umbrella' organisations and Goldsmiths' College. The initial list of amateur arts organisations included a number of groups which were to be excluded from the statistical analysis either because they were professional companies or professionally-administered community arts initiatives. One choir, the Sydenham Chorale, and a music promoting group, the Blackheath Music Society had disbanded over the course of the last few years. Excluding carnivals and festivals, some 41 amateur groups were identified; usable responses

LW1 Lewisham: responses to questionnaire

	Number identified	Number responded
Performing groups		
Drama	4	1
Operatic/light operatic	6	4
Choirs	7	2
Brass bands	–	–
Orchestras/wind bands	3	1
Folk dance	4	3
Other performing	3	3
University-run music groups	2	1
Non-performing groups		
Art	3(a)	3
Photography	1	1
Poetry	1	1
Music promoting	1	1
Other	4	2

(a) Excludes two groups covering South East London as a whole. See text.

were received from 23 of them. This represented a response rate of 61 per cent.

Relative to the size of the resident population, Lewisham had fewer individuals involved in formal amateur groups than any of the other case study areas. It has been noted in Chapter 3 that London in particular, and urban areas generally, recorded fewer societies per head of resident population than in less densely populated areas. There are a number of possible explanations for this. London is of course a major centre for professional arts and entertainments, and it is possible that the extent of professional arts provision in London acts as a disincentive to active participation in the arts. Secondly, the existence, until recently, of the Inner London Education Authority's extensive provision in adult education, combined with classes offered by Goldsmiths' College, may have acted against the establishment of free-standing arts organisations. Again, in spite of attempts to make the survey of amateur arts as wide ranging as possible, the list of amateur arts organisations has been dominated by established and predominantly European-style organisations. 'Amateur' ethnic minority arts groups either do not exist in any numbers or have been very hard to identify in Lewisham. Finally, it may be that the dormitory and transient nature of the resident population makes it harder to establish formal local groups. But although there appeared to be fewer 'amateur' groups active within the borough, there were many groups which fell more readily under a 'community arts' heading.

LW2   Lewisham amateur performing groups: membership, performances and attendances, 1989/90

Type of organisation	Number responding	Total Member- ship	Total perform- ances	Average attendance per perf.
Drama	1	15	6	400
Operatic/light operatic	4	129	28	303
Choirs	2	107	7	125
Dance	3	42	29	..

Table LW2 gives details of the membership, performances and attendances for the principal categories of performing arts group.

By far the best represented group in Lewisham were the opera/musical comedy societies, 4 out of 6 of which returned the questionnaire. The two largest operatic societies were both members of the National Operatic and Dramatic Association (NODA). Restricted access to alternative performing venues in Lewisham is an important issue for groups in the borough and two of the responding operatic societies expressed concern over the future of Lewisham Theatre. Over the years this had become their regular performing base but, as one society's secretary put it, the venue

is becoming more expensive to hire... which always causes concern. If Lewisham Theatre becomes privately run, this may affect the company radically.

Whether amateur or professional, opera is an expensive art form to mount, and consequently, in simple financial terms, amateur operatic societies are the largest of all non-professional societies. Three of the four societies in Lewisham mounted 2 productions each in 1989/90 and generated just under three quarters of their total income through box office sales (table LW3). The second largest contribution came from members' subscriptions (11 per cent). Three societies charged between £30 and £35 per member per year, but one charged its members £50. None of the societies received any income from business sponsorship and only one received a small grant from the local arts council in 1989/90.

LW3 Lewisham: opera companies, sources of income, 1989/90 (a)

	£s	Percentages
Box office income	33,657	73
Subscriptions	4,885	11
Fund-raising	6,562	14
Other earned income	602	1
Public funding	100	*
Total	45,806	100

(a) Based on replies from 4 opera companies.

All three of the responding folk dance groups had been formed within the last ten years; they had a combined membership of 42. Tylers Men, the only one of the three groups not affiliated to the Morris Federation, stated that its principal motives were 'to operate a member-friendly morris side [for] mixed ability performers... NOT to pursue a nebulous stardom policy [and] to perform only traditionally collected dances'.

Three groups were linked by the common aim of providing entertainment to the elderly and other disadvantaged groups. Some of this activity was the direct consequence of the work of Doreen Jackson, the Leisure Activities Organiser for Age Concern Lewisham. The Rolly Oldies Tap Dance Group is made up of six volunteer pensioners aged between 66 and 74. The group, formed in 1986, acts on behalf of Age Concern to 'entertain the elderly in clubs, old peoples' homes...' The main aim of the Strollers Concert Party is also to entertain disadvantaged audiences with 'traditional London entertainment', and although it is an independent group, the Strollers Concert Party did receive a small grant from Age Concern Lewisham in 1989/90. Lewisham Variety Club is a 17-strong voluntary group. In 1989/90, it gave 40 performances, mainly to audiences of senior citizens. The Club also puts on a main variety show at the Lewisham Theatre in aid of a local hospice which attracts a paid audience of around 400. Age Concern Lewisham also organises a number of annual events specifically designed to encourage the elderly to expand their involvement in the arts: an art and craft exhibition (held in the foyer of the Council's Civic Suite and provided free of charge) is open to all Lewisham residents over the age of 60; and Lewisham Theatre is the venue for a senior citizens' talent contest. This is also open to all residents over 60.

Compared to either Aberdeen or Exeter Universities, Goldsmiths' College had fewer arts-based student societies and only 2 of the 5 identified returned completed questionnaires. With some 2,700 students, Goldsmiths' has a somewhat smaller student population than either Aberdeen or Exeter. But the smaller number of Goldsmiths'-based arts societies can also be explained by the fact that some societies exist to cover the whole of the University of London's student population (in 1991 the University of London Union listed the following arts societies: Asian Arts, Black Arts, Chorus, Drama, Music, Orchestra and Opera Group). Goldsmiths' does have its own drama and music departments and the former is endowed with a 200-seat venue, the George Wood Theatre, and smaller drama studios. As well as productions by the Goldsmiths' Drama Society and students on the drama and theatre arts course, the theatre is used for performances by visiting professional companies, NXT and other groups.[2]

The Music Department runs its own orchestra and choir, the Goldsmiths' Sinfonia and Chorus, which have a combined membership of 200. Although the ensembles are mainly designed to cater for undergraduate students in the Department, 'in trying to forge links with the local community we open membership by an informal audition to anyone reaching the relevant standard', and in this respect the orchestra and choir are advertised as part of Goldsmiths' short course programme. The present conductor of the Goldsmiths' Sinfonia, Mark Shanahan, provides a good illustration of the inter-relationship between amateur and professional sectors in music for the training of young professionals. He spends part of his time conducting a variety of amateur and student orchestras in London and the South East, but increasingly his work is made up of a significant number of professional engagements including, most recently, a run of performances at the English National Opera.

Although part of Lewisham's musical activity is centred around Goldsmiths' College, much goes on outside. Lewisham Concert Band, a member of the British Association of Symphonic Bands and Wind Ensembles, is, in terms of performances, the most active amateur music group based in the area. It attracts a playing membership from across London and gives around 10 concerts a year, including a number of radio broadcasts. Partly as a consequence of successful competition appearances, Lewisham Concert Band has built something of a reputation nationally. However, although the Band regularly rehearses within the Borough, the majority of its performances are given elsewhere. In 1990/1, the Band gave one performance at Lewisham Theatre, but otherwise, performances were given in neighbouring boroughs or further afield.

The two responding choirs – Lewisham Choral Society and the Ascension Choir – were members of the National Federation of Music Societies. The choirs had many similar characteristics. Both had a membership of around 55; they gave 3 or 4 concerts in churches or cathedrals; they met to rehearse on average, 33 times a year; both were entirely self-financing; and they each engaged two professionals per rehearsal. However, there was one significant difference between them: whilst Lewisham Choral Society was a free-standing association, in 1989/90 the Ascension Choir operated as an adult education class, although it clearly had an independent artistic life outside the realms of its regular meetings. Table LW4 sets out details of performances by venue type for performing arts groups.

Only one questionnaire was returned from a festival or carnival group. The Trinidad and Tobago Carnival Club is a Lewisham-based carnival band, one of more than 100 bands that take part in the Notting Hill Carnival.

Lewisham has a range of free-standing groups which meet to encourage the work of amateur visual artists in the Borough. There are at least five amateur groups which are active in the locality: the Blackheath Art Society, the South London Photographic Society, the

LW4   Lewisham performing groups: number of performances at each type of venue, 1989/90

	LEA school	College	Arts venue	Church	Other
Drama	-	-	-	6	-
Operatic/light operatic	-	-	26	-	-
Choirs	-	-	2	3	2
Orchestras	2	1	-	3	-

South London Artists, the South East London Art Group and the Lewisham Society of Arts. The Society undertakes 2 exhibitions per year and, on the 16 occasions that they met in 1989/90, regularly engaged the services of a 'professional'. The Blackheath Art Society, active since the 1950s and with some 230 members, puts on around 4 exhibitions a year but meets less regularly (4 to 5 times a season).

Two of the groups, although drawing members from Lewisham, cover a much larger area of South London. South London Artists, with a membership of 180, has been organising an annual exhibition since 1929. This group has closer connections with Southwark than Lewisham; until two years ago its exhibitions were held at the Camberwell School of Art, but they currently take place at the Blackheath Conservatoire for Music and the Arts. The South East London Art Group dates from 1947, and has around 120 members. In addition to arranging 2 exhibitions a year – which take place at Blackheath Village Library – the Group meets about 6 times a year for demonstrations, still life sessions and discussions. All of the free-standing fine arts groups shared a number of similar features: they all had a mixture of amateur and professional members; they all undertook exhibitions; there was a degree of overlap between the membership of the societies (one person was a member of all four groups); and their members were drawn from a wide catchment area. This last point reinforces the problem of assessing the extent of amateur activity *within* Lewisham. According to the Society's secretary, Lillian Taylor, three-quarters of the membership of the Lewisham Society of Arts live in the borough, whilst the members of the Blackheath Art Society were drawn largely from Greenwich. The South East London Art Group and the South London Artists had members from across South London.

Adult and youth provision

Adult education provision in Lewisham is based on a complex series of structures. Community Education Lewisham (CEL) run two adult education centres in the Borough, but in addition Goldsmiths' College, the University of the Third Age, the Horniman Museum, and the Albany make contributions to adult and community education in the borough. But just as tensions have developed over the funding of the independent amateur sector (see below), so they have also surfaced in adult education. Even prior to the disbanding of the ILEA, there was a noticeable reduction in traditional group-based performing arts classes in Lewisham. These classes have not been reinstated since CEL took over the running of adult education in 1990. Furthermore, the current constraints on CEL financing have brought about further reductions in the number of courses on offer. In the *CEL 1991-1992 Prospectus*, Margaret O'Neill, Director, writes 'We have had to make considerable changes in what we can offer in the coming year because of the significant reduction in our budget'. One practical consequence of these changes was the closure of 9 adult education branches as from 1991/2. Even at a reduced level, CEL still manage to offer a range of arts and crafts courses, although there is a preponderance of courses in the visual arts, crafts and dance.

Lewisham is fortunate in having Goldsmiths' College within its boundaries. The College has a large Department of Continuing and Community Education, an Extra Mural Department funded entirely by the Universities Funding Council (it had support from the ILEA before that organisation's demise in 1990). Goldsmiths' considers itself to be the principal provider of university-based adult education in South East London.

LW5   Goldsmiths' College short course programme, 1991: arts-related courses

Art (one-day, weekend or week-long courses only)	6
Creative writing and poetry	10
Drama (theatre/performance skills and technical course)	3
Dancing (Scottish)	1
Video production	2
Music	42
Total	64

According to Malcolm Barry, the Director of Continuing Education at Goldsmiths' since 1985, there has been a sea-change in the type of adult education courses run by Goldsmiths'. It has tended to pull out of much of its original programme of adult education in the performing arts and its courses are more closely related to training and the obtaining of professional qualifications. This move anticipated more detailed guidelines from the Universities Funding Council on the purposes of, and priorities for, continuing education.

Barry estimates that between 1985/6 and 1990/91, the number of classes offered in the arts fell by around half. In music the adoption of a skill-enhancing approach to adult education is epitomised by the switch from instrumental classes to those offering skills in 'musicianship'. For drama, the change in emphasis has been from straightforward participation and production to courses such as 'theatre skills'. Whilst a production may sometimes be one by-product of such a course, it is not considered to be the *raison d' être*. The aim is to develop participants' skills regardless of their background.[3]

The Lee Centre, opened in 1975, was also part of Goldsmiths' operation, and was designed to provide community education for young adults. Goldsmiths' ceased funding the Centre at the end of the financial year 1990/91 and it has now closed. In its final year, the Lee Centre offered three arts-based classes – sewing and textile crafts, community photography and creative arts. But the Centre was also occasionally used by University of the Third Age (U3A) South London. U3A is an educational initiative for mature people 'with time on their hands or without paid work'. It is volunteer-run and its members – there are some 300 in U3A South London – pay an annual fee of £5 which entitles them, without having to pay further charges, to attend any of the classes, all of which take place during the day. Tutors offer their services free or receive only travel expenses. In the Spring 1991 programme, 4 classes with a practical arts element, as well as a number of art appreciation classes, were programmed. U3A South London receives support in kind from both Goldsmiths' and Lewisham Borough in the form of access to venues and printing facilities.

The 1980s has witnessed a remarkable growth in youth-based community arts provision in the Borough and one of Lewisham's strengths lies in the provision of opportunities for youth music-making. This is achieved principally through the Lewisham Academy of Music, a Deptford-based youth music project, originally set up in 1981 (as part of The Combination at the Albany Empire). The Academy, which has been independent since 1986, is a highly individual establishment which does not fall neatly into any description of formal youth or adult arts provision. Writing in the introduction of the 1989/90 annual report, the Academy's former chair, Andy Benson, describes the place as 'fast and noisy; it's exciting and stimulating; it's an open door'.[4] Located in unlikely premises – a former morgue and coroner's court – the Academy provides daily classes and workshops, taken by professional musicians, in a range of musical styles such as Reggae, Afro-Caribbean, Latin and Jazz. To attend any of the range of classes costs £3 for one month (£2 for under-18s and £10 for waged members). The membership varies between 300 to 450 and, where necessary, instruments are provided. The Academy also operates an outreach service to local schools, youth groups and those with special needs. Several shows are organised throughout the year to provide a wider platform for the Academy's workshops. And whilst the Academy is primarily aimed at 'a young membership', this goes well beyond 16, covering an age group from around 5 to 25 years. Those attending the Academy range from the complete beginners to established professionals hoping to improve particular aspects of their technique. The Academy places special emphasis on equality of access. Andy Benson estimates that half of the Academy's users are white and half are black; and women are particularly encouraged (see Figure 4, p.26). The Academy's annual report states that it places no special emphasis on music as a vocation. In 1990/1, the Academy incurred running costs of around £140,000, of which 81 per cent (84 per cent in 1989/90) was covered by grants from Lewisham Borough, GLA and the Youth Service of the former Inner London Education Authority.

A more traditional form of musical training is provided by the Blackheath Conservatoire for Music and the Arts. Located just outside the borough, the Conservatoire is an independent school operated by a charitable trust (the former Blackheath School of Art was formally combined with the Conservatoire as from the summer of 1991). The Conservatoire has a long history, dating back to 1881, and in 1990/1 had around 600 students, of whom one-third were adults. As well as providing individual tuition, the Conservatoire offers group and class tuition across a range of musical and artistic forms.

Lewisham also has a number of active youth theatre and dance projects such as Lewisham Youth Theatre, Impact Young Women's Drama Group and South East London Youth Dance, all of which have been set up during the 1980s. Lewisham Youth Theatre currently operates under the auspices of CEL with an allocation of 6.5 tutor hours per week, although the budgetary problems facing CEL may place that allocation in jeopardy. Impact was originally set up as part of the Young Lewisham Project but is now an independently organised group. With the Laban Centre, an international centre for the study of dance and dance training, based at Goldsmiths', and a dance animateur on the Borough Council's community arts team, community dance has a high profile. A number of other youth arts projects – Basement and Second Wave – have operated under the auspices of the Albany Empire.

Public funding for the amateur arts

The history of Lewisham Arts Council provides a good illustration of the tensions which can arise over the provision of public funds for the amateur arts. Traditionally, the Arts Council received a small annual grant (£4,400 in 1988/9) from Lewisham Borough Council which the Arts Council then allocated principally to a small number of established amateur arts groups. For much of the Arts Council's existence, its management was in the hands of these amateur groups. However, the nature of the Arts Council changed dramatically when new members from local community arts groups were elected to a majority of seats on the Management Committee. The Leisure Services grant was withdrawn in 1989/90 and subsequently the Arts Council was reclaimed by the original amateur societies. The latter have managed to find a commercial sponsor, the Royal Mail, which has sustained the role of the Lewisham Arts Council as a grant-giving body; the Council currently has 18 member groups.

The Borough Council has for some time made limited funds available to small arts organisations through the Small Grants Scheme. Since the Council ceased making grants to Lewisham Arts Council, this has become the principal means of support for non-professional arts bodies in the borough. No amateur or professional distinction exists for applicants to the Small Grant Scheme. The only restrictions are that the recipient, if a membership organisation, should have more than 50 per cent of its members resident in the borough and that groups already in receipt of revenue funding are barred from applying. Of the annual budget of £8,000, the majority goes to non-professional bodies. A large part of funding through the scheme is devoted to special events. The Council provides various means of indirect support for all kinds of community groups, including a free-equipment loan scheme and a 'festival package' which provides assistance with the design and production of festival publicity material.

Conclusion

Arts participation in Lewisham provides a good illustration of the four forms of participation identified in Chapter 2: an established and active amateur core; adult education engaged in a process of change; and a range of more recent community and youth initiatives, inspired by those professionally-involved in the arts. Tensions can well up between the groups involved, as the history of Lewisham Arts Council illustrates.

But if the amateur and community arts worlds can, at times, appear somewhat adversarial, they are at least united by pressures of funding. Through an unfortunate coincidence of events, many of the structures upon which arts participation has developed in the borough seem insecure in the current climate. Amateur access to venues; adult and community education; funded-youth arts projects: all would appear to be vulnerable.

On a more positive note, the Lewisham Academy provides a good example of how funding bodies can usefully act together as facilitators within the participatory arts. The experience in the Borough also serves to highlight the fact that there is no clear boundary between amateur arts and community arts. In Lewisham, a number of amateur arts groups were involved in community-based entertainment for disadvantaged groups.

References

1. John Haskey, 'The ethnic minority populations in private households – estimates by county and metropolitan district of England and Wales', *Population Trends*, No.63, Spring 1991.

2. NXT (New Cross Theatre) – is described as a 'professional theatre company located within [the College] and operates as a performance and research facility for staff and graduates', *Goldsmiths College Graduate Prospectus*.

3. Conversation with Malcolm Barry, Director of Continuing Education, Goldsmiths', 17 December 1990.

4. 'The Lewisham Academy of Music Annual Report 1989-1990'.

4   Powys

The county of Powys – once described as 'the waistcoat of Wales' – is a creation of local government reform in the early 1970s. It consists of three districts: Montgomeryshire (population 53,500), Brecknock (population 41,700), and Radnor (population 23,200). The county covers almost one quarter of the land mass of Wales, running for an average of 30 miles east to west and 70 miles north to south. There are less than 60 people for every square mile, and about 60 times more sheep than people; agriculture is still the main economic activity, although tourism appears to be growing fast.

About one quarter of the population speaks Welsh as either a first or second language. The strongest Welsh-speaking communities are in the west and north of the county; little first-language Welsh is spoken in the east. There is no traditional Welsh-speaking in Llandrindod Wells, the administrative headquarters of Powys County Council, but a great deal spoken in and around Machynlleth.

In terms of the financing and administration of the arts, two of the three districts (Brecknock and Radnor) fall within the South-east Wales Arts Association area; Montgomeryshire is within the North Wales Arts Association area.

The Development Board for Rural Wales has been important in the social and economic development of the area in the last 15 years. From its headquarters in Newtown it operates in the whole of Powys, as well as in parts of two neighbouring counties.

Cultural traditions and characteristics
Powys is a county of two cultures. Welsh-language culture is growing fast. In one primary school in Newtown (an overwhelmingly English-speaking area), about 100 out of the 300 pupils are receiving most of their tuition through the medium of Welsh and the percentage of parents opting to have their children taught through Welsh is

growing each year. The 'learners ethos' has affected adults as well as children. The demand from adults – including immigrants from England and elsewhere – for courses in the Welsh language has been increasing steadily for years.

Poetry, stories and song lie at the heart of Welsh-language culture, for which there are two crucial networks: the network (or rather pyramid) of eisteddfodau – from the small and local to the Royal National Eisteddfod; and the Urdd Gobaith Cymru (the Welsh League of Youth) which organises a remarkable range of cultural, sporting, and other activities. In the Montgomery (Maldwyn in Welsh) area alone, there are 50 Urdd branches, involving nearly two thousand youngsters. Most of these branches are based at schools, and the majority of the branches are busy between January and March preparing for the Urdd area eisteddfodau. These are the preliminary rounds for the Urdd national eisteddfod, which is held each summer, and which is one of the main youth culture events in the Welsh calendar.

The Urdd groups include choirs, chamber groups, pop/rock, folk, brass and wind bands, and youth theatres, and also cover the following subjects: contemporary and folk dance, art and craft, photography, amateur film-making and video, recitation, penillion singing, and literary competitions.

More information about eisteddfodau and the other festivals in Powys is given later in this chapter. The growth of a variety of different kinds of festivals has been one of the most striking characteristics of the English-speaking culture in Powys in the last decade or so.

'Do it yourself' has long been the hallmark of the arts in the rural areas of the United Kingdom – the traditions of poetry and music-making, and the skilled practice of a wide range of crafts, have very deep roots in Powys. The Young Farmers' Clubs are also important in providing opportunities to practise and enjoy the arts in rural Wales.

Main arts venues and institutions

There are four arts centres in Powys. Three are now well-established. Theatr Hafren, which is part of Coleg Powys in Newtown; the Wyeside Arts Centre in Builth Wells, which was formerly a public meeting hall and market place; and the Guildhall in Brecon which puts on a mixture of professional touring groups and local companies. In Machynlleth, the Tabernacle Trust has been organising an annual arts festival and other regular events in a converted chapel with a wonderful acoustic; in April 1991 the Trust opened a small art gallery and further building work is planned to develop an arts centre for the Machynlleth area. In addition the Ystradgynlais Miners Welfare Hall, near the most south-westerly point in Powys, has been refurbished under the Valleys Initiative, and will open towards the end of 1991 as a 600-seater venue to be used for amateur as well as professional activity.

Though their full-time paid staffs are tiny in number, or non-existent, these arts centres act as essential resources for a wide range of arts activities in the county. For example, without the support of Theatr Hafren, it is unlikely that Mid-Wales Opera (a classic example of professional/amateur collaboration) and the Mid-Wales Folk Festival, would have been as successful as they have been; and the organisation of the 1989 Powys Eisteddfod was greatly assisted by staff and facilities at the Machynlleth Tabernacle.

The other major all-the-year-round professional arts organisations in the County are the two Oriel galleries – at Newtown and Welshpool – which are subsidised by the Welsh Arts Council and the North Wales Arts Association and which present an ambitious and imaginative programme of exhibitions; and Theatr Powys and the Powys Dance Project based in Llandrindod Wells.

The management panel of Theatr Powys/Powys Dance Project is a sub-committee of the County Council Education committee's Community, Leisure and Recreation Sub-committee (oh yes!). Theatr Powys was founded in 1972; it currently employs 15 members of staff of whom five are actor-teachers, three are administrators, two are artistic directors, two are stage managers; there is also a writer-in-residence, a designer and a wardrobe supervisor. The company's brief is to provide theatre-in-education (TIE) projects for the county's 130 schools and also to provide theatre for the community which can involve performances in a variety of spaces from church halls to theatres. The company played a major part in the community play in Llanidloes in 1989. The company also offers training opportunities to schools, communities and colleges; workshops and residencies; and it has been heavily involved in initiating and supporting youth theatre in the county. The Powys Dance Project is the umbrella name that covers the work of the Powys Dance Centre (which opened in 1988) and the Footloose Dance Company (which was established in 1981).

Footloose comprises three dancer-teachers who take responsibility for a wide range of community dance projects; typically Footloose will work with a school or community group for four weeks, and the residency will be completed by a performance. Theatr Powys/Powys Dance Project have played a major part in encouraging interest in drama and dance, and in raising the standard of work performed in Powys in the last twenty years.

The Mid-Border Community Arts Association is a good example of a community based promoter in a rural area operating with a population base not much larger than a big village. Run entirely by volunteers, it not only has supported the development of the Presteigne Festival until last year (when the festival was hived off) but it also promotes a year-round programme of professional and amateur arts activity using small grants from the local authorities and the South-East Wales Arts Association.

Amateur arts and crafts groups

The number of different amateur arts and crafts groups that were identified in the course of the research are shown in Table P1.

Two-thirds of the responding drama societies have been founded since 1970. The oldest and most active of the drama societies – Newtown Amateur Dramatic Society – was founded in 1934. It presented four productions in 1989/90, giving a total of 24 performances. The Society has its own theatre, a church school which was converted by the Society's members into the Powys Theatre. The Society's general secretary writes:

> We have received support from the Town Council, the Development Board for Rural Wales and the Welsh Church Acts Fund, but this has been financial aid for specific purposes – e.g. major roof repairs, purchase of new lighting and sound equipment, and recently the construction of a lighting and sound control room and the conversion of the roof space into a well-equipped wardrobe room.

> We receive no subsidy from any of the Arts Associations, and we are completely independent and self-supporting. We do have a very good working relationship with Theatr Hafren, the professional theatre run by Powys County Council. We lend each other equipment and this works very well.

P1 Powys: responses to questionnaire

	Number identified	Number responded
Performing groups		
Drama	13	9
Orchestra and brass bands	1	1
Choirs	20	8
Operatic and light operatic	2	2
Brass and silver bands	5	3
Folk music and dance	2	2
Non-performing groups		
Arts and crafts	6	4
Photography/camera clubs	6	6
Film societies/cinema clubs	2	1
Writing groups	2	1
Music promoting	7	3

> This theatre provides a very necessary function for people of all ages
> to gain skills in amateur drama in all sections – e.g. acting, directing,
> stage management, stage design, scenic painting, costume design etc
> as well as being the centre for the many other groups – YFC, WI,
> school drama groups, etc to obtain advice and help with their
> productions, and they make great use of our extensive wardrobe.

Almost every town in Powys, large or small, has an amateur
dramatic society – many put on pantomimes and other entertainments
as well as 'straight' plays.

Powys probably has more youth theatres per head of population
than most parts of England and Wales, but the secretary of the
Montgomeryshire Community Drama Association, a local networking
organisation, writes:

> There seems to be a barrier between the established Groups and the
> Youth Groups, perhaps because, by their very nature, they are
> transient. Sadly some very promising youngsters do not make the
> transition to an established Group.

The Mid Powys Youth Theatre is dependent on the professional organisation of Theatr Powys – and is not included in the tables in this section. In 1989/90 the Mid Powys Youth Theatre was able to spend £3,643 on professional help. The company describes its principal motives as being 'to raise the self-awareness and self-esteem of the community through the arts as a process to bring out the individual's voice and ability to work collectively'. The company relies on Theatr Powys for rehearsal space, wardrobe and the use of vehicles. Grant applications are made with the help of the assistant administrator of Theatr Powys, who is also treasurer of the Mid Powys Youth Theatre.

The North Powys Youth Theatre, founded in 1983, also receives significant public financial support. £2,813 of its total income of £3,848 in 1989/90 came from public sources, and the company's director writes that because of the reliance on limited but necessary sums of public money 'our only future problems are likely to be financial'.

Another remarkable organisation with considerable achievements to its name, but also an organisation whose future is far from clear, is Cwmni Theatr Ieuenctid Maldwyn or Maldwyn Youth Theatre, which works in the Welsh language. One of the group's three co-directors, Penri Roberts, a primary school headteacher in Newtown, writes:

> Our aim is to bring musical drama to the people of Wales. Up to now we have produced and performed 4 full-length musicals in theatres, 2 smaller productions at local community level and one Oratorio performed in chapels and churches. In two chapels we had audiences of a thousand plus. We filled Theatr Clwyd to capacity twice on one night with our last musical.

Three of Maldwyn Youth Theatre's productions – which can be up to two years in preparation – have been televised. The company employs professional sound and lighting technicians for each production as well as a professional choreographer. Originally the company was nearly all under 30. Now, while 60 per cent of those singing or performing are under 20, the age range of the company as a whole is 16-44 – but there is a high turnover with a new company formed for every production. The company is highly dependent on the stamina and creative energy of its co-directors.

Five brass bands were identified in Powys, of which three sent information. The bands span the generations. The oldest member of the Knighton Town Silver Band is 87 and the youngest 7. The principal issue affecting the future of the Llandrindod Wells Silver Band, which was reformed in 1964, is the need to recruit new members. The Newtown (W.R. Davies Motors) Band, which was founded as the Newtown Silver Band in 1880, rehearses about twice a week and performs once a week, and is particularly concerned to maintain its high standards. Indeed for two out of three respondent bands, 8 out of 9 choirs, both the operatic/musical societies, but only 4 out of the 9 respondent drama societies in Powys, the achievement of artistic quality is very important to the life of the organisation.

In addition to the expressed concern with high artistic standards, 'pleasure' and 'enjoyment' are words that recur frequently in the responses from choirs to the PSI questionnaire. As with the bands, membership of many choirs spans three or four generations. Six of the 9 choirs responding were founded between 1966 and 1976, which suggests some revival of choral music in Wales in that decade. (The Welsh Amateur Music Federation has confirmed that many male voice choirs were founded in the 1960s and 1970s.) The Machynlleth and District Choral Society, which was founded in the early 1920s, reported that 'the biggest threat to our success as an organisation is the increasing age of our membership and the lack of interest amongst young people in continuing our tradition of choral singing. We are also hampered by a chronic lack of men's voices; most men seem to prefer the easier option of singing in male voice choirs'.

P2 Powys amateur performing groups: membership, performances and attendances 1989/90

	Number responding	Total member- ship	Total perform- ances	Average attendance per perf.
Drama	9	487	74	230
Operatic/light operatic	2	120	18	444
Choirs	8	347	97	..

The eight respondent choirs had a total membership of 348, but there are about 120 members of the Ystradgynlais Male Voice Choir (not one of the respondents) when it is at full strength. The

P3 Powys amateur performing groups: professional input to rehearsals and performances

	Number responding	Groups with some professional input to rehearsals	to performances
Drama	9	1	–
Operatic/light operatic	2	1	1
Choirs	8	2	3

Ystradgynlais Male Voice Choir, was formed in 1947. The choir has performed extensively throughout England and Wales, has visited Germany on three occasions, and toured Ontario, Canada and Pennsylvania, USA. The choir's musical director, Leighton Jenkins, was for many years the head of music at the local comprehensive school. He still refers to his choir (average age about 60) as 'my boys'.

In all there are about one thousand members of the 22 amateur performing arts groups in Powys from which membership figures were received. Grossing up for non-respondents, this gives a figure of 1,920 as the total membership of the orchestras, bands, choirs, and operatic and dramatic societies identified in the course of this study. This figure excludes all regular participants in folk music, in all forms of dance, and all who participate in the arts in Young Farmers' Clubs (see below) and branches of the Women's Institute (WI). However, in the Brecknock area, none of the 39 WI branches is regularly involved in the performing and visual arts and crafts. There are however two separate WI craft clubs in Brecknock (not included in Table P5), and in 1990, as part of the seventy-fifth anniversary of the WI movement, the Powys- Brecknock Federation of WIs organised a two-day drama festival in which eight different branches presented a variety of sketches, speeches, entertainments and short plays. Elsewhere in Powys, WI involvement in the arts is also very patchy, though a couple of WI choirs were identified, and the WI in Montgomeryshire also organises a drama festival.

It is hardly surprising that in a county as rural as Powys a large number of plays and concerts are put on in village halls; but the importance of the network of theatres/arts centres can be seen from Table P4.

P4   Powys amateur performing groups: number of performances at each type of venue 1989/90

Type of organisation	School (LEA)	Church/ chapel	Arts centre/ theatre	Community centre/ village hall	Other
Drama	9	–	31	30	4
Operatic/light operatic	2	2	14	–	–
Choirs(a)	21	12	26	16	11

(a) Information for 7 choirs only.

Camera clubs in Powys are of recent origin. All five of the clubs where the date of foundation was reported are less than 12 years old. The clubs are small (average membership:18), and as one of the club secretaries put it their success 'depends on informality and disciplined participation'.

Four art clubs and societies were identified in Powys, with an average membership of 47 for the two from which replies were received.

P5   Powys: visual arts and crafts groups

Type of organisation	Number responding	Groups with paid tutors	Total members	Number of exhibitions held 1989/90
Painting	2	2	94	4
Crafts	2	2	72	2
Camera clubs/ photographic	6	3	110	10

Eisteddfodau

Information was received from seven eisteddfodau. Six of these were local one-day events each involving between six and 32 people in its organisation, and each attended by between 100 and 300 people – the majority of whom were also competitors. At least two of these local eisteddfodau have been held annually for more than a century. Total expenditure of these six eisteddfodau was approximately £4,300 – most of which goes on adjudicators, accompanists, and prizes. Income comes from admission fees, donations, fund-raising activities and small grants from community, district and town councils.

The Powys Eisteddfod is on a different scale. Held annually since 1820, the 1990 Powys Eisteddfod took place in a marquee in Llanfair Caereinion. Dozens of competitions are held for all age-groups covering a very wide range of arts and crafts. 1,500-2,000 people were actively involved as performers, exhibitors and behind-the-scenes helpers in the weekend-long event, which was attended by more than 5,000 people. Income for the Powys Eisteddfod (approximately £25,000 in 1990) comes from trusts, from the Development Board for Rural Wales, from HTV, from Montgomeryshire District Council, as well as from admission charges and fund-raising.

Festivals

The Montgomeryshire Music Festival was first held in 1921. It used to be a huge event held in a converted aircraft hangar. Now it consists of a single concert, usually involving a number of local choirs in a major choral work. Other major arts festivals in Powys are shown in Table P6.

P6 Arts festivals in Powys

	Year of first festival	Professional administration	Paid attendances 1990
Llandrindod Wells Drama Festival	1933	No	1,500-2,000
Llanfyllin Festival	c 1970	No	1,500
Llandrindod Wells Victorian Festival	1981	Yes	40,000
Presteigne Festival	1983	Yes	4,000
Brecon Jazz Festival	1984	Yes	30-40,000
Machynlleth Festival	1987	Yes	..
Gregynog Festival	1988	Yes	1,300
Hay-on-Wye Literature Festival	1989	Yes	20,000
Mid-Wales Folk Festival	1989	No	3-5,000

It can be seen that seven out of the nine festivals listed started in the 1980s. Some – the Gregynog Festival, the Hay-on-Wye Festival of Literature, and the hugely successful and popular Brecon Jazz Festival ('one of the highlights of the jazz outdoor season' according to the *Financial Times*) – are largely or entirely professional events, but all depend to a greater or lesser extent on the work of volunteers (see Appendix E). The most traditionally amateur of the festivals in the list is the oldest of them: the 58th Annual Drama Festival was held in the Albert Hall, Llandrindod Wells, in May 1991. The festival, which is a competitive festival for full-length plays, depends almost entirely on box-office income to pay the adjudicator's fees, travelling expenses for the competing companies, and the costs of using the theatre.

The Llandrindod Wells Victorian Festival, held each August, is as much a social event as an arts festival – and is designed with more than one eye on the tourist trade. The Town, District and County Council put in £16,250 to the 1990 Festival, and the Development Board for Rural Wales contributed £26,000 – so that more than half the costs of the festival came from public funds. But then there is a huge amount of voluntary input from the citizens of Llandrindod Wells, many of whom spend the week in Victorian dress. Certainly the Victorian Festival is a classic slice of 'Heritage Industry' – with eminent Victorians like Glenn Miller ('When there is music like this to be heard, who would quibble about the odd 50 years or so?') and the Pasadena Roof Orchestra both contributing in recent years. As one commentator has pointed out 'The point is for everyone to have a good time, and for the tourist trade to increase its turnover'.[1] With a Welsh folk evening, a daily craft market, a street organ festival, bands and male voice choirs, there is a great deal of amateur arts activity in the Victorian Festival.

The smaller festivals – Machynlleth, Presteigne, Llanfyllin – combine opportunities for local people to be involved with a chance to see and hear some top-class professional work. One of the highlights of the Presteigne Festival is what has become an enormously successful local arts and crafts exhibition. In 1990 there were 320 entries for the exhibition, nearly all of which were sold during the course of the Festival for sums ranging from £1 to £250.

Five of the festivals listed have benefitted from financial support from the Development Board for Rural Wales. The Mid-Wales Folk

Festival received £1,000 from the DBRW in 1989, £3,000 in 1990 and £6,000 (towards a total budget of £14,500 in 1991). The Festival Organiser, Phil Freeman, admits that, without the help and support of Theatr Hafren, the festival could not have got off the ground. Phil Freeman notes 'the traditional underfunding of the folk-related arts' and describes the principal motives of the festival as 'encouraging the re-discovery of traditional culture as a focus for community life'.

The arts in youth and adult education provision

Adult education in Powys is provided by the County Council at three college sites, and at eleven smaller centres throughout the County. At the college sites in Newtown, Llandrindod Wells, and Brecon a range of visual arts and crafts classes are on offer, and in 1990/91 you could learn tap dancing at Brecon, practise creative writing at Llandrindod Wells, and social dancing and sequence dancing at Newtown. Most of the smaller centres also offer painting and craft classes. The WEA also organises a limited number of classes throughout the county; one of the 'writers and writing' groups originally organised by the WEA in the mid-1980s continues to meet on an informal basis.

Eight full-time professional youth workers cover the county, and although there is some arts work in the county youth service, more arts activity is probably generated through the Urdd Gobaith Cymru groups (see above), the 'independent' youth theatres, and the Young Farmers' Clubs. In Powys there are three YFC federations based on the pre-1974 counties. The YFCs are particularly important in Powys; although Powys accounts for less than 5 per cent of the population of Wales, 27 per cent of YFC members in Wales (approximately 2,100 out of 7,700) live in Powys. The age range of YFC members is 11-26, and at least half the members are not young farmers. The YFC movement has a full bi-lingual policy throughout Wales. Bi-annual competitions are held in drama and entertainment (a half-hour entertainment suitable for family watching) – with the county winners going on to compete at a national level; in Radnorshire alone in 1990, 220 members from eight of the 14 YFCs were involved in the entertainment competition. In addition there is an annual YFC eisteddfod, and during the Royal Welsh Show held each year at Builth Wells, there are YF folk dancing and disco dancing competitions.

Conclusion

Given the small and scattered population there is an extraordinary amount of arts activity in Powys. The powerful roots of Welsh-language culture and the revival of that culture, thanks partly to S4C and the coming of the national curriculum; the enlightened attitude of Powys County Council towards Theatr Powys and the Powys Dance Project, and the sustained high quality work of those companies with schools and communities; the all-the-year round service provided by the county's arts centres; the support provided for the arts, in particular for arts festivals, by the Development Board for Rural Wales; the crucial role of schoolteachers in Wales in organising and directing arts activity out of school; all these have been important in encouraging the huge amount of volunteer effort that sustains the arts in this most rural of counties. In all the arts in the county, the last decade or two have brought new and fruitful collaborations between part-timers and full-timers, amateurs and professionals. Indeed Powys provides a striking example of how, with a limited amount of public support, and limited arts venues, a rich programme of amateur and professional activity can be developed. It is important that there is sufficient continuity of funding and sufficient concentration on the arts at all levels of the education system to ensure that that programme is further developed in the 1990s. It is also important that the number of key organisational posts is increased; for example, the work of the Maldwyn Youth Theatre would certainly be more secure if it had one full-time worker.

Reference

1. Nicholas Murray, 'Back to the future', *New Statesman and Society*, 18 August 1989.

5 Stoke-on-Trent and Newcastle-under-Lyme

The City of Stoke-on-Trent is an amalgam of six towns. The Borough of Newcastle-under-Lyme, generally more leafy-laned and middle-class, lies to the west of the six towns, and on the western fringe of the Borough sits Keele University, just a little remote from the life of the Potteries. Geographically Stoke-on-Trent and Newcastle-under-Lyme are one area, sharing many facilities and services. They have a combined population of about 360,000 of whom two-thirds live in Stoke-on-Trent district.

The six 'Potteries' towns each specialises in different types of ware – bone china in Longton, Fenton, and Stoke, earthenware in Hanley and Burslem, bricks and tiles in Tunstall – and each has developed a separate identity 'with strong parochial attitudes, a pattern which to some extent still prevails today'.[1] The industrial revolution exploited the environment of north Staffordshire with utter ruthlessness; since then the Potteries have suffered from being roughly half way between Birmingham and Manchester, without the political pull and economic muscle of these regional centres. However the National Garden Festival in 1986, on the site of the former Shelton steelworks, attracted more than two million visitors, and acted as a catalyst for some substantial new developments in retailing and other service industries. But Stoke has never been accorded assisted area status, which has meant, among other things, that reclamation of the many derelict areas is proceeding at a slower pace than could otherwise be the case.

Cultural traditions and characteristics

In 1989 Comedia consultancy was commissioned by the Director of Museums, Arts and Heritage of Stoke City Council to undertake a cultural audit of Stoke-on-Trent, and, on the basis of its findings to develop a cultural strategy. Comedia's report was approved by the City Council in 1990, but because of the constraints on local government expenditure, most of its recommendations have remained 'on ice'. The report noted the poor salaries for designers in the ceramics industry in Stoke-on-Trent, and remarked that 'the bulk of the output is still historical patterns with little attention paid to innovation' and 'the city's industry has few links with Stoke's arts communities; this is to the detriment of both industry and the arts.[2] One link between the ceramics industry and the artistic life of Stoke and Newcastle is provided by the Sir Henry Doulton School of Sculpture, which, each year since 1986, and thanks to the support of Royal Doulton Ltd, has given a small group of students a chance to develop their talents for figurative sculpture.

Indeed although because of the ceramics industry the city brands itself 'a creative city', the number of independent practising craftspeople in the city and county wanting to sell their work through the county's main crafts gallery is tiny. John Rhodes, who is both Staffordshire's County Arts officer, and responsible for the Stafford Art Gallery and crafts shop, has said that of the 300 or so craftspeople applying to sell their work through the crafts shop in the last ten years, only three have been resident in Staffordshire. At the same time, it is striking that many designers of pottery do not regard their work as artistic. 'This area has no record of being enthusiastic about cultural activities and cultural facilities' says Lee Corner,[3] who for years ran Art Link (an organisation that arranges for artists to work in a variety of institutional settings) from an office in Newcastle-under-Lyme.

The musical life of Staffordshire is fed and reinforced by the activities and achievements of the Staffordshire County Music Department, the music wing of the local education authority. Ten thousand schoolchildren are learning a musical instrument – including about a thousand learning the clarinet – in Staffordshire; this is a free service in school hours, and as yet remains unaffected by the innovations of the Education Reform Act. Outside school hours about 3,000 schoolchildren are regularly involved in bands, choirs and orchestras; this again is a free activity with free transport provided. But the staff of the County Music Department are well aware that many children give up playing music once they have left school; many leave the area for work or further studies. But moves are afoot to start community bands to cater for those school-leavers wanting to continue with some organised musical activity. At the same time the Deputy Director of Music argues that the Department should be more concerned with the emotional education of children than with whether they continue playing after leaving school.

The brass band tradition is less strong in Staffordshire than in other parts of the Midlands and North. However, the Royal Doulton Band, one of Britain's leading bands, is based at the company's works in Burslem. The band's director receives a full-time salary from the company's public relations budget. The band has 50 engagements each year, only three or four of which are in the Potteries. The bandsmen, not one of whom works for the company, come from all walks of life, and travel from far and wide to rehearse (twice each week) and to perform. The bandsmen are supplied with instruments and with free uniform, but otherwise only receive their travel expenses.

As in other cities of similar size there is a great deal of popular musical activity – jazz, indie, rock, rhythm and blues, etc. In a special study for this report, Jill Ebrey identified 20 rock bands, 13 rhythm and blues bands, 25 indie/pop bands, 14 jazz bands, 19 punk and thrash, 2 soul, one reggae, two dance, and four folk bands in the study area. These bands frequently form and reform, but assuming that the average size of a band is six instrumentalists and singers, there are about 600 people, nearly all young men, involved in making various forms of pop, rock and jazz sounds in Stoke and Newcastle. Most of these bands are unknown outside the city, but

> most felt they had a professional attitude towards their music even if they didn't earn a living from it. Bands and their entourages generally ally themselves with a style and philosophy associated with a particular musical type... Within these communities, there may be people who earn their living from making music, but the majority have full-time jobs in non-related areas or are students. The bond of expression through a particular style far outweighs distinctions around amateur and professional.[4]

The choral and operatic traditions are also strong in north Staffordshire, and more is said about these later in this report.

It is clear that the various Asian, Afro-Caribbean and eastern European communities in the Potteries – of which only the Asian community can be numbered in thousands – are constrained by the inadequate meeting places for social and cultural activities. The Hindu Cultural Centre, founded in 1985, now has 125 members, and, with some financial help from West Midlands Arts, organises a number of music, drama and dance events each year.

Main arts venues and institutions

A recent visitors' guide to Stoke-on-Trent lists eight 'Ceramic Museum and Visitor Centres' and a further four museums in Stoke and Newcastle.

With a staff of about eighty, the City Museum and Art Gallery is important both for its permanent collection of English pottery and porcelain, and for its wide range of temporary (mainly fine arts) exhibitions. From a recent survey of a large sample of visitors it is clear that the City Museum and Art Gallery has a lot of regular and satisfied customers. 94 per cent said that they thought that the museum was successful in its main task, and 90 per cent said that it was likely or very likely that they would visit the museum again.[5] Other public galleries include those at Keele University and at North Staffordshire Polytechnic.

The two main theatres in Stoke and Newcastle are the New Victoria Theatre in Newcastle-under-Lyme, and the Theatre Royal, Hanley. The New Vic is a well-equipped purpose-built theatre-in-the-round that can seat about 600 people. There is a resident repertory company, and a wide ranging programme, including concerts, both professional and amateur. The New Vic received £273,000 from the Arts Council of Great Britain in 1989/90 as well as considerable grant-aid from the local authorities. By contrast, the 1,424-seater Theatre Royal, Hanley is run on purely commercial lines, promoting and receiving shows and hiring its facilities to local amateurs. Another heavily used theatre is the Mitchell Memorial Youth Theatre, owned by Staffordshire County Council and operated by the area Youth and Community Office.

A local record shop-owner, Mike Lloyd, via Stoke and Newcastle Music, promotes concerts at the Victoria Hall, which is owned by the City Council, and the Keele Concerts Society promotes an annual series of classical concerts. In recent years the Stoke and Newcastle Arts Project(SNAP), which works for increased opportunities for the community to participate in the arts, has organised an annual small-scale professional dance festival. SNAP has in the past worked with Beavers Arts, a theatre group with a substantial track record of community-based performances, residencies and workshops. And it has supported the work of Ziggy Dance Company, an organisation that involves young people in experimental dance performances. Ziggy Dance Company has had grants from the Regional Arts Association, but its work seems to be more valued outside Staffordshire than in Stoke and Newcastle.

Amateur arts organisations in Stoke and Newcastle

78 active amateur arts groups – and 8 festivals and carnivals – were identified in the Stoke and Newcastle area. Of these 43 groups and 6 festivals and carnivals replied to our questionnaire. The response rates are shown in Table SN1.

SN1 Stoke and Newcastle: responses to questionnaire

Type of organisation	Number identified	Number responded
Performing groups		
Drama	18	7
Orchestras and wind band(a)	5	4
Choirs(a)	13	8
Keele Philharmonic Society(b)	1	1
Operatic/light operatic	5	1
Brass bands	3	–
Folk music and dance	4	2
Contemporary dance	1	1
Other music making	3	3
Music hall	1	–
Non-performing groups		
Arts and crafts	10	6
Photography/camera clubs	5	3
Literary/writing groups	2	1
Amateur cine and video	2	1
Film societies	1	–
Recorded music	2	2
Music promoting	1	1
Other	1	–

(a) Excludes Keele Philharmonic Society.

(b) Keele Philharmonic Society comprises three choirs, orchestra and a concert band.

Of the performing groups, half have been founded since 1970. The North Staffs Operatic Society was founded in 1892 and the North Staffordshire Symphony Orchestra in 1904; of the non-performing groups the longest standing is the Newcastle and District Camera Club, which dates back to 1907.

If those responding to the questionnaire are representative of the amateur performing arts in Stoke and Newcastle, and assuming that this study has managed to identify all (or most) of the groups and companies involved, there are about 30,000 attendances each year at adult amateur choral and orchestral performances in Stoke and Newcastle; a total of about 40,000 attendances at about 180 drama performances; and about 50,000 at about 60 operatic and light operatic performances. These exclude performances by groups and organisations operating wholly or largely within the framework of the Youth and Community service; they also exclude work organised by the Staffordshire County Council Music Department, and they exclude initiatives taken by community artists, adult educators, and others paid to take initiatives.

SN2 Stoke and Newcastle amateur performing groups: membership, performances and attendances 1989/90

Type of organisation	Number responding	Total member- ship	Total perform- ances	Average attendance per perf.
Drama	7	362	70	220
Orchestras(a)	4	127	34	156
Keele Philharmonic Society(b)	1	222	9	200
Choirs	8	354	109	125
Operatic/light operatic	1	200	14	900

(a) Includes one wind band; excludes Keele Philharmonic Society.

(b) Comprises three choirs, an orchestra and a concert band.

Eight of the 21 performing groups have some professional help at rehearsals, but only four of the groups employed professionals for performances in 1989/90. The choirs and orchestras, operatic and dramatic groups have varied aims and ambitions – many stress that they are out to enjoy themselves and to bring enjoyment to others. A

SN3 Stoke and Newcastle amateur performing groups: professional input into rehearsals and performances

Type of organisation	Number responding	Groups with some professional input into rehearsals	into performances
Drama	7	2	–
Orchestras	4	1	1
Keele Philharmonic Society	1	1	1
Choirs	8	3	2
Operatic/light operatic	1	1	–

large number of the choirs are church-based, and, as can be seen from Table SN4, perform in churches more than in any other venue. The existence of the Mitchell Memorial Theatre enables many of the drama societies to perform in a proper theatre. In addition, the Stoke-on-Trent Repertory Theatre, the one amateur theatre company in Stoke and Newcastle that is affiliated to the Little Theatre Guild, has had its own home (a 191-seater theatre) since 1933. It is now 'busily involved in (frighteningly!) ambitious plans to improve even further not only the scope and range of our productions but also the facilities available to our patrons'.[6]

SN4 Stoke and Newcastle amateur performing groups: number of performances at each type of venue(a)

Type of organisation	School (LEA)	Arts centre/ theatre/ concert hall	College/ Univ.	Church	Other
Drama	–	33	28	–	9
Orchestras(b)	2	4	–	4	–
Keele Philharmonic Society	–	–	9	–	–
Choirs	5	12	–	68	12
Operatic/light operatic	–	14	–	–	–

(a) Some incomplete returns from choirs and orchestras.

(b) Includes one wind band; excludes Keele Philharmonic Society.

More than half of the performing groups in Stoke and Newcastle say that the achievement of artistic quality is very important to the life of the group. The North Staffordshire Symphony Orchestra aims 'to give local amateur instrumentalists the opportunity to perform orchestral music to the highest possible standard' – and it is generally agreed that the quality of the orchestra's work has been greatly improved since they started to employ a professional conductor. The Stoke-on-Trent Bedford Singers aim 'to sing extremely well'. And the intention of the Keele Philharmonic Society is 'to provide the best amateur music available... we do use professionals when the requirements and standards of the works performed demand it'.

In drama, a competitive youth and adult drama festival has been organised in every year since the Second World War. In 1991 eight adult groups were competing in the adult section, five of which were from Stoke and Newcastle.

There is very considerable enthusiasm for putting on musicals and light opera in north Staffordshire, and usually sizeable audiences for the productions. The Centenary Amateur Operatic Society presents one musical each year, nearly always a Gilbert and Sullivan; a professional producer is employed and a cast of 50-60 with a full orchestra usually manages to fill the Mitchell Memorial Theatre for seven performances. The North Staffordshire Operatic Society 'completely run the theatre' when they put on their productions at the Queen's Theatre, Burslem. But although the number of musical productions in the area has increased – including some musical productions by drama groups – audiences are not quite what they used to be. The North Staffordshire Operatic Society used to attract 15-20,000 people to their main productions 15 years ago; total audiences for their top shows now are more likely to be in the 10-12,000 range – still a sizeable audience by any standards. The youth section of the Stoke-on-Trent Operatic Society has been one of the success stories of the last decade; it can usually fill the Mitchell Memorial Theatre for six nights with its productions; and some of its leading performers have gone on to success with the adult amateur operatic societies. The adult societies usually audition for their lead parts; and some of the principal performers in the area have worked with all the main adult operatic societies. One perennial problem for the operatic societies is to find useful employment for some of the older members – some of whom continue to appear in the chorus as much for their ticket-selling capacities as for their continuing vocal quality.

So much for the performing arts. Some basic figures for visual arts and crafts groups are given in Table SN5.

The art groups – mainly watercolourists – tend to be informal groups employing their own tutor or adviser. The camera clubs and art groups depend entirely on subscriptions for their income. The Staffordshire Patchworkers and Quilters (which has more than 50 members) is involved in fund-raising and other income generating activities to enable it to book tutors for workshops, pay for excursions to quilt shows, build up a library for members' use, and subsidise students' fees. Many of the members also belong to the Quilters' Guild, a national organisation. The 30 members of the North Staffordshire Guild of Craftsmen received a small grant from West Midlands Arts to help meet the costs of organising displays and craft fairs.

SN5 Stoke and Newcastle: visual arts and crafts groups

	Number responding	Groups with paid tutors	Total members	Number of exhibitions held 1989/90
Painting	4	3	150	4
Crafts	2	1	80	4
Camera clubs/photographic	3	1	135	3

A good deal of work done by local artists is exhibited at the City Museum and Art Gallery, at Keele University and at the North Staffordshire Polytechnic's Flaxman Gallery, where the work of former students of the Poly's art and design course are sometimes exhibited. Angela Drakakis Smith, who runs the gallery at Keele University started the Staffordshire Women's Artists' Network (SWAN). SWAN aims to encourage women artists in the county partly through the provision of more opportunities to exhibit their work. Ms Drakakis Smith says that 'there is quite a lot going on in the visual arts in the area, but it is not co-ordinated and it is not well-publicised or adequately funded. Those who can leave the area for the larger cities where it is easier to get funding for projects do so, thus denuding the area of talent'.[7]

The great majority of amateur arts and crafts events and activities in Stoke and Newcastle are organised without any direct public funding. Between them the Borough of Newcastle-under-Lyme and the City of Stoke-on-Trent give grants totalling about £3,000 each year for amateur musical activities. In 1990/1 the largest grants went to Newcastle Operatic Society (£500 from the Borough of Newcastle-under-Lyme) and the North Staffordshire Symphony Orchestra (about £800 from the Stoke-on-Trent City Council).

The main arts content in the local carnivals – popular voluntarily-organised one-day or weekend events in various parts of the Potteries – characteristically comprises marching bands and/or dance troupes. Carnival organisers also tend to lay on even more traditional or exotic attractions like Carnival queens, civic dignitaries or – as featured at the Fenton Carnival in 1990 – 'The Auto Space Kings – Motor Cycle Entertainment on the High Wire'.

More down-to-earth entertainment is provided by the Potteries Folk Festival, which has been an annual event since 1988. The Festival, which is grant-aided by Stoke-on-Trent City Council, is organised by a committee drawing on about another 20 unpaid volunteers; but the organisers state that 'most artists are professional as are sound engineers'.

The arts in youth and adult education provision in Stoke and Newcastle

The following information about adult education classes has been compiled by Jill Ebrey, a lecturer at Stoke-on-Trent College:

There are five 'providers' of adult education in Stoke and Newcastle; these are (a) the Workers Educational Association (WEA) (b) the University of Keele (c) Newcastle-under-Lyme College, a tertiary college (d) Stoke-on-Trent College, which has both Further and Higher Education status (e) Staffordshire Youth and Community Service. The latter administer a wide range of recreational and vocational classes and activities that are held in a network of Youth and Adult Centres, most of which are in school buildings. Each centre has a warden, manager, youth and community worker or co-ordinator. A few of these are full-time; most are paid on a part-time or sessional basis. Between them in 1990/1 the Youth and Adult centres in Stoke and Newcastle acted as host for 151 classes in the performing, literary and visual arts and crafts; the classes employed 99 tutors and attracted a total of 2,385 students. More than half of the classes (88 in all attended by 1,112 students) were in miscellaneous crafts, of which dressmaking was the most popular. 23 classes attended by 285 students were in painting, drawing and sculpture, 13 attended by 361 students were drama classes, and 13 classes for which there were 464 students consisted of sessions of ballroom/Latin/sequence and old time dancing. Many of the dancing classes, and some in the other categories, were self-programming, that is the class operated without a paid tutor, and organised its own meeting times in rooms where the hire charges were waived. It is clear that classes at Youth and Adult Centres are almost all in traditional categories; for example there were no classes in contemporary dance. Of the other providers of adult education in Stoke and Newcastle, the University of Keele and the Workers Educational Association each organised six classes in the arts and crafts, Stoke-on-Trent College scheduled 14 such classes and Newcastle-under-Lyme College 12, of which three were photography classes.

The Youth and Community Service also operates the Mitchell Memorial Theatre in Hanley, runs drama workshops and organises an annual youth and adult drama festival (see above). The theatre seats 380 and is programmed for 46 weeks each year. Eight drama groups and three operatic societies are affiliated to the Youth and Community service in Stoke and Newcastle. This affiliation gives these organisations a number of benefits: firstly they are provided with free rehearsal space; secondly, some of the groups have an adult tutor or director paid on a sessional basis by the Youth and Community service; and thirdly affiliated groups have limited free use of the Mitchell Memorial Theatre should they wish to use it, which most of them do. The groups take all the box office to plough back into future productions.

The most remarkable work initiated by one of the adult education providers in the area in the 1989/91 period was the Silverdale Community Play, the catalyst for which was a WEA local history series. The play's author, Joyce Holliday, and Zoe Munby, tutor organiser for the WEA in north Staffordshire and south Cheshire, helped to establish the Silverdale Community Play Association in 1989; eleven performances of the play, which focussed on the life and work of a legendary local Communist councillor, Fanny Deakin, were given in May 1991. Zoe Munby put together a budget of £74,000, including grants of £19,000 and £6,000 respectively from West Midlands Arts and Staffordshire County Council. A full-time professional director and a part-time professional musical director were both employed on the project for several months each, as well as a professional composer, a professional designer, a professional production manager and three or four other paid staff, including a disability co-ordinator. Well over one hundred residents of Silverdale, a former mining village, were involved in a direct way in the production – about 20 on sewing, about 20 on front-of-house work, and a further 85 in the cast, some drawn from local amateur drama societies, but many making their first public appearance in any kind of play. One critic described the production as 'a powerful tale, powerfully told' and the collective energy of those involved as 'both thrilling and moving'.[8] It is planned that a number of activities built up around the play will continue – these include a quilt-making workshop, photography, and an annual carnival.

Conclusion

It could be argued that the Staffordshire County Council does a good deal for the amateur arts in north Staffordshire through the provision of the Mitchell Memorial Theatre;and does a great deal for music through its Music Department, which forms part of the local authority. The Mitchell Memorial Theatre is certainly a useful facility, but is far from ideal – particularly, for example, for small-scale dance. Perhaps what is needed in the Potteries more than any other cultural facility is an attractive arts centre with an appropriate small performance space.

Other priorities suggest themselves. Firstly, to provide financial inducements to encourage more of the well-established performing arts organisations to take on the challenge of more adventurous work, as well as the constant repetition of old favourites. The comment that the amateur drama groups and amateur operatic groups in the area tend to perform to an undemanding audience was frequently heard; if true such a state of affairs is hardly very exciting or artistically healthy. Secondly, to provide more training opportunities for all age groups, so that more people can derive practical help and inspiration from experienced practitioners. Thirdly, to provide more opportunities for young people; the Staffordshire Music Department's possible plans for establishing community bands for those who have left school suggests a promising development. Finally the formation of a local arts association or local arts council to build on the work of the Stoke and Newcastle Arts Project and to encourage more communication and collaboration between amateur arts groups should do more good than harm.

References

1. E. Hambrook, *Portrait of a city*, Penrhos publications, 1989, p.9.

2. Comedia, *A Cultural Strategy for Stoke-on-Trent*, April 1990, p.20 and p.5.

3. Conversation with Lee Corner, 25 October 1990.

4. Jill Ebrey, 'Played in Stoke', March 1991, mimeo.

5. City Museum and Art Gallery, 'Museum Visitor Survey', March 1991, mimeo.

6. *Little Theatre Guild of Great Britain Yearbook 1989/90*, p.88.

7. Conversation with Angela Drakakis Smith, 16 April 1991.

8. Robin Thornber, 'Go See Fanny Deakin', *The Guardian*, 13 May 1991.

6 Teignbridge

The district of Teignbridge in Devon is distinguished by varied topography. The impressive coastline and seaside resorts of Teignmouth and Dawlish encompass a lowland area primarily devoted to farming. In the north east of the district is the rugged landscape of Dartmoor National Park. Teignbridge has a population of 110,500, a quarter of whom live in the market town of Newton Abbot, the administrative centre of the district. The towns of Teignmouth and Dawlish together make up a further 25 per cent of the district's population. A number of smaller centres – Bovey Tracey, Kingskerswell, Kingsteignton, Chudleigh, Heathfield and Exminster – account for a fifth of the population whilst the remainder are scattered across numerous smaller settlements which typify the rural nature of this part of the West Country.

The attraction of Teignbridge as a part of the country to retire to has been one factor which has led to a high degree of in-migration. Between 1981 and 1989, the population of the local plan area grew by 16 per cent, a higher growth rate than any other district in Devon (the rate for the county as a whole over the decade was just under 7 per cent). This has resulted in the resident population having a distinctly ageing profile: 26.6 per cent of residents are of retirement age.[1]

The district has a range of industries; some 70 per cent of total employment is in the service sector, much of it in tourist-related industries. Manufacturing accounts for 20 per cent of employment and, although the numbers employed in agriculture have fallen in recent years, this still constitutes a significant part of the rural economy (4.4 per cent of total employment in 1987). Average wage rates remain well below the national average.

Main arts venues and institutions

There are no resident professional performing arts companies in Teignbridge. The principal receiving venue for professional arts companies touring the area is the Dyrons Centre, a dual-use (sport and arts) leisure centre in Newton Abbot, operated jointly by the District Council and County Council. The most prestigious of its visitors is the Royal Shakespeare Company which has given a number of performances over the last ten years, most recently during its 1988/9 and 1990/1 seasons. But with the exception of the RSC, and annual visits by the Bournemouth Sinfonietta, middle and large-scale professional performances in the area are all but non-existent.

The District Council owns a number of small arts facilities which it leases out to other organisations. In Newton Abbot, the Alexandra is used for showing films but it also doubles as a venue for musicals and pantomimes. The Carlton Theatre in Teignmouth, a purpose-built venue dating from the 1930s, but rebuilt in 1964, is leased by the Council to the Teignmouth Players, an amateur drama group. North along the coast to Dawlish, the Shaftesbury Theatre started life as a nineteenth century Temperance Hall. In 1959, the Hall – which had fallen into use as a furniture store – was purchased by the Dawlish Repertory Company and was subsequently converted into a 135-seat theatre. Spread around Teignbridge are five town halls and more than 50 village halls which from time to time host small-scale arts events. Local arts activities have been invigorated by the District Council's appointment of an Arts and Events Officer in 1988. There has been a range of community-based arts initiatives – crafts, music, and video animateurs, and a literature residency.

Although the District is poorly provided for in terms of established arts venues, Teignbridge does have a number of specialised arts and crafts institutions, which reflect the cultural traditions of the area. The Devon Guild of Craftsmen is a membership organisation of professional craftspeople which promotes the work of its members by allowing them access to the Riverside Mill Gallery in Bovey Tracey. The Guild has been in existence since the mid-1950s but the Gallery has only been functioning since the end of 1980s. More recently, the Guild joined forces with South West Arts and Teignbridge District Council to appoint a craft animateur to develop craft activities, particularly in the more rural parts of the district.

Amateur arts activities

The limited provision of professional arts venues and events in the Teignbridge locality tends to place a much greater emphasis on the role of the amateur. Relative to the size of its resident population, Teignbridge has a large number of functioning amateur arts organisations. Newton Abbot, Dawlish, Teignmouth and the smaller centres of Bovey Tracey, Buckfastleigh, Kingsteignton and Ashburton each had their own localised networks of amateur arts organisations.

TB1 Teignbridge: responses to questionnaire

Type of organisation	Number identified	Number responded
Performing groups		
Drama	12	8
Operatic/light operatic	5	4
Choirs	8	6
Brass bands/orchestras	2	1
Folk and country dancing	9	4
Other	3	3
Non-performing groups		
Painting/drawing	4	5
Crafts	5	3
Camera clubs/photography	3	2
Music promoting/appreciation	4	4
Amateur cine	1	1
Other	3	–

Table TB1 breaks down the responses into their appropriate categories. Table TB2 gives details of the performances, audiences and memberships of the principal categories of performing groups.

Only one of the operatic and musical comedy societies was not affiliated to NODA. By contrast, all but one of the responding drama societies are not affiliated to a national organisation, although some drama groups identified were members of the South Devon Drama Federation. The Federation, which was established in the mid-1960s, was set up to provide a focus for amateur talent by organising an annual

TB2 Teignbridge amateur performing groups: membership, performing attendances, 1989/90

Type of organisation	Number responding	Total member- ship	Total perform- ances	Average attendance per perf.
Drama	8	345	47(a)	96(a)
Operatic/light operatic	4	277	48	177
Choirs	6	203	13(b)	67(b)

(a) Figures relate to only 6 of the responding drama groups.

(b) Excludes attendances at performances by men's or ladies' barbershop choirs.

competitive festival and providing courses and demonstrations. It has 18 members, 10 of which entered the 1990 festival. As the Federation's name implies, member societies come from the neighbouring districts of Torbay, Exeter and East Devon, as well as from Teignbridge, and the festival finals are held outside the Teignbridge district, in Torquay.[2]

Of the dramatic societies identified, 60 per cent have been established over the last two decades. But statistics cannot convey the contribution that the performing groups made to the life of the various villages around Teignbridge. Whilst the pleasures of performing were clearly important to the members of the various groups, many mentioned that they felt the group helped to contribute to the life of the village or the local community. Lilian Woolnough, the chair of Tedburn St Mary Drama Society, which dates from the 1950s and is one of the longer established drama societies, referred specifically to 'the keeping alive of the traditional village pantomime'. Three drama groups used their performances as a means of fund-raising for local charities.

Only one drama group, the Haytor Area Players, was part of the Women's Institute, and according to the Players' secretary, there were no other WIs in Teignbridge regularly involved in drama. The group rehearsed at the local WI Hall in Haytor but gave their regular performances in the village hall. In fact a large part of amateur theatrical activity is sustained in the network of village halls and community centres across the district. As table TB3 shows, 63 per cent of recorded drama performances in 1989/90 were undertaken in

TB3 Teignbridge amateur performing groups: number of performances at each type of venue, 1989/90

Type of organisation	Total	School (LEA)	Arts centre/ theatre	Village hall/ comm. centre	Church	Other
Drama	47	–	2	28	14	3
Operatic/light operatic	48	10	32	6	–	–
Choirs	13	–	–	–	13	–
Rehearsals(a) (percentages)	100	–	12	59	18	12

(a) Based on an analysis of 16 responding societies.

village halls. Only the societies based in and around Teignmouth, Dawlish and Newton Abbot had the luxury of more specialist performing venues, although one musical comedy society in Ashburton used the local school hall. All choir performances were undertaken in churches.

Generally, professional input into productions was found to be limited. Whilst the findings from the other case studies suggested this might be expected for the dramatic societies, even the responding operatic and music societies tended to function with a minimum of paid professional input (Table TB4). But although *direct* input was virtually non-existent for most groups, there were other avenues for

TB4 Teignbridge amateur performing groups: professional input into rehearsals and performances(a)

Type of organisation	Number responding	Groups with some professional input	
		into rehearsals	into performances
Drama	8(a)	2	–
Operatic/light operatic	4	3	2
Choirs	6	3	4

(a) Two responding drama societies did not answer this question.

professional/amateur collaboration. The Devon Shakespeare Project runs various courses at the South Devon College (in Torquay, outside Teignbridge) which provide opportunities for anyone involved in amateur dramatics to work with professional directors.

However, one group that did benefit from direct professional involvement was the Manaton and East Dartmoor Theatre, established as an informal group in 1984 and formally constituted as a charity in 1989. Mark Beeson, the theatre's founder and artistic director explained that:

> The main aim... is the promotion of an indigenous imaginative theatre tradition through the production of verse plays about the Dartmoor area... The plays are entirely home-grown, with text, music, movement and scenery created by local people usually on a professional basis, while the acting is done by local people on a non-professional basis. We also run training workshops, particularly for children, in order to enhance skills for the future, and put on subsidiary performances such as a mini-musical (again composed by local musicians). The difficulty of categorising the Manaton and East Dartmoor Theatre makes it hard for us to attract funds from mainstream arts-funding bodies. We are hoping that a less rigid divide between professional and amateur theatre may emerge, which would be to our benefit.

The theatre did indeed have a substantial professional input; one or two professionals are engaged per session, and three quarters of its expenditure goes on professional fees.

Table TB5 gives details of the income structures of the three principal categories of performing arts group in 1989/90. The figures for the drama societies are heavily influenced by the Manaton and East Dartmoor Theatre. Contributions from public funding bodies were minimal for all three categories of society. The choirs' income came from a range of sources – subscriptions and fund-raising accounted for 71 per cent of all income and consequently they relied much less on funds generated from ticket sales than either the drama or light operatic societies.

With only one orchestra and one silver band, music groups in Teignbridge were found to be predominantly vocalist. Of the six responding choirs, 2 were members of the National Federation of Music Societies. The Teignbridge Ladies Barbershop Singers ('The Chordettes') and Harmony Exe are members of their respective

TB5 Teignbridge: light operatic, drama societies and choirs, sources of income, 1989/90

	Light operatic(a)		Drama(b)		Choirs	
	(£s)	%	(£s)	%	(£s)	%
Box office	22,286	84	9,558	62	1,312	10
Subscriptions	1,604	6	575	4	4,932	39
Sponsorship	–	–	195	1	268	2
Fund raising	1,134	4	1,212	8	4,041	32
Other earned	1,365	5	1,135	7	1,500	12
Public/grant making bodies	300	1	2,800(c)	18(c)	700	5
Total	26,689	100	15,475	100	12,753	100

(a) 4 Societies of which three were members of NODA.

(b) 7 societies.

(c) Includes one grant of £2,500 from a Trust.

'umbrella' organisations – the Ladies Association of British Barbershop Singers (LABBS) and the British Association of Barbershop Singers (BABS). Two choirs, each with around 20 members, were not affiliated to any national bodies.

Barbershop singing has a strong competitive dimension and the national organisations for barbershop singers partly reflect this. The Chordettes have been in existence since 1975 and the group was one of the seven founder members of LABBS (see Chapter 4). The Chordettes has 62 members, 10 of whom are under the age of 30. Although, as with many amateur groups, social motives underpin creative activity, the wish to compete and improve means that the achievement of artistic quality is accorded a high priority. As a result, entry to the choir is closely controlled; new members are auditioned and are required to show their competence in 'holding a tune' against the other parts and learning new songs. Margaret Westlake, a founder member of the group, described The Chordettes as 'very serious fun'. This fun requires a high degree of self-financing; members of group have to pay a subscription of £20 per annum to LABBS. As well as undertaking competitions, the group receives fees from engagements. These help to defray the cost of commissioning a freelance theatrical costumier to create a new set of performing costumes for each year's convention. These costume sets cost between £5,000 and £6,000 and generate an estimated 6 weeks of work for the costumier.[3]

4 non-performing music societies returned questionnaires. Two were recorded music societies and one was a recently started 'music appreciation society' in Moretonhampstead. The recorded music societies both dated from the 1970s, and in each case their youngest member was 50 years old. The most established – and largest – of the non-performing music groups was the Newton Abbot and District Society of Arts. In 1989/90, the Society promoted 8 concerts of chamber music by professional artists. Artists' fees accounted for 58 per cent of the Society's expenditure in 1989/90. Although one-fifth of their income comes from public sources, an equivalent amount was generated from business sponsorship.

The survey brought responses from 7 arts and crafts societies located in the Teignbridge district. Of the 6 groups that gave details of their date of foundation, only one had been in existence prior to 1970. 3 belonged to regional affiliations of societies: 2 were members of the Association of Devon Arts Societies and one group was a member of the West Country Embroiderers. The Hon. Secretary of the Newton Abbot Art Group expressed concern about a reduction in the group's membership. But this was not the result of declining interest, rather the result of the competing attraction of an adjacent group: 'the recent success of the Bovey Tracey Art Group has led to a drop in numbers'.

Exhibiting was a feature of virtually all of the arts, crafts and photography societies and, between them, the groups independently arranged some 12 exhibitions during 1989/90. Only one art group and one camera club did not organise any exhibitions, whilst the group based in the village of Ilsington existed for the singular purpose of running an annual exhibition to raise funds for the village hall. Table TB6 gives details of the arts and crafts societies activities.

All the arts and crafts groups are entirely self-financing, mainly through members' subscriptions and the profits from exhibitions or other fund-raising ventures. The Teignmouth Art Society charges a submission fee for exhibitors at its self-promoted exhibitions and charges for admission. The largest part of exhibition income comes from the commission on woodturnings and pictures sold during the course of the exhibition. The chairman of the Society, Rod Clark, felt

TB6 Teignbridge: visual arts and crafts groups

	Number responding	Groups with paid tutors	Total members	Number of exhibitions held 1989/90
Painting and drawing	3	2	83	2
Crafts	4	2	233	9
Camera clubs/photography	2	–	73	1

that although the Summer Exhibition and the introduction of new and younger members to the group had improved the quality of the work, the main restraining factor on further improvements was the lack of a suitable venue for exhibiting.

Arts festivals
Arts festivals are held in the seaside towns of Dawlish and Ashburton. Both are organised and run by committees of volunteers but engage a range of professional and amateur groups. The Ashburton Festival, established in 1980, is not an annual event. However, its organising committee is active, and a festival was planned for two weeks in the summer of 1991. The Dawlish Arts Festival has a longer and less interrupted history, dating from 1953. The Festival combines professional and amateur events. This enables the Festival organisers to cross-subsidise their professional promotions, including one performance by the Bournemouth Sinfonietta, with income generated from amateur performances. In addition to these more regular events, amateur participation is also a significant feature of one-off celebrations, such as 'Teignmouth 300' which featured a range of participatory arts events.

Teignbridge has few public museums and galleries and is one of five Devon districts which does not incur any direct expenditure on a museums service.[5] However, apart from the Riverside Mill Crafts Gallery, Dawlish, Newton Abbot and Teignmouth all have small independent museums run by the local history societies. With the exception of one part-time paid member of staff at Newton Abbot and nominal payment for the cleaning of the Dawlish Museum, the three museums are entirely dependent upon voluntary staffing.

Adult education

Adult education provision in Teignbridge splits into two categories: there are three adult/community education centres in Teignmouth (Community College), Dawlish and Newton Abbot (Adult Education Centre). The WEA also has a branch in Newton Abbot, but according to Tony Hincks, the South Devon Tutor Organiser for the WEA, these are all limited to art, music and literature appreciation. In the outlying parts of the district, two community education officers are responsible for the development of community education initiatives. County Council-run adult education is covered by a block grant to cover the cost of administration, rather than provide specific funding for the costs of putting on classes. To some extent, the provision of adult education is demand-led. The two community education officers encourage individuals to approach the County Council to arrange specific classes which are provided in local schools and village halls. A flexible approach to classes is also in evidence at Teignmouth Community College. Established classes have been encouraged to set up as free-standing clubs having access to premises at a reduced rate. Hence, some of the 'independent' societies listed in the survey actually meet on adult education premises. But generally, there is a considerable variation in the provision of adult education even within Teignbridge, in part because of the different factors influencing rural provision, but also because of the varied approaches adopted by heads of centres.[5]

Public funding

Since Teignbridge acquired an Arts and Events Officer, Renee Smithens, in 1988, there has been a considerable increase in community-based arts activity. Apart from the Crafts Animateur, one of the most interesting projects funded by the Council is a grant for Actiontrack Performance Company to work with young people in bands in the remote rural areas of the area. But apart from a grant of £2,000 towards 'Teignmouth 300', only £850 in grants was made available to independent amateur organisations identified in the district in 1989/90; the remainder was dispersed in small grants to professional community arts initiatives. However, 1990/1 did see a substantial increase in grants to local amateur arts groups (£5,500 including Teignbridge Craft Development Project). Significant support for the amateur arts was provided through maintaining venues leased to non-professional organisations, namely the Carlton Theatre in Teignmouth and both Dawlish and Teignmouth Museums. This was estimated to be worth in the region of £5,000.[6] Furthermore, the Council has recently purchased £15,000 worth of rostra, chairs and exhibition equipment for use by local arts groups.

Conclusion

Teignbridge sustains a rich and diverse network of organised amateur arts activity. In the smaller villages, local arts groups of all kinds attached significance to the contribution that participatory activities of an artistic kind made to the sense of community, and in most instances outside the towns, it was the village halls which provided the focal points of this activity. Teignbridge had a particularly high number of art societies. Some of the societies felt they were hindered by the lack of a suitable permanent exhibiting area for community use.

The significance of amateur arts activity was considered to be even greater due to the limited nature of professional arts activity in the area and it serves to provide a reminder that there is little professional arts activity in most rural areas. Professional/amateur collaboration was generally more limited than in the other case study areas. The appointment of an Arts and Events Officer was already having a considerable impact on artistic provision in the area. The District Council's contribution, in monetary terms, was most significant as a provider of facilities rather than grants.

References

1. Figures taken from draft local plan.

2. Mrs A. Broom, 'South Devon Drama Federation', Bovey Tracey Players, mimeo., undated.

3. Conversation with Margaret Westlake, 19 December 1990.

4. *Leisure and Recreation Statistics 1990-91 Estimates*, Chartered Institute of Public Finance and Accountancy, 1991.

5. Meeting with Community Education Organisers in South Devon, November 1990.

6. Letter from Renee Smithens, Arts and Events Officer, Teignbridge District Council, 18 October 1990.

7 Telford New Town

Telford, in Shropshire, was established as a new town in 1968 by a government decision to incorporate the earlier Dawley New Town, the town of Wellington, and a number of other towns and villages, into one major settlement. The Head of Public Relations for Telford Development Corporation (TDC), which was wound up in September 1991, has written that before its designation as a New Town:

> the place was as dull as a felt boot. It isn't popular to say this. Some local people, with memories dimmed by the mist of time, indignantly remember some arcadian paradise between the pit mounds and the decaying remains of a once-great coalfield and iron-making area. But it was a mess and several millions of pounds have been spent on filling pit-shafts and reclaiming around two thousand acres of derelict land which would hardly support a goat. Ironbridge alone, a key part of Telford's image, needed a vast programme of building restoration which came just in time to save much of that Town from inevitable closing orders and demolition notices.[1]

During the 1980s, the population of Telford grew by 15,000 to over 117,000 in 1989. The local authorities' plans are for continued growth, and a population of 140,000 in Telford by 2001. Both in terms of population and area, Telford New Town forms a large part of Wrekin District, which had a total population of 136,100 in 1989, and Wrekin District Council is inheriting many of the responsibilities of the Development Corporation.

Cultural traditions and characteristics
Telford is located between the Black Country, from where much of its population has been drawn, and Wales; influences from both directions, as well as a wider range of cultural traditions – there are,

for example, a flourishing Caledonian Society and a popular steel band – are woven into its culture.

At the southern end of the New Town lies the Severn Gorge, the birthplace of the Industrial Revolution. With considerable backing from the Development Corporation, the Ironbridge Gorge Museum has been created around a unique series of industrial monuments spread over about six square miles of the Gorge, which has now been declared a World Heritage Site. The Ironbridge Gorge Museum attracted 350,310 visitors in 1989.[2] A completely separate initiative, the Ironbridge Open Air Museum of Steel Sculpture opened in June 1991 as a result of collaboration between this new Museum's Trustees and the Development Corporation.

Much of the amateur artistic life of Telford is rooted in clubs and societies formed in the old urban areas, such as Wellington, Dawley, and Oakengates, during or soon after the Second War. The Telford Ladies Choir began as a mixed voice choir in the 1940s, Wellington Theatre Company was formed in 1940, the GKN Sankey Male Voice Choir (now only loosely connected with GKN Sankey) in 1941, the Horsehay Amateur Dramatic Society in 1944, and the Donnington Garrison Amateur Dramatic and Operatic Society (subsequently re-named the Little Theatre, Donnington Society) in 1954. But there are two much more venerable groups still performing in the area: the Jackfield Band was formed as a pipe and drum band in 1893 and the Hadley and District Orpheus Male Voice Choir started in 1901. The visual arts, crafts and literary groups tend to be of more recent origins: one of the older such groups, the Telford Art Society, started in 1965; its entire membership now consists of senior citizens.

For fifteen years Telford Community Arts, a dedicated group of professionals, was substantially funded by West Midlands Arts, TDC and Wrekin District Council. Telford Community Arts became nationally known for its work; the organisation made a significant contribution to cultural life in the New Town. In its own potted history, Telford Community Arts stated its priorities as to

> work in the interests of the working class and to organise our activities accordingly... Since 1974 one of our main contributions to the cultural life of our area has been the weekly workshop. Each year up to 20 groups of local residents have met together once or twice a week to do community arts. They have worked on banners, with clay and

textiles, on murals, video films, plays, music, photography, books, magazines, sculpture, dance, posters – indeed most art forms;[3]

The nature of Telford Community Arts' work resulted in problems with political antagonists and funding agencies; the Development Corporation withdrew its grant because of the political content of some projects, and in 1989 a decision to wind up the company was made by the Management Council and members of Telford Community Arts.

One spin-off from the work of Telford Community Arts was a group that produced some attractive posters for two national youth organisations – Youth Clubs UK and the National Youth Bureau – and then turned its attention to video. Between 1986 and 1990 the Dead Honest Soul Searchers (DHSS) – young people who trained at Birmingham Film and Video Workshop and Wolverhampton Polytechnic – made video programmes about, with and for, young people. They saw their task as using video to articulate the point of view of the under-represented.

More recent approaches to community arts in the town have included the appointment of a community dance animateur, funded for three years by West Midlands Arts and Wrekin District Council; Kiki Gale occupied the post for 18 months (until June 1991) and in that time widened the range of opportunities for people, young and old, to practise and enjoy many types of dance activity, and to give dance performances in different parts of Telford. Fiona Hay was appointed to work as dance animateur from June 1991.

Main arts venues and institutions

Wrekin District Council employs an arts and entertainments officer and an assistant, who is responsible for administering Wrekin and Telford Arts, the arts association for the area. Wrekin and Telford Arts grew out of the Wellington Arts Association; it is funded by Shropshire County Council and West Midlands Arts as well as the District Council; it organises the annual Wrekin and Telford Festival (see below), gives grants to local groups as well as to individual artists, and promotes small-scale professional theatre and other events.

Wrekin District Council owns and runs what for many years was called Oakengates Town Hall, but was re-named Oakengates Theatre in June 1991. The 650-seater 'Town Hall' opened in 1968 and was refurbished in 1984. (In April 1991, the programme at Oakengates Town Hall included wrestling, Ironbridge Lions Club presenting the

Bryan Jones Big Band playing music from the forties to the sixties, Telford and District Light Operatic Society performing 'Calamity Jane', and Jimmy Smith Promotions presenting the sensational Australian comedian Kevin 'Bloody' Wilson – 'if easily offended please stay away'.) Wrekin District Council also gives grant aid to local organisations, and promotes events in other areas of the Wrekin in addition to the programme described above.

The Academy of Saint Nicolas, an orchestra named after a church in Newport, Shropshire, but whose core members are drawn from all over the Midlands – and indeed sometimes play as the Midlands Symphony Orchestra – has frequently given classical concerts in Oakengates Town Hall. The Town Hall is certainly far from ideal for such events, because the acoustics are not good, and the ambience outside the building leaves much to be desired. Indeed there is no satisfactory sizeable multi-purpose arts facility in the new town area, and apart from the theatre at Madeley Court School, little in the way of facilities for the performing arts in the southern half of the town. The Hayward Arts Centre, part of New College, the sixth form college in Wellington, opened in November 1990; it has a performing area, with accommodation for 150 people on movable rostra, as well as an exhibition area; in recent months 'performances have taken place regularly, with lunchtime and evening student concerts and plays... the arts centre is also proving to be an excellent attraction to professional companies.'[4] The Princes Street Arts Centre (see below) is also an important facility for those living in north Telford.

Wrekin College Centenary Theatre, which seats 250, has been used for chamber orchestras, soloists and theatre companies.

At the end of the 1980s the Visual Arts Trust came into being as a result of discussions between officers of TDC, West Midlands Arts and a number of Shropshire based artists. The Trust has promoted some successful exhibitions and events and done much to promote collaboration between professionals and amateurs; but to date has got nowhere in its attempts to achieve one of its main original purposes: the establishment of a gallery for the visual arts in Telford.

Apart from a general reference to libraries, 'building societies' windows and solicitors' windows', and village halls, a recent report on the crafts in Shropshire was unable to recommend one suitable exhibition space for displaying arts and crafts in the New Town area. However a map in the report showed 28 crafts workshops in the

Telford New Town area, with a particular concentration in and around Ironbridge.[5] The Green Wood Trust, founded in 1984 and based in Coalbrookdale, is a small, but unique and impressive organisation which promotes the traditional woodland crafts of coppicing, and basket, coracle and furniture making. The Trust has a museum, runs courses and holds exhibitions.

Amateur arts and crafts

Excluding the youth theatres and youth bands (of which more below), 29 amateur arts groups were identified in the New Town area, as shown in Table T1.

T1 Telford New Town: responses to questionnaire

Type of organisation	Number identified	Number responded
Performing groups		
Drama	5	4
Light operatic	1	1
Choirs	9	5
Brass bands	3	2
Orchestra	1	1
Folk and county dancing	2	2
Non-performing groups		
Painting and drawing	2	2
Crafts	2	2
Camera clubs/photography	2	2
Poetry/writing groups	2	2

In addition to the long-established choirs, brass bands and amateur drama companies, there are a number of groups founded more recently, as well as the inevitable casualties. Two of the casualties serve to indicate the precarious nature of much amateur arts activity. The New Town Singers started in 1972 and have recently disbanded. The group used to meet once a week – and usually put on a Gilbert and Sullivan production in the summer, and a carol concert at Christmas. But the choir failed to attract younger members – while some of its members died, some gave up, and others joined other choirs. The Brookside Amateur Dramatic Society took an 'enforced rest' in 1990 after more than a decade of activity. There were difficulties with premises, some people changed their jobs, and others left. There was an offer of the use of the theatre at Madeley Court School, but some members were reluctant to go there because it was too far from Brookside – in fact it is a couple of miles! The Society has now re-formed.

But what is striking, in Telford as elsewhere, is the resilience of many of the long-standing groups. For example, the secretary of the Hadley and District Orpheus Male Voice Choir, which has won over a hundred male voice championships, says that the group has achieved and maintained a high standard of performance 'through comradeship and dedication and regular rehearsals'. The same, no doubt, could be said of the GKN Sankey Male Voice Choir, which in 4 of the last 5 years has been invited to compete in the major All England Male Voice Choir competition at Huddersfield.

The Jackfield Brass Band has been in continuous existence since 1893. One of the band's long-standing members writes:

> This October we compete at the National Brass Band Championships in London for the third time in four years... During the same period we have produced two successful cassette recordings and played to a packed audience at Oakengates Town Hall in a joint concert with the British Open Champions – Sunlife Band. We are at present planning a short concert tour to Switzerland in 1992.
>
> On the non-playing side we have replaced nearly all our instruments, purchased new uniforms, bought our own wooden bandroom and are in the process of buying a brick building to provide additional practice facilities and ultimately to be used as a recording studio to enable us to produce our own cassettes.
>
> All this has been achieved by the efforts of players, committee and supporters and without a regular sponsor from industry or commerce.[6]

In its 27 years of existence the Wrekin and Telford Choral Society has presented between 50 and 60 different oratorios and concert versions of opera 'to an area starved of this kind of music'. For more than 40 years the Telford Caledonian Society, whose main activity is Scottish country dancing, has maintained 'the traditions and customs of Scotland' hundreds of miles from home.

The two main amateur drama companies – the Little Theatre, Donnington and the Wellington Theatre Company – occupy buildings that they do not own. But the members of both groups put a great deal of effort not only into their artistic activities, but also into the upkeep of their buildings. At the Little Theatre, Donnington, they rehearse 'almost daily' – with an estimated 275 rehearsal sessions in 1989/90. At the Wellington Theatre Company 'we "live" in our theatre'; there are usually three rehearsals each week, and the aim is to work to 'a standard as professional as possible by non-professional cast and crew'.

Some of the performing groups – for example the Telford Light Orchestra and the Donald Morris Singers – have been 'raising money for charities' as a supplementary motive to the primary concern of entertaining others.

T2 Telford amateur performing groups: membership, performances and attendances 1989/90

Type of organisation	Number responding	Total member-ship	Total perform-ances	Average attendance per perf.
Drama	4	207	81	109
Light operatic	1	112	14	350
Choirs	5	241	55	..
Brass bands/ensembles	2	47	..	..
Orchestra	1	36	7	..

The Little Theatre, Donnington frequently engages professional musicians for its productions, but it is the Wrekin and Telford Choral Society and the Telford and District Light Operatic Players that probably make most regular use of professionals: the Light Operatic Society engages a professional pianist for rehearsals and 20 musicians for the week of the show; and the Choral Society has three professionals involved in its rehearsals and usually about six in its performances. Over half its income of £7,643 in 1989/90 went on fees for professional soloists, accompanists and conductor. In 1990 the Society raised £6,000 to buy a 'state-of-the art' Domus Viscount opera organ.

T3 Telford amateur groups: professional input to rehearsals and performances

Type of organisation	Number responding	Groups with some professional input into rehearsals	into performances
Drama	4	1	1
Light operatic	1	1	1
Choirs	5	4	4
Brass bands	2	–	–
Orchestra	1	–	–

(a) 'Professionals' may be directors, conductors, singers or musicians; they include tutors.

The Princes Street Arts Centre, a converted primary school, built before the first World War, houses the Belfrey Theatre, home of the Wellington Theatre Company, as well as the Wrekin Art Society, the Wrekin Arts Photographic Club, and the Wrekin Pottery Group. The Pottery Group has 10 members; the Photographic Club, which organises numerous competitions each year, has visiting lecturers, and arranges trips to other clubs and to exhibitions, has 58 members; and the Art Society has 87 members. The Wrekin Art Society describes its principal motivation as being 'the promotion of the visual arts in the Telford and Wrekin areas where there is at present a lack of such facilities – encouraging non-professional artists to maintain and develop their interest, talents and skills in drawing and painting in

T4 Telford amateur performing groups: number of performances at each type of venue 1989/90

Type of organisation	School (LEA)	Theatre/ arts centre/ town hall	Community centre/ village hall	Other
Drama	–	60	14	7
Choirs (a)	7	5	3	16
Orchestra	2	2	–	3
Light operatic	–	14	–	–

(a) Figures only available for 3 choirs.

various media, and holding at least two exhibitions each year.' From 1977 to 1991 the Princes Street Arts Centre building was owned by TCD, which invested considerable sums in repairs and maintenance, and charged the users only modest levels of rent; but with the demise of the Corporation, a Trust has been established to take over responsibility for the building. Although the principal users will be represented on the Trust, they are naturally concerned about the prospect of future rising costs in an 80-year-old building that was not originally built as an arts centre.

T5 Telford visual arts and crafts groups

Type of organisation	Number responding	Groups with paid tutors	Total members	Number of exhibitions held 1989/90
Painting and drawing	2	1	92	3
Crafts	2	1	20	6
Camera clubs/photography	2	2	78	..

There are two literary organisations in Telford – the Salopian Poetry Society, founded in 1976, and the Wrekin Writers Group, which started in the mid-1980s, and which now has 30 members. Of the Wrekin Writers Group its chairman writes:

> As a group with two professional writers as members and with several others who have had work published, we aim to give help and guidance to those who have aspirations to see their work in print, whether it be poetry, short stories, novels or articles. Time throughout the year is given to each of these aspects and a criticism service is in operation.

The Salopian Poetry Society has 117 members in all parts of the UK, though the committee members all live in or around Telford. The Society works to 'promote the love of poetry'; it holds an annual open poetry competition and issues a quarterly magazine, but will not print anything 'which is considered to be too political, religious or pornographic in nature'.

Youth arts and the arts in adult education

A brief, but ill-fated, experiment in community education took place at Madeley Court School at the end of the 1970s. Robert Petty, who was teaching at the school at the time, writes:

> In 1978 the Madeley Court complex was completed with a theatre that linked the school building and the sports centre. The then headmaster, Philip Toogood, used this moment to establish a full programme of evening activities... These activities included:
>
> - a wide range of evening classes (650 enrolments in the first year) that included art and crafts.
>
> - a Film Society programme. The Court Film Society ran for over ten years, run by a voluntary committee, until the arrival of the town's multiplex.
>
> - an amateur theatre group – Link Theatre – which pre-existed this enterprise, but which had previously been homeless.
>
> Lack of resources resulted in a struggle to survive the second year, after which the teacher, who had been brought in to establish the programme, left. After that, various aspects of it continued independently for some years, but there is now no trace of any of it.[7]

Most adult education in Telford goes under the name of community education and is organised by Telford College of Arts and Technology, the further education college for the area. Regular evening classes offered commencing in September 1990 at six different centres throughout the new town area included 12 classes in crafts of various kinds (including calligraphy and flower arranging, but excluding machine knitting), 2 in photography, 6 in painting and drawing, as well as regular sessions of creative writing, circle dancing and 'ladies choral'. At the Phoenix Centre, Dawley, classes in clarinet, keyboards, flute, piano, folk guitar, and singing were on offer.

The youth service in Telford has also been active in promoting the arts, though the pressures on local government finance have forced some cutbacks in 1991.

For three years until its closure in May 1991, the Lion Street Cultural Centre was based in an old United Reform Chapel in Oakengates. The building was owned by Telford Development Corporation, leased to Shropshire County Council, who sub-let it to a

Management Committee, of whom – under the organisation's constitution – half were aged under 25. In a report written for a conference in November 1990, Andrew Bengrey, then the Centre's arts co-ordinator, wrote:

> The original group that started the campaign for the Lion Street Cultural Centre formed out of a group of young people that were promoting live music at a club in Wellington, Telford, called the Gemini.
>
> Lion Street is trying to develop links with Asian young people in Telford. Telford has a very large Asian population, but no facilities that cater for their needs and culture directly. Lion Street is trying to develop a regular Bhangra night. Bhangra is the name which describes the combination of traditional Indian music with contemporary rock music of the West.
>
> The project has always tried to keep its independence from the youth service and to involve young people directly in decision making and the overall running of the centre.[8]

The Centre has had to live with having a 'punk' image; it opened with two full-time staff – an administrator and a caretaker; with support from the Gulbenkian Foundation, an arts co-ordinator was appointed in 1990. The building has been used in a great variety of ways including numerous arts workshops as well as musical events. However the Centre was funded as an Urban Programme project on the understanding that employment would be created by using the basement for crafts workshops and a recording studio; but because of essential work treating dampness in the basement, this aspect of the project has never been brought to fruition with a consequent loss of potential income. When the Centre's severe financial problems were brought to light in May 1991, officers of the County Council's youth service were forced to close the building, although it is hoped to re-open it in due course on a somewhat different financial and managerial basis.

The County Council's youth service was also responsible in the mid-1980s for establishing the Madeley Music Project and the Dawley Workshop Project – both of which have worked to create a musical environment within which young people can support each other, develop musical skills, and exchange ideas; because of constraints on

County Council budgets the future of both these projects was brought into question in 1991. It is clear that these projects, and many of the activities at the Lion Street Cultural Centre have been valued by the young people who have been involved in them.

Outside the youth service, the Telford Schools Brass Band, which is run and financed by the education authority, at least three youth drama groups, and the Ebony and Ivory Steel Band, which is part of Telford West Indian Association, are all active. But the majority of participants in all these groups tend to be under sixteen, so that, strictly speaking, they fall outside the scope of this study.

However, mention should be made of the youth theatre (for youngsters up to the age of 18) run by the Little Theatre, Donnington and the Wellington Theatre Company, which have provided an introduction to drama, as well as considerable experience of working in the theatre, for many young people, some of whom have subsequently entered the profession.

Festivals

In addition to a number of community festivals and community celebrations, which in the 1970s and 1980s Telford Community Arts did much to initiate and support, there are now five regular arts festivals in Telford: the Wrekin and Telford Festival; All Folk Around the Wrekin; the Ironbridge Bluegrass and Roots Festival; the Wellington Drama Festival, and the Wrekin Dance Festival.

The Wrekin and Telford Festival was first held in 1973 and has been held annually since; the 1991 festival consisted of twenty different events – including Humphrey Lyttleton's band, a formal demonstration, 'An evening with the Company of Storytellers', a gospel concert, and much else involving both amateur and professional performers. There were also two exhibitions and displays by a regimental band and by Morris and Country dancing teams. The festival is promoted by Wrekin and Telford Arts, and events are planned to 'suit all tastes, using venues in all parts of the Wrekin'; the festival administrator works half-time for Wrekin District Council, and half-time for Wrekin and Telford Arts. In 1990, 19 unpaid volunteers were involved in the organisation of the festival, and attendances totalled about 4,500. The festival's total expenditure was £22,860 of which £14,493 went in professional fees. The Festival receives financial support from Wrekin District Council, Shropshire

County Council and West Midlands Arts; but at the opening of the 1991 Festival, its chairman said that 'five years ago the festival committee had twice the money to spend it had now.'

'All Folk Around the Wrekin' is a weekend folk festival held each June at the Court Centre, Madeley. The festival, which was first held in 1976, attracted 8-900 people in both 1990 and 1991. It is organised by a group of about 10 people, and, in 1991, received grants totalling £1,900 including £900 from Madeley Parish Council to pay for a children's programme. The 1991 festival produced a loss of about £4,000, which is being underwritten by a number of individual committee members. The festival has operated as a fairly traditional folk festival. It is the policy of the organising group, that, in future years, the festival should become more of a community-based event – possibly linked by a week of activities to the Ironbridge Bluegrass and Roots festival.

The Ironbridge Bluegrass and Roots festival was first held in 1988, and the fourth festival was held at the Maws Craft Centre from Friday 21 to Sunday 23 June 1991. About 1,500 people attended the festival that was very largely organised by volunteers. Subsidies for the 1991 festival totalled £2,300 from West Midlands Arts, Wrekin and Telford Arts, and the Shropshire County and Wrekin District Councils. Leading American and UK Cajun and Bluegrass groups performed throughout; there were also performances by international folk dance troupes, and music workshops, fringe shows and children's entertainment. The festival sees itself as 'a small national festival', which engages the services of professional musicians and dancers from all over the world. in 1990 the festival spent approximately £5,000 on professional artists' fees. Mal Salisbury, the festival's founder and principal organiser, was one of the people instrumental in forming the British Bluegrass Music Association (BBMA) in 1991.

The Wellington Drama Festival (WDF) is held at the Princes Street Arts Centre each year, and is hosted under the rules set by the National Drama Festivals Association. The WDF, which was first held in 1983, is open to one-act, youth and full-length plays, and, in November 1990, companies from Bristol, Bath, Staffordshire and Shropshire took part in the eight nights of the festival (total attendances: approximately 480). The Festival Co-ordinator is a member of the main committee of the Wellington Theatre Company. The Committee provides support to the Co-ordinator, but most of the organisational work is carried out by the Co-ordinator, and during the run, by the Festival Stage Manager, and front of house management. The Festival Co-ordinator writes:

> The logistics of hosting performances by so many different groups performing so many different plays are daunting, but the pleasure of groups being able to meet one another and discuss highlights and problems alike, make a drama festival a very worthwhile occasion and a learning experience for all concerned – the winning of an award is 'icing on the cake'.

The Wrekin Dance Festival was first held in 1987. It is a competitive festival that takes place at the end of November each year. In its first year it was promoted by Wrekin District Council which subsequently handed over responsibility for the organisation of the Dance Festival to an independent committee which promotes the Festival with the help of a diminishing grant from the District Council.

Conclusion

Telford Development Corporation, which was wound up in September 1991, has been highly successful in attracting Japanese and other inward investment, resulting in the creation of several thousand jobs, which has helped keep the unemployment level close to the national average. However, the town does not have the facilities or investment in the arts to be found in many other new towns of similar vintage.

Wrekin District Council has an experienced, energetic and capable arts officer, and this report has described a good deal of well-established amateur arts activity in the town, much of which has been assisted over the years by the TDC. Nevertheless, as with Stoke-on-Trent, Telford appears to behave as a series of discrete estates, villages or small towns, with little central focus to the new town's cultural life. When it comes to provision for the arts, the twenty-three years of the Development Corporation, seem something of a missed opportunity.

Telford will continue to grow for many more years, and the local authorities need to look elsewhere for good examples of the kind of facilities that should exist near the heart of any large town. In short, there is a need for an arts centre, including a gallery capable of showing painting, sculpture and crafts of the highest quality. But also the participatory side of arts activities in Telford seem to rest too heavily on some admirable, but venerable, organisations – for example while the work of the dance animateurs is helping to expose a considerable potential interest in contemporary dance, there are no proper facilities for such dance activity in the whole of the new town. Question marks hang over the future contribution of the youth service to provision for the arts in Telford, and the links between adult education and the arts in the town are not noticeably strong. Again, the Wrekin and Telford Festival, which has been important in offering an intense programme of arts events each spring and in bringing amateurs and professionals together, appears to have lost its way, and has perhaps been straining too hard to be all things to all people. In sum: there is little regular professional arts activity in the town, much that is strong in the amateur arts, but also a good deal of parochialism. However, the District Council is in process of developing a new arts strategy.

References

1. David Everington, 'Telford Development Corporation', *Business Times*, August 1990.

2. *Sightseeing in the UK 1989*, BTA/ETB Research Services, 1990.

3. Telford Community Arts, *Not the Royal Opera*, 1989.

4. Bob Wysome, 'The Hayward Arts Centre', *Arts in Schools*, Shropshire Arts Education Project, July 1991, No.6.

5. See Annabel Stratton, 'Shropshire Crafts Marketing Initiative' Shropshire Leisure Services, 1991.

6. P.D. France, Letter to the *Shropshire Star*, 13 July 1991.

7. Letter from Robert Petty, 29 July 1991.

8. Andrew Bengrey 'Lion Street Cultural Centre, a report', written for The Arts Post-16: School, College and Community Conference, Shrewsbury, November 1990.

9. 'Concern for festival future', *Shropshire Star*, 4 May 1991.

Appendix A

Selected 'umbrella' organisations: membership by English region and county, 1990

The table has been compiled from the directories and membership lists of five of the principal 'umbrella' organisations in the performing arts. For the National Operatic and Dramatic Association (NODA), the National Federation of Music Societies (NFMS) and the National Association of Choirs (NAC) figures relate to the number of affiliated clubs in a given county. For the English Folk Dance and Song Society (EFDSS) and the British Federation of Brass Bands (BFBB), the figures refer to *all* groups listed in the directories that they publish rather than only affiliated societies or bands. There are minor variations in the determinant of 'location' between the different 'umbrellas'. Brass bands are listed by the county in which their rehearsal room is located. Folk dance and song societies are listed by the county in which they meet, as are members of the NAC. NFMS-affiliated societies have been analysed by the address of the federal representative. The various means of identifying the location of societies is likely to make relatively little difference to the general pattern of regional distribution of societies. In the case of NODA, however, there may be a significant understating in the number of London-based societies (and a corresponding overstating in the number of societies in the home counties) because NODA's London membership is limited to those societies whose NODA-representative lives in a London postal district.

Selected 'umbrella' organisations: membership by region and county, 1990

	EFDSS (a)	BFBB (a)	NAC	NFMS	NODA	Total	Total per million population
North							
Cleveland	15	7	6	11	7	46	83.2
Cumbria	27	14	11	25	26	103	210.5
Durham	18	17	11	9	28	83	139.1
Northumberland	7	3	4	9	11	34	112.8
Tyne and Wear	15	8	11	11	34	79	69.8
Total	82	49	43	65	106	345	
Total per million population	27	16	14	21	34	112	
Yorkshire and Humberside							
Humberside	16	8	9	14	10	57	67.0
Yorkshire	130	68	60	80	182	520	128.0
Total	146	76	69	94	192	577	
Total per million population	30	15	14	19	39	116	
East Midlands							
Derbyshire	31	20	12	13	28	104	112.5
Leicestershire	39	16	5	9	27	96	108.4
Lincolnshire	14	9	4	24	14	65	111.6
Northamptonshire	23	5	1	11	21	61	105.2
Nottinghamshire	24	14	8	16	11	73	72.4
Total	131	64	30	73	101	399	
Total per million population	33	16	8	18	25	100	
East Anglia							
Cambridgeshire	34	8	1	16	20	79	121.2
Norfolk	21	9	–	12	19	61	82.0
Suffolk	29	4	1	25	26	85	133.1
Total	84	21	2	53	65	225	
Total per million population	41	10	1	26	32	110	
South East							
Bedfordshire	13	5	1	11	19	49	92.3
Berkshire	31	5	3	31	18	88	117.8
Buckinghamshire	26	8	1	20	24	79	125.9
East Sussex	36	8	–	18	25	87	122.1
Essex	64	15	4	59	61	203	132.7
Hampshire	43	14	6	44	45	152	98.5
Hertfordshire	56	3	1	94	45	149	151.1
Isle of Wight	5	–	–	–	8	13	99.6
Kent	64	8	1	74	58	205	134.8

	EFDSS (a)	BFBB (a)	NAC	NFMS	NODA	Total	Total per million population
Oxfordshire	38	17	–	24	12	91	157.2
Surrey	31	12	–	68	47	158	158.0
West Sussex	26	4	–	24	25	79	112.3
Total	433	99	17	417	387	1,353	
Total per million population	41	9	2	39	36	127	
South West							
Avon	54	9	–	15	39	117	122.6
Cornwall	34	34	6	14	28	116	251.8
Devon	44	12	–	30	58	144	141.0
Dorset	24	7	–	18	23	72	109.8
Gloucestershire	39	6	–	22	11	78	147.9
Somerset	29	7	–	17	20	73	159.4
Wiltshire	23	7	–	12	18	60	107.7
Total	247	82	6	128	197	660	
Total per million population	53	18	1	28	42	142	
West Midlands							
Hereford & Worcs.	37	3	–	27	27	94	139.2
Shropshire	17	1	8	13	9	48	119.8
Staffordshire	31	6	12	17	28	94	91.0
Warwickshire	17	9	5	10	–	41	84.6
West Midlands(c)	37	15	16	27	82	177	67.6
Total	139	34	41	94	146	454	
Total per million population	27	7	8	18	28	87	
North West							
Cheshire	47	8	9	33	54	151	158.0
Greater Manchester	48	37	10	10	50	155	60.1
Lancashire	57	13	21	31	101	223	161.4
Total	173	62	42	87	222	586	
Total per million population	27	10	7	14	35	92	
Greater London	98	5	5	106	46	260	38.6
Total per million population	15	1	1	16	7(b)	38	

(a) For the English Folk Dance and Song Society and the British Federation of Brass Bands, figures relate to entries in their respective directories rather than affiliated groups.

(b) See accompanying text.

(c) The area of the former West Midlands Metropolitan County.

Appendix B

The National Federation of Music Societies (NFMS)

The NFMS is the 'umbrella' body for non-professional choirs, music societies and orchestras in the UK. The NFMS agreed to provide access to its mailing list to allow a full survey of its membership to be undertaken. The structure of the survey reflected the different types of society in membership. Separate questionnaires were designed for choirs, orchestras and music-promoting societies (or music clubs) respectively. The principal function of music societies can be described as arranging and promoting concerts. Questionnaires were distributed in November 1990. A reminder letter was sent to all members as part of the quarterly mailing to NFMS members.

Using the NFMS mailing list, adjusted to exclude member societies within the seven case study areas, a total of 1,240 questionnaires were sent (762 to choral societies, 202 to orchestras and 276 to music societies). In the course of receiving replies, the sample was reweighted. Five professionally-run promoting societies were taken out of the sample.

The response to the survey was good. Usable questionnaires were returned by 441 choirs, 157 promoting societies and 120 orchestras. These accounted for 57.3 per cent, 58.1 per cent and 61.2 per cent respectively of the reweighted samples, an overall response rate of 58.1 per cent. Details of NFMS members' expenditure on professional musicians and other details on the relationship between amateur music and the professional world are given in Chapter 12. This Appendix considers some of the other areas covered by the survey.

Britain has a long tradition in formal amateur music. But although 9 NFMS choirs are more than 140 years old, three-quarters of NFMS choirs have been established since 1940. Music societies represent an even more recent phenomenon; 85 per cent of responding societies in that category have only functioned since 1940.

Table NFMS 1   Date of foundation, by type of society(a)

Numbers

	Choirs	Music societies	Orchestras
1800 - 1850	9	–	–
1851 - 1900	37	2	15
1901 - 1939	60	20	20
1940 - 1960	115	57	29
1961 - 1970	79	24	17
1971 - 1980	69	26	19
1981 - 1990	33	18	7

Percentages

	Choirs	Music societies	Orchestras
1800 - 1850	2	–	–
1851 - 1900	9	1	14
1901 - 1939	15	14	19
1940 - 1960	29	39	27
1961 - 1970	20	16	16
1971 - 1980	17	18	18
1981 - 1990	8	12	7

(a) Base: All societies answering the question (402 choirs, 147 music societies and 107 orchestras).

Status and membership

The majority of choirs and orchestras in NFMS membership function as free standing voluntary-run associations; few exist as part of an adult education class. In spite of the high participation rates recorded for students in full-time education (see Chapter 3), only a very small number of student societies were affiliated to the NFMS. The case studies revealed that, for the amateur arts as a whole, student societies largely operated outside the 'umbrella' movement. Two-thirds of all NFMS members had charitable status.

Table NFMS 2   Choirs and orchestras, by status

	Choirs		Orchestras	
	Numbers	Percentages	Numbers	Percentages
Free-standing voluntary organisation	402	91	92	84
Adult education class	33	7	19	17
Student society	4	1	–	–
Corporate	2	*	–	–

Table NFMS 3   Membership: subscriptions and numbers

	Choirs	Music societies	Orchestras	Total
Average annual subscription per person(£s)	23.1	20.3	23.5	..
Average membership	75	137	50	83
Total membership	32,678	21,140	5,946	59,764
Grossed up estimate for all NFMS	56,860	36,380	9,720	103,000

With a combined membership of 56,860, choral societies and choirs make up 62 per cent of total estimated individual membership of the NFMS; the total estimated membership of member orchestras was smaller, accounting for less than 10 per cent of NFMS individual membership. With an average membership of 137, music societies are the largest of the three categories of society, but their members are concert-goers rather than concert-givers.

For performing groups, the issue of accepting new members is often complicated by a number of different considerations: the physical limitations on size of orchestra or choir; the inertia of incumbent members; and a desire to maintain or improve standards. So while it may be social needs that underpin the existence of a society or group, the desire to achieve quality can be equally important for many societies and groups. For whatever reason, the majority of choirs and orchestras exercise some form of control on the acceptance of new members. Significant differences were found to exist between choirs and orchestras. While 38 per cent of choirs functioned without any membership restrictions, the figure for orchestras was much lower, at less than 10 per cent of respondents. Just under half the orchestras adopted a mixed approach to new members depending on the section that the new member wished to join.

Table NFMS 4   Restrictions imposed on the entry of new members(a)

Column percentages

	Choirs	Orchestras
New members admitted by:		
Invitation	4	14
Audition	41	8
Trial	7	23
Varies by section/mixed	10	48
No membership restrictions	38	8
Total	100	100

(a) Base: 441 choirs and 120 orchestras.

Rehearsals, performances and attendances

The rehearsal and performance characteristics of choirs and orchestras were similar. Choirs undertook an average of 36.5 rehearsals in 1989/90, marginally higher than the figure for orchestras (32.5). On average, choirs and orchestras gave a total of 4.5 and 4.6 performances respectively during the 1989/90 season. Performances fall into two distinct categories: engagements and own/joint promotions. The latter account for the largest number of performances by both choirs and orchestras: 'engagements' made up only 9 per cent of UK choral performances and a slightly higher proportion of orchestral performances. Grossed up estimates of performances and attendances are given in Table NFMS5. In total, the combined output of all NFMS member societies in 1989/90 was an estimated 6,060 concerts, attracting an audience of over 1.36 million. To put this figure in to perspective, attendances at the South Bank Halls and Barbican combined were 1.42 million in 1988/9.

Table NFMS 5   Rehearsals, performances and attendances(a)

	Choirs	Orchestras
Rehearsals		
Annual average	36.5	32.5
Total	16,085	3,873
Performances		
Own promotions:		
Unaccompanied	827	na
Accompanied		
Full-time professional	137	na
Ad hoc professional orchestra	330	na
Semi-professional orchestra	300	na
Amateur orchestra	159	na
Total own promotions	1,753	451
Engagements	175	94
Total UK performances	1,928	545
Overseas performances	56	1
Total performances	1,984	546
Estimated total attendances	485,995	160,417
Grossed-up estimate for all NFMS:		
Performances	3,460	890
Attendances	847,600	262,100

(a) Music societies promoted a total of 994 concerts (an annual average of 6.30), drawing an audience of 146,707. Grossed up estimates for 1989/90 give a total 1,711 performances and an audience of 252,500.

Income

Subscription income provides the financial basis for most voluntary groups.[1] Performing societies are no exception to this general rule. There are two striking features about the income structures of responding organisations within all three categories of society: their reliance on public funding is limited; and the funding structures that have evolved rely on a diversity of income sources, ie they have a broad plural funding base. This contrasts somewhat with dramatic and operatic societies identified in the case study areas which tend to rely to a greater extent on income from the box office.

Table NFMS 6   Choirs: income by type

	Total (£ thousands)	Average (£s)	Number receiving	Percentage of all income
Box office	1,498	3,492	429	37
Engagement fees	78	923	85	2
Subscriptions	1,184	2,716	436	29
Sponsorship	276	1,400	197	7
Donations	421	1,029	409	10
Other income	259	978	265	6
Public funding				
Local authority/local arts council	139	594	234	3
RAAs	159	800	199	4
Total income	4,014	9,102	441	100

Overall, funds mainly come from self-generated or private income sources. The total value of the contribution from Regional Arts Associations has fallen substantially in recent years, even before allowing for inflation (see Chapter 9). This is further born out by comparing an analysis of 581 NFMS choirs and orchestras which applied for RAA funding in 1982/3 with figures for choirs and orchestras *in receipt* of RAA funding in the PSI survey.[2] Although it is not possible to provide a more detailed categorisation of income, it is clear from the figures that choirs and orchestras are less reliant on direct public funding now than they were in 1982/3.

Table NFMS 7   Orchestras: income by type

	Total (£ thousands)	Average (£s)	Number receiving	Percentage of all income
Box office	402	3,469	116	45
Engagement fees	48	1,079	45	5
Subscriptions	117	1,055	111	13
Sponsorship	98	1,583	62	11
Donations	87	863	101	10
Other income	55	667	83	6
Public funding				
Local authority/local arts council	59	755	78	7
RAAs	33	601	55	4
Total income	901	7,505	120	100

Table NFMS 8   Music societies: income by type(a)

	Total (£ thousands)	Average (£s)	Number receiving	Percentage of all income
Box office/subscriptions	530	3,374	157	58
Other earned income	44	368	119	5
Sponsorship	63	641	119	7
Donations	77	570	135	8
Other	58	540	107	6
Public funding				
Local authority/local arts council	63	579	109	7
RAAs	79	686	115	9
Total income	914	5,815	157	100

(a) Excludes professionally-run music societies.

Table NFMS 9   Income from public sources, 1982/3 and 1989/90

	1982/3	1989/90
Choirs and orchestras in sample	581	244
Percentage of income from public sources	17	10
Percentage of income from other sources	83	90

Source: PSI/NFMS survey; *Facts about the Arts 2*, PSI, 1986.

Orchestras earn half of their income from the box office or engagements and, partly on account of their smaller size, receive a smaller proportion of their income from subscriptions. The reverse is true of choirs, nearly one quarter of whose income comes from subscriptions. Similar proportions of choirs and orchestras earned income from sponsorship and the combined value of this income was not inconsiderable. The grossed-up estimate for the value of sponsorship income from all three categories of society was £0.75 million. Table NFMS 10 gives details of box office income by size for responding choirs. 18 per cent of choirs generated more than £5,000 at the box office and 6 per cent earned more than £10,000. But the majority of choirs earn much smaller sums, 67 per cent receiving less than £3,000.

Table NFMS 10   Size of choir, by box office income

Box office income (£s)	Percentage of responding choirs in each category
Less than 499	13
500-999	15
1,000-1,499	16
1,500-1,999	11
2,000-2,999	12
3,000-4,999	15
5,000-9,999	12
10,000 and over	6

Few choirs or orchestras rehearse in dedicated arts venues. Local education authority (LEA) schools are the single most important rehearsal venues for both choirs and orchestras. The close links that exist between traditional choral music and the church is apparent in the pattern of both rehearsing and performing; just under a third of all choirs undertook their rehearsals in churches or church halls; more than half gave their self-promoted performances in churches or cathedrals.

Orchestral performances were more evenly spread across different types of venue. The most frequently used premises for orchestral concerts were local authority arts venues, accounting for over one-third of all self-promoted orchestral performances. Music society concerts were also promoted in a variety of venue types, although like orchestral performances, local authority arts venues were most popular. Relative to either choirs or orchestras, music societies put on a higher proportion of concerts in non-local authority arts venues, state and independent schools.

Table NFMS 11   Premises: rehearsals

		Column percentages
	Choirs	Orchestras
School - LEA	33	43
School - independent	8	6
College	5	6
Local authority arts venue	3	5
Other local authority venue	2	8
Non-local authority arts venue	1	2
Church	17	4
Church hall	25	15
Community centre	4	6
Other	2	7
Total	100	100

Table NFMS 12   Premises: self-promoted performances

Column percentages

	Choirs	Music societies(a)	Orchestras
School (LEA)	6	19	7
School (independent)	4	8	4
College	3	7	6
Local authority arts venue	16	23	36
Other local authority venue	6	9	11
Non-local authority arts venue	3	7	5
Church	51	14	28
Church hall	4	2	1
Community centre	4	3	1
Other	3	9	1
Total	100	100	100

(a) Excludes 36 performances promoted by societies at more than one venue.

References

1. Jeff Bishop and Paul Hoggett, *Organising around Enthusiasms*, Comedia, 1986, p.104.

2. John Myerscough, *Facts about the Arts 2*, PSI, 1986.

Appendix C

Youth theatre in the UK

The information below is based on computer print-outs provided by the National Association of Youth Theatres. NAYT estimates that there are 700 active youth theatre groups in the UK, and it has up-to-date information about the year of foundation, membership, age-range, staffing, finance, facilities and equipment, of approximately 280 of these groups, most of which are full members of NAYT.

Year of Foundation
There are 265 groups of which NAYT has a record of their year of foundation – the oldest was founded in 1944. The number of currently active groups founded in each of the last five decades is as follows:

1940s	3
1950s	5
1960s	20
1970s	54
1980s	179

Age of members
Members of youth theatre groups are of every age from nought to 80. The great majority are teenagers. Over half the groups have an upper age limit between 18 and 25. The most common age span for membership of youth theatre groups is 14 to 18, but 37 per cent of the groups for which NAYT holds information about the age span of members have an upper age limit of 16 or less.

Total membership
Excluding one company on Tyneside which has a total membership of 2,000 organised into a number of different groups, the average number of members of a youth theatre group is 71. So if there are about

700 groups in the UK, the total membership would be approximately 50,000. 60 per cent of all youth theatre groups have 50 members or fewer.

NAYT 1   Youth theatres in the UK: public sector funding

	Number in each area	Number stating sources of finance	Number receiving funds from L.A. youth service	RAA	Theatre/ arts centre
English Regional Arts Association areas (1990)					
Eastern	23	21	11	2	3
East Midlands (inc. Bucks)	25	24	11	2	–
Greater London	38	36	24	8	6
Lincs and Humberside	6	5	2	–	1
Merseyside	13	12	9	1	2
Northern	13	13	7	3	2
North West	16	15	13	4	1
Southern	15	14	10	3	–
South East	12	11	5	1	1
South West	31	31	11	5	7
West Midlands	29	27	13	1	5
Yorkshire	15	13	8	1	1
Wales	15	13	7	2(a)	2
Scotland	20	18	4	4(b)	2
N. Ireland	4	4	–	4(b)	–
Total	275	257	135	41	33

(a) In Wales one group received funding from the Welsh Arts Council.

(b) In Scotland and Northern Ireland, where there are no RAAs, the groups received funding from the respective Arts Councils.

Sources of finance

Table NAYT1 shows the number of youth theatre groups in the countries and regions of the UK that received some funding from different sources. 52 per cent of groups recorded that they received funding from local authorities/the youth service; 16 per cent received some funding from Regional Arts Associations or national Arts Councils; and 13 per cent received some financial support from a parent theatre company or arts centre. In a few cases, financial support is also received from some community schools and colleges and from business sponsors. But, to supplement their box-office income and grants-in-aid, many groups have to go in for a range of other fund-raising measures; and often they are subsidised out of the pockets of their directors or organisers.

Staffing

Most youth theatre groups do not have any paid full-time staff. About one-third of all paid staff in youth theatres are working in youth theatre in Greater London. After London, Merseyside is the area where paid staff are most likely to be found working in youth theatre. The NAYT figures give a total of 178 full-time staff, 397 part-time staff, and 1,054 volunteers working in the 249 groups in the UK that have supplied information.

Appendix D

Local art clubs and societies

In June 1991 a short questionnaire was sent from PSI to 180 local art clubs and societies throughout the UK. The clubs and societies were selected at random from a list of 1,077 names and addresses of local art clubs and societies provided by The Artists' Publishing Company (APC), publishers of the magazines *The Artist* (circulation 17,000) and *Leisure Painter* (circulation 23,000).

L1 Geographical distribution of sample and respondents by country and by English Regional Arts Association areas

	Number of clubs in area	Number in sample	Number responding	Not known/ gone away
English Regional Arts Association areas (1990)				
Eastern	81	15	3	–
East Midlands	55	10	5	–
Greater London	85	12	4	3
Lincolnshire and Humberside	32	3	–	1
Merseyside	20	5	2	–
Northern	90	18	7	1
North West	54	8	5	1
Southern	92	18	14	–
South East	83	9	3	–
South West	142	27	13	2
West Midlands	53	12	5	4
Yorkshire	96	16	10	1
Northern Ireland	20	5	1	1
Wales	76	8	4	1
Scotland	98	14	9	2
Total	1,077	180	85	17

It became clear that the mailing list provided was not completely up-to-date. 17 of the questionnaires (9 per cent of the total sample) were returned as the addressee had died, gone away, was not known, or had parted company with the club or society in question. Nevertheless, after one reminder letter, 85 responses were received (a 47 per cent response rate).

Although out-of-date in places, the mailing list provided by The Artists' Publishing Company does appear to be reasonably comprehensive. For example, it contains 53 out of 63 art clubs and societies included on a list provided by Yorkshire Arts – as well as 43 clubs and societies not on that list. It does not include 10 art clubs and societies included in the Yorkshire Arts' list – five of them groups set up by members of the Asian communities in Yorkshire. The great majority of art clubs and societies that came to light in the course of the seven area surveys conducted for this study are included in the APC list.

L2   Date of formation of local art clubs and societies

	Number of respondent clubs and societies founded in each period
Before 1900	8
1900 - 1939	10
1940 - 1949	10
1950 - 1959	9
1960 - 1969	20
1970 - 1979	15
1980 - 1989	11
1990	1

It has also been possible to compare the APC list with a list of local art clubs and societies provided by the Welsh Arts Council and a list published in the Scottish Arts Council publication, *Helping the Arts* (second edition, 1990). A total of 28 local art clubs and societies appear on the lists produced by the Scottish and Welsh Arts Councils and Yorkshire Arts but not on the APC list. This represents a 10 per cent addition to the numbers of local art clubs and societies in these

L3   Membership numbers in local art clubs and societies(a)

Number of members	Number of respondent clubs and societies of each size
1 - 49	30
50 - 99	22
100 - 149	20
150 - 199	5
200 - 249	5
250 - 299	–
300 - 349	3

(a) A total of 7,984 members in 85 groups.

areas to the 270 such clubs and societies on the APC list. However it can also be estimated that approximately 15 per cent of the clubs and societies on the APC list are not strictly local art clubs and societies or are no longer in existence. Allowing for these additions and subtractions produces a figure of 1,025 as the estimated total number of freestanding local art clubs and societies in the UK, that is those with a continuing existence that operate wholly or largely outside the framework of adult education provision, the youth service, women's institutes, townswomen's guilds, etc.

Table L2 shows that 32 per cent of local art clubs and societies have been founded since 1970, and that 21 per cent (18 out of 84 respondents) were formed before the Second War.

The median membership size of local art clubs and societies is 75 (see Table L3) which suggests that there are approximately 76,900 people subscribing to local art clubs and societies. The average subscription is £9.10p (see Table L4).

Characteristically local art clubs and societies meet monthly or fortnightly – though about a quarter meet weekly or more frequently. 28 clubs and societies (33 per cent) regularly engage a paid tutor, demonstrator or lecturer(s), and seven do so occasionally. 30 of the 85 respondents (35 per cent) are affiliated to a local or regional association – 13 to a local arts council or arts association, 9 to a regional federation of arts societies, and 8 to a regional arts association. Table L5 shows the variety of meeting places for local art clubs and societies.

L4 Annual subscriptions (full members only)

	Number of clubs and societies in each category
Nil	2
£3 or less	7
£3.01 - £5	26
£5.01 - £10	32
£10.01 - £20	12
£20.01 - £30	3
£30.01 - £40	1
£40.01 - £50	2

68 of the 85 respondents (80 per cent) accepted 'amateur artists' as an adequate description of their members. 11 described themselves as a mixed group of amateurs and professionals, and a further five said that they had a few or a 'handful' (in one case quite a handful) of professionals. The Ionist Art Group, which was founded in 1987, is special in that its members consist of professional scientists with an amateur interest in art, and professional artists with an amateur interest in science.

L5 Meeting places for local art clubs and societies(a)

	Number of respondents meeting in each type of venue
Village hall or church hall	17
Community or civic centre	12
Gallery/museum/arts centre	8
College	7
Rented studio	6
School	5
Youth centre	4
Adult education institute	4
Private house	4
Library	3

(a) Many art clubs and societies meet outdoors in the summer.

21 out of the 85 respondents (25 per cent) received some financial support or support in kind from public bodies in 1990/1. 14 received help from a local authority, 8 from a local arts council, 2 from the Scottish Arts Council, and one from a Regional Association. However, more than three-quarters of the local art clubs and societies had a total income of less than £2,000 in the last financial year.

Appendix E

The role of the volunteer

This appendix brings together existing research findings on the extent of volunteering in the arts backed up with selective examples from the case study areas.

Estimates of the contribution of volunteer input are difficult to evaluate and are often highly subjective. The amount of time contributed by a single volunteer (and the quality of the work) varies between individuals. This was one finding of a series of *General Household Survey* questions on volunteering undertaken in 1987. Of the 23 per cent of the adult population who claimed to have been engaged in some form of voluntary work in the previous twelve months, 23 per cent had spent under 5 days, whilst 15 per cent had spent over 100 days involved in voluntary work in the previous 12 months.[1] So there are serious difficulties involved in evaluating the relative significance of volunteering simply by a head count of volunteers in different organisations.

Having accepted that 'number of volunteers' is a crude measure of volunteer activity, it does provide a starting point for estimating the pattern of volunteering across different categories of arts organisations. Table V1 draws together information on employment from the case studies of *The Economic Importance of the Arts* study. A general pattern emerges which indicates that volunteering in the professional arts is not evenly spread across the art forms. Rather, the statistics indicate how three sectors of the arts – museums, arts centres, and festivals – rely particularly heavily on unpaid, volunteer assistance.

Museums and galleries
The various surveys of volunteering in museums all present different pictures of the extent of volunteering. The most recent of the annual surveys conducted by British Tourist Authority/English Tourist Board Research Services (1989) estimates the number of volunteers active

V1 Volunteers in professional arts organisations

	Glasgow	Ipswich	Merseyside
Performing arts			
Producing theatres	8	–	9
Receiving theatres	–	na	–
Touring companies	–	–	–
Opera/ballet companies	7	na	na
Orchestras/other music	4	–	40
Festivals	38	60	..
Arts centres/other small companies	102	111	124
Museums & galleries			
Local authority	6	6	148
Independent	55	3	135
Galleries/studios	50	..	..
Heritage/other	..	c325	..

Source: *Economic Importance of the Arts in Ipswich,* PSI, 1988; *Economic Importance of the Arts in Glasgow*, PSI, 1988; *Economic Importance of the Arts in Merseyside*, PSI 1988.

in UK museums at around 11,400, with volunteers being engaged by 41 per cent of all museums. This is a grossed-up estimate for all museums based on a sample of 927 museums. Jenny Mattingly's survey of volunteers in museums and galleries in 1982/3 was based on a much smaller sample of 103 museums, of which 91 per cent claimed to use volunteers. However, a survey undertaken by the Museums Association in 1982/3 reported only 52 per cent of responding museums as using volunteers. There seems no way to resolve these diverging estimate of the significance of volunteering in museums. The context of the survey and the sample size are all likely to be important influences on the reported use of volunteers.[2]

In addition to volunteering, many museums (and performing arts venues) have 'friends' organisations. This was particularly true of the larger independent, local authority and national museums. However in some instances, the distinction between a friend and a volunteer was somewhat arbitrary. The former are usually identified by their supportive and largely fund-raising role, but this is not always the case.

In her report for the Office of Arts and Libraries, *Volunteers in Museums and Heritage Organisations*, Sue Millar identified three types of friends: members who pay a subscription and occasionally attend events; members who are active in that they participate in fund raising activities; and those friends who provide more 'hands on' assistance. The number involved far exceeds the notional figure for museum volunteering. The British Association of Friends of Museums (BAFM), set up in 1972, has some 216 member organisations representing over 150,000 individuals.[3]

Two things are clear: volunteers make a major contribution to the running of museums and galleries in the UK; and the extent of volunteering in museums is spread unevenly between categories of museum. Both Sue Millar's report and the recent inquiry into collection management, *The Cost of Collecting,* noted that it was the independent museum sector which recorded the highest incidence of volunteer input relative to total staffing. Replies from 61 museums surveyed show how the significance of volunteers varies between type of museum. Although volunteers accounted for only 2 per cent of the staff of national museums and 14 per cent of staff at local authority museums, independent museums relied most heavily on the contribution of volunteers, accounting for one third of all individuals engaged.[4] This is further confirmed by a PSI/Association of Independent Museums survey. One-third of the 241 independent museums responding to the PSI/AIM survey engaged some volunteer help; 23 per cent of independent museums function with no paid staff.[5] So in addition to providing assistance to museums with paid staff, whether independent, local authority or national, volunteers are wholly responsible for running a small but significant number of museums.

Museums and galleries located within four of the case study areas were asked to assess the importance of volunteer input. In Teignbridge, Teignmouth Museum and Dawlish Museum are examples of the volunteer-run museum. Both museums represent typical examples of this type of independent museum: founded in 1978 and 1969 respectively, their collections are concerned primarily with the history of the surrounding locality. In addition to a governing committee of 8, Dawlish Museum has a 'display team' of up to 6 volunteers. The museum, open daily from May to September, is staffed by two stewards. This involves 26 individuals per week, drawn from a pool of around 80. Other members of the Society assist with fund-raising. The only paid labour is for the cleaning of the museum.[6] A third museum in Teignbridge, the Newton Abbot Town Museum, although benefitting from one paid part-time member of staff, nevertheless relies extensively on the assistance of 14 volunteers. They are involved in a variety of tasks, acting as 'guides' to the museum, security staff and 'a few choose to help with the catalogue index and to sort the collections'. Curator, Felicity Cole, stated that without them 'our museum would only be open for 10 hours a week'.[7]

A similar pattern of smaller museums relying heavily on volunteers was repeated in Aberdeen and Exeter. Both cities boast regimental museums (the Gordon Highlanders and the Devonshire and Dorset Regiments) which have small permanent staffs. The contribution made by volunteers in both regimental museums was more directed towards specified areas of activity such as cataloguing, research and conservation, rather than to general, all-round tasks. Major Carroll, curator of the Devonshire and Dorset Regiment Museum in Exeter put the case bluntly: 'In short, without this volunteer labour our collections would deteriorate faster and remain undocumented'.[8] Here, assistance was largely in the form of monthly visits from two volunteer groups of the National Association of Decorative and Fine Arts Societies (NADFAS).

NADFAS was established in 1968 to increase the enjoyment, knowledge and care of the arts and to stimulate interest in the preservation of the cultural heritage. It has 250 autonomous societies in the UK with a combined membership of over 60,000. Although there is a strong educational dimension to NADFAS, about 5 to 10 per cent of NADFAS membership actively volunteer. Sue Millar notes:

> NADFAS volunteers make a major contribution in the area of preventive conservation. Their formalised procedures, training methods, and approach to working with paid staff are exemplary. At the Horniman Museum... their assistance in preparing objects for exhibition or storage under the instruction of paid conservators...has released paid staff to undertake more specialist tasks.[9]

Diverging views were expressed by some of the larger local authority museums and galleries on the use of volunteers. Hilary McGowan, Exeter's Assistant Director for Leisure and Tourism with responsibility for Museums and Arts noted that 'the Museums Service depends greatly on volunteers to carry out curatorial work and raise money through the Friends. The work is extensive and we could not function without them'. This was not the case in Aberdeen, where the Council did not condone the use of volunteers except where the work is preparatory to undertaking further education in the arts field.[10]

There were other examples of vocationally orientated volunteering. For much of 1991, the Spacex Gallery in Exeter engaged a graduate who intends to start a BA course in Museums Management the following autumn; the then director of the Spacex, Ann Jones, considered this sort of contribution as 'invaluable'. But in addition to the practical assistance provided by volunteers, it is the specific contribution in the field of fund-raising that is much valued. As well as specific schemes such as an arts-raffle, Spacex runs a Friends scheme which invites individuals to support the Gallery financially and in doing so to become 'actively involved in the gallery's events'.[11]

In Powys, the two principal galleries – the Oriel Gallery in Welshpool and the Davies Memorial in Newtown – rely on teams of volunteer stewards. The Welshpool Gallery has 20 people who each contribute half-a-day each month; the gallery in Newtown has a team of seven regular volunteers, of whom 5 undertake half-a-day each month and two half-a-day each week.

Arts centres and festivals

A full survey of arts centres undertaken in 1986 confirmed the significance of volunteering in this area of arts provision. Four-fifths of arts centres responding to the survey recorded using volunteers. Some were entirely dependent on volunteers with 10 per cent of responding arts centres functioning without any paid staff at all. The findings also confirm the variations in time committed by individual volunteers. Over 80 per cent of volunteers gave less than 5 hours per week, whilst a small proportion, 2 per cent of volunteers, devoted more than 20 hours per week.[12]

A comprehensive survey of arts festivals is being undertaken by PSI in autumn 1991. The findings of *The Economic Importance of the Arts* study illustrated that volunteers frequently play an important role in organising festivals. As with museums and arts centres, included under the generic heading of festivals is a diverse group of activities which range widely in size, content and professional/voluntary input. Indeed, as the case studies show, arts festivals demonstrate a wide range of amateur/professional collaboration in both an administrative and artistic sense.

V2 Festivals and carnivals in case study areas: status and volunteers, 1990

	Paid admin.	Artistic programme	Volunteers involved in organisation
Aberdeen			
Aberdeen Alternative Festival	Yes	Prof/am	16
Aberdeen Arts Carnival	Yes	Prof/am	..
Aberdeen Bon Accord	Yes	Prof/am	..
Aberdeen Drama Festival	No	Am	..
Aberdeen and North East of Scotland Music Festival	No	Am	..
Aberdeen International Youth Festival	Yes	Am	..
Exeter			
Exeter Festival	Yes	Prof/am	–
Devon and Exeter Competitive Festival	No	Am	20
Powys			
Llandrindod Wells Victorian Festival	Yes	Prof/am	500
Llandrindod Wells Drama Festival	No	Am	60
Hay-on-Wye Festival of Literature	Yes	na	75
Brecon Jazz Festival	Yes	Prof	300
Machynlleth Festival	No	Prof	10
Powys Eisteddfod	No	Am	100
Stoke and Newcastle			
Cheadle Carnival	No	Am	25/30
Werrington Carnival	No	Am	26
Hartshill Festival	No	Am	12
Fenton Carnival	No	Am	86
Potteries Folk Festival	No	Prof/am	30
Teignbridge			
Ashburton Festival	No	Prof/am	12
Dawlish Arts Festival	No	Prof/am	12
Telford			
Wrekin & Telford Arts	Yes	Prof/am	19
Wellington Drama Festival	No	Am	15

Note: Although featuring amateur performers, competitive festivals usually engage professional adjudicators.

14 of the 23 festivals and carnivals listed in table V2 engaged no paid staff at all. But the fact that they are volunteer-run does not mean that they promote only amateur artists. For instance, the 1989 Dawlish Arts Festival consisted of a mixture of professional and amateur concerts including one performance by the Bournemouth Sinfonietta; and any profits from the amateur events are used to underwrite concerts by young professionals.

This appendix has sketched out those areas of the arts which have developed strong relationships with volunteers. But problems can arise in the use of volunteers in conjunction with paid staff. As Sue Millar observes:

> the realisation by paid professional staff in museums that volunteers have a significant place within the museum community... has created a climate whereby voluntary activity is no longer equated with amateurism. Volunteers and volunteer-led museums are no longer on the fringes of the museum movement. Nevertheless, the delineation of paid and unpaid posts and the definition of appropriate volunteer tasks remains an area of sensitivity.[13]

Certainly, the difficulties which can arise from paid staff/volunteer relations are not limited to museums with a core of paid staff. *Arts Centres in the UK* also identified a range of views over the use of volunteers. More recently, a study of seven arts centres in the Southern Arts area examined the contribution of volunteers. The report highlighted ways in which volunteers are excluded from the decision-making process and are sometimes considered for only the

V 3 Estimated number of volunteers in arts centres, museums and heritage sites

	Arts centres	Museums	Heritage sites
Year of survey	1986	1989	1989
Estimated total number of volunteers	3,710	11,400	13,600
Percentage of respondents using volunteers	80	41	32

Source: Robert Hutchison and Susan Forrester, *Arts Centres in the UK*, PSI, 1987; *Sightseeing in the UK*, BTA/ETB Research Services, 1990.

most menial and basic tasks. It recommended ways in which the role of volunteers – or participants – could be enhanced so as to maximise their contribution. Clearly, for volunteering to be successful, it requires effective aims and objectives, management and training.[14]

To sum up, volunteers make a significant contribution to the running of many kinds of arts establishments and events, but that contribution is most evident in museums, arts centres and festivals. It is worth noting that one feature common to these three categories of organisation is that they have all expanded considerably in numbers over the last two decades. Over 77 per cent of non-local authority arts centres opened between 1970 and 1985; 70 per cent of independent museums have opened since 1970. The evidence from our case studies would suggest that there has been a considerable increase in the number of arts festivals over the last two decades. Given this, volunteers would appear to have played a crucial part in facilitating new developments in the organisation of the arts and museums over the last 20 years.

References

1. Jil Matheson, *General Household Survey 1987 Voluntary Work*, HMSO, 1990.

2. Jenny Mattingly, *Volunteers in Museums and Galleries*, The Volunteer Centre, 1984.

3. Office of Arts and Libraries, *Volunteers in Museums and Heritage Organisations – Policy, Planning and Management*, HMSO, 1990.

4. Barry Lord, Gail Dexter Lord and John Nicks, *The Cost of Collecting – Collection Management in UK Museums*, HMSO, p.115.

5. *Cultural Trends 4:1989*, PSI, 1990, p.22.

6. Letters from K.W. Rixon 9 December 1990 and Mrs D.Todd, 7 December 1990.

7. Letter from Felicity Cole, 11 December 1990.

8. Letter from, Major J. Carroll, 5 December 1990.

9. Office of Arts and Libraries, *op.cit.*, p.19.

10. Letters from Hilary McGowan, 18 July 1991 and Mr A. Hidalgo, 26 June 1991.

11. Letter from Ann Jones, 30 November 1990.

12. Robert Hutchison and Susan Forrester, *Arts Centres in the UK*, PSI, 1987.

13. Office of Arts and Libraries,*op.cit.*, HMSO, 1990, p.3.

14. Robin Gorna, *Volunteering and Participation in Arts Centres*, Windsor Arts Centre, 1990.